NEW MERMAIDS

General Editors:
William C. Carroll, Boston University
Brian Gibbons, University of Münster
Tiffany Stern, University College, University of Oxford

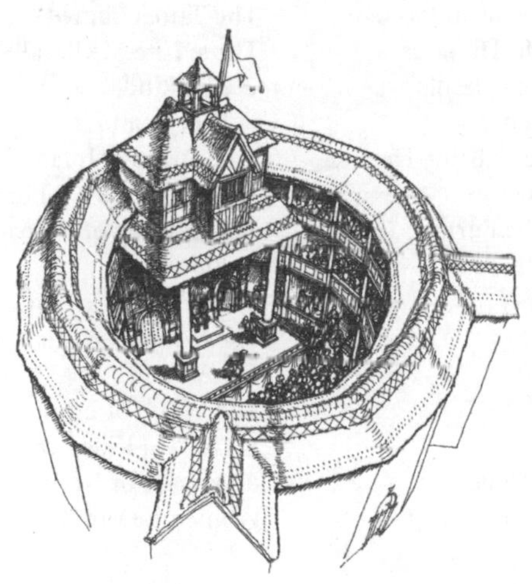

Reconstruction of an Elizabethan Theatre
by C. Walter Hodges

NEW MERMAIDS

The Alchemist
All for Love
Arden of Faversham
Arms and the Man
Bartholmew Fair
The Beaux' Stratagem
The Beggar's Opera
The Changeling
A Chaste Maid in Cheapside
The Country Wife
The Critic
Doctor Faustus
The Duchess of Malfi
The Dutch Courtesan
Eastward Ho!
Edward the Second
Elizabethan and Jacobean Tragedies
Epicoene, or The Silent Woman
Every Man In His Humour
Gammer Gurton's Needle
An Ideal Husband
The Importance of Being Earnest
The Jew of Malta
The Knight of the Burning Pestle
Lady Windermere's Fan
London Assurance
Love for Love
Major Barbara
The Malcontent
The Man of Mode
Marriage A-La-Mode
Mrs Warren's Profession
A New Way to Pay Old Debts
The Old Wife's Tale
The Playboy of the Western World
The Provoked Wife
Pygmalion
The Recruiting Officer
The Relapse
The Revenger's Tragedy
The Rivals
The Roaring Girl
The Rover
Saint Joan
The School for Scandal
She Stoops to Conquer
The Shoemaker's Holiday
The Spanish Tragedy
Tamburlaine
The Tamer Tamed
Three Late Medieval Morality Plays
  Mankind
  Everyman
  Mundus et Infans
'Tis Pity She's a Whore
The Tragedy of Mariam
Volpone
The Way of the World
The White Devil
The Witch
The Witch of Edmonton
A Woman Killed with Kindness
A Woman of No Importance
Women Beware Women

NEW MERMAIDS

THOMAS MIDDLETON &
WILLIAM ROWLEY

THE CHANGELING

edited by Michael Neill

Professor of English
University of Auckland

Bloomsbury Methuen Drama
An imprint of Bloomsbury Publishing Plc

BLOOMSBURY
LONDON • OXFORD • NEW YORK • NEW DELHI • SYDNEY

Bloomsbury Methuen Drama
An imprint of Bloomsbury Publishing Plc

Imprint previously known as Methuen Drama

50 Bedford Square
London
WC1B 3DP
UK

1385 Broadway
New York
NY 10018
USA

www.bloomsbury.com

BLOOMSBURY, METHUEN DRAMA and the Diana logo are trademarks of Bloomsbury Publishing Plc

First published 2006 by Bloomsbury Methuen Drama
Reprinted 2008, 2009, 2011, 2013, 2015, 2016

British Library Cataloguing-in-Publication Data
A catalogue record for this book is available from the British Library.

ISBN: PB: 978-0-7136-6884-1
ePDF: 978-1-4081-4453-4
ePub: 978-1-4081-4454-1

Library of Congress Cataloging-in-Publication Data
A catalog record for this book is available from the Library of Congress.

Series: New Mermaids

Printed and bound in Great Britain

CONTENTS

ACKNOWLEDGEMENTS

My principal debts are necessarily to those whose generosity has given me the time to complete this project: to the Master and Fellows of Trinity College, Cambridge, and to the Folger Shakespeare Library for the award of visiting fellowships; to the University of Auckland for research funding and a period of sabbatical leave. It goes without saying that in the course of preparing this edition I have frequently relied on the scholarship and insight of others – not least the previous Mermaid editors, Joost Daalder and his predecessor Patricia Thomson. I am particularly grateful to Douglas Bruster, editor of *The Changeling* for the forthcoming *Oxford Middleton*, and to its general editor, Gary Taylor, who allowed me access to their unpublished work; to my colleague, Mac Jackson, whose knowledge of the Middleton canon is unrivalled; to my general editor, Brian Gibbons for his wise and good-humoured supervision of the project; and to the editorial staff at A & C Black, especially Jenny Ridout and Katie Taylor, for their patience and expertise. The librarians of Trinity College, Cambridge, the Cambridge University Library, the Folger Shakespeare Library, the London Theatre Museum, and the Auckland University Library, have been unfailingly helpful. For their many personal and professional kindnesses I owe more than I can easily express to Anne Barton and Adrian Poole at Trinity, to Gail Paster, Barbara Mowat, Betsy Walsh, and Carol Brobeck at the Folger, and to my colleagues in Auckland, especially Terry Sturm, Albert Wendt, Peter Simpson, and Andrew Sharp. Without the help of the people and institutions I have named this edition would never have seen the light of day; but its remaining errors and imperfections belong, I fear, to me alone.

Finally, of course, I must thank my wife, Kubé Jones-Neill, for her constant love and support. This edition is dedicated to her.

Auckland, 2006 M.N.

INTRODUCTION

About the Play

'The next good mood I find my father in, / I'll get him quite discarded' – with these chillingly offhand words, Beatrice-Joanna, the spoilt daughter of a powerful nobleman, plans to destroy the livelihood of Deflores, the family servant who has crossed her once too often (II.i.92–3). In the following scene, she will plot the murder of an inconvenient fiancé with equal *sang froid.* Locked in the absolute self-centredness of late adolescence, fortified by the vanities of high-rank and youthful beauty, and utterly confident of the indulgence of a doting father, Beatrice simply has no inkling of the reality of other human beings, discarding them at need like so much trash. In their beguilingly deceptive simplicity, her lines are representative of the technical mastery that makes *The Changeling* one of the most compelling tragedies in English. Thomas Middleton, who wrote the scene in which they appear, had a wonderful ear for the psychological and social nuances of colloquial speech; and here, in little more than a dozen words, he allows his heroine to reveal as much about herself as another dramatist might convey in an entire soliloquy.

For those who come to it with expectations shaped by the writings of Shakespeare, Middleton and Rowley's tragedy may at first seem anomalous. Although, in its treatment of the treacherous servant Deflores, it self-consciously recalls *Othello,* and although the murderous *folie à deux* that consumes Beatrice and Deflores sometimes seems like a rewriting of *Macbeth,* it is conspicuously without the poetic grandeur and metaphysical resonance of those plays. *The Changeling* belongs to that slightly paradoxical genre known as 'domestic tragedy': cast in the same bourgeois mould as the anonymous masterpiece *Arden of Faversham* (c. 1591) or Thomas Heywood's *A Woman Killed with Kindness* (c. 1603), it acquires a sharper edge of social observation from its authors' familiarity with the conventions of city comedy – the genre that satirised the mores of the urban middle-class. Despite its seemingly narrow domestic focus, however, *The Changeling* has much to reveal about the gathering social and political tensions that were to plunge England into a destructive civil war within twenty years of its first performance; and in the unblinking insight with which it explores the psychology of its twin protagonists, it is recognisably ancestral to the realist theatre pioneered by Ibsen and others at the end of the nineteenth century – and thus to styles of representation that, through the medium of cinema and television, continue to shape the dramatic experience of modern audiences.

Authorship

Although *The Changeling* is nowadays reckoned amongst the finest tragedies of an exceptionally prolific era, it is a work that challenges some of our culture's most deeply rooted assumptions about the nature and genesis of high art: its colloquial style, its psychological naturalism, the violent generic contrasts of its double-plot design, and even the circumstances of its composition, are difficult to reconcile with the lofty claims of what Sir Philip Sidney characterised as 'the high and excellent Tragedy'.[1] Like many popular dramas of its period, moreover, it was not the product of a single artistic vision, but emerged from the partnership of two writers whose history of collaboration with a whole range of contemporaries is an eloquent testament to the commercial nature of their enterprise. Such collaboration was characteristic of a profession which, as the term 'playwright' suggests, was kin to the humble crafts of cartwright, wheelwright, and shipwright. Indeed the business of supplying new material for the voracious playhouses of Elizabethan and Jacobean London may best be compared with scriptwriting for an entertainment factory like modern Hollywood: just as film-scripts are often commissioned from a team of writers, so a theatrical entrepreneur like Christopher Beeston, if he wished to obtain a new play in a hurry, might assemble a group of jobbing playwrights and suggest a subject to them; and just as screen writers are subordinate to directors and actors, their identity remaining largely unknown to the cinema-going public, so the name of a play's author (as title-page advertisements reveal) was often assumed to be of less interest than that of the company that performed it. Although we think of a play as being, like any literary work, the property of its creator, in the Elizabethan and Jacobean theatre a playscript belonged, for most practical purposes, to the players as soon as they received it from the playwright, whose relative insignificance was reflected in the niggardly fee he usually received.

By the time Middleton and Rowley wrote *The Changeling*, it is true, the theatrical world had witnessed the beginnings of a significant shift in the status accorded to dramatic texts. Key markers of this change were the publication of Ben Jonson's and then Shakespeare's *Works* in prestigious folio volumes (1616, 1623); and from the second decade of the seventeenth century a growing number of plays were published with the addition of elaborate prefatory material calculated to flatter the social

1 Sir Philip Sidney, 'An Apology for Poetry', in Edmund D. Jones (ed.) *English Critical Essays (Sixteenth, Seventeenth, and Eighteenth Centuries)* (London 1947), p. 26.

and cultural self-esteem of writers and readers alike. Just a year after *The Changeling*'s debut, Middleton and Rowley themselves contributed admiring verses for *The Duchess of Malfi*, echoing the sentiments of Webster's dedicatory epistle on the immortalising power of dramatic poetry; yet the two seem to have taken no more than intermittent interest in the publication of their own plays, a great many of which – including *The Changeling* itself – appeared only after their deaths.

In the case of William Rowley (1585–c.1625) this is perhaps not altogether surprising, since what little we know of his life suggests that he was first and foremost an actor – a leading member of the Prince's Men, specialising in comic roles[2] – for whom playwriting (mainly as a collaborator) was a sideline.[3] By contrast, Thomas Middleton (1580–1627) seems to have earned his livelihood entirely by his pen. Born to prosperous lower middle-class parents, and educated at Oxford,[4] he was nearing the end of a long career, during which he had written pamphlets and verse satires, in addition to his numerous plays for both elite and popular playhouses, and a variety of city pageants and entertainments. He had collaborated with a wide range of contemporaries, including Shakespeare, Webster, Ford, Dekker, Heywood, Munday, and Rowley himself, but had achieved prominence on his own account with a succession of outstanding city comedies, mocking the vices and foibles of urban life, and a small number of satiric tragedies, including the greatly admired *Women Beware Women* – probably written just a little before *The Changeling*. The most recent count credits Middleton with sole authorship of some eighteen surviving plays, perhaps a dozen collaborations, and at least ten pageants, masques and entertainments. It was, no doubt, his standing as a writer that won him appointment as London's first city chronologer in 1620; yet there is little evidence of concern to secure the kind of lasting literary reputation that mattered so much to Jonson. He seems to have taken some pride in the publication of his civic pageants and entertainments; but only eleven of his independent dramas were printed in his lifetime – several of them, including his early masterpiece, *The Revenger's Tragedy* (1607), anonymously; and he bothered to

2 See Bawcutt (1998) p. 2 for the suggestion that Rowley wrote the part of Lollio as a showcase for his own talents, though there is no conclusive proof that it was his.

3 Rowley's handiwork has been claimed in parts of up to fifty plays; but, of the sixteen plays widely accepted as his, no more than two or three appear to have been his unaided work (see David Gunby, 'William Rowley', *Oxford Dictionary of National Biography*).

4 Middleton matriculated at Queen's College in 1586, though there is no record of his having taken a degree.

supply dedicatory epistles for only two plays, *The Roaring Girl* (1611), co-written with Dekker, and *The Witch*, which survives only in manuscript.

The Changeling, then, is the work of two men for whom playwriting was less a vocation than a trade. We have no means of guessing the circumstances under which they began work on the script, but it may very well have been Beeston who commissioned them to adapt its sensational story of lust and murder. Certainly the manner in which the two set about dividing up their task suggests that, initially at least, the project was driven by no great personal investment: a variety of verbal and metrical tests concur in suggesting that Rowley undertook the composition of the comic underplot, while Middleton had primary responsibility for the tragic main plot; however the same tests have shown that Rowley (presumably to ensure a roughly equal distribution of labour) was also allocated the task of writing the crucial opening and closing scenes, as well as the first sixteen lines of Act IV, scene ii. This may seem an odd arrangement to anyone devoted to notions of authorial integrity; but to two seasoned professionals whose collaboration on at least four earlier works had made them thoroughly familiar with each other's way of working, it must have seemed an entirely practical solution. The result, against the apparent odds, was a text which, despite its superficially divergent plots, is distinguished by a remarkable imaginative coherence. It is clear that, as their writing progressed, the two playwrights must have exchanged ideas, read each other's contributions, and perhaps even worked over portions of one another's scripts. Indeed it would be surprising if Middleton did not claim some oversight of the crucial scenes which his collaborator provided for what was otherwise his own portion of the play; and there are passages in each where Middleton may either have revised Rowley's work, or even contributed some speeches of his own.[5]

5 The presence of certain stylistic markers, especially a relatively high number of feminine endings, suggest that Middleton may have had a hand in the opening exchange between Alsemero and Jasperino (I.i.1–45), as well as in Beatrice's death speech (V.iii.153–65) whose poetic intensity is uncharacteristic of Rowley. Other pointers to Middleton's presence include 'inclination' (I.i.27) – a word that occurs in several of his plays, but nowhere in Rowley – and the characteristic use of 'it' as a 'potentially vague substantive' at V.iii.102, 109, 227 (see Bruster, pp. 5, 9, 13, and cf. Commentary, V.iii.138). Roger Holdsworth, 'Notes on *The Changeling*', *N&Q* 234 (1989), 344–6, suggests that Middleton may also have been responsible for the first 122 lines of the last scene.

Date and Sources

Closely worked though their script appears to be, Middleton and Rowley seem to have worked on *The Changeling* with the rapidity expected of seasoned professionals: their principal source, John Reynolds' collection of 'Tragicall Histories', *The Triumph of God's Revenge*, was itself relatively new, having appeared only in 1621, while a secondary source – Leonard Digges' translation of G. de Sespedes y Menses' novel, *Gerardo The Unfortunate Spaniard* – was not entered for printing on the Stationers' Register until 11 March 1622; yet the play itself seems to have been ready by 7 May, when it was licensed for performance by Lady Elizabeth's Men.

The story of Alibius and Isabella, which makes up the sub-plot of *The Changeling*, resembles numerous folk-tales in which an aged husband is cuckolded by his beautiful young bride, but in its present form it seems to have been entirely of Rowley's invention. By contrast, the main plot is closely based on Reynolds, whose History IV, 'Alsemero and Beatrice-Joana', the dramatists followed with considerable fidelity, especially in the first half of the play – even picking up and elaborating his favourite metaphors of eyesight and blindness.[6] Such changes as the dramatists made to their source material seem to have been mainly prompted by considerations of dramatic economy, by a wish to clarify the moral patterns of the narrative, or by a concern for psychological plausibility. Thus, for example, where Reynolds' characters move between Valencia, Briamata, and various locations in Alicant, *The Changeling*'s tragic action is confined (after an opening scene at the castle gate) within the claustrophobic walls of Vermandero's fortress; where the original narrative stretches over several months, the play's action unfolds in a matter of days;[7] where Reynolds' indictment of the adulterous Beatrice-Joana is complicated by her jealous husband's complicity in the killing of one Piracquo brother and his cowardly murder of the other (for which he is tried and executed), Middleton and Rowley make Alsemero the blameless victim of his wife's treachery; and where in the original Alsemero's jealousy of Beatrice-Joana seems curiously unmotivated, the play grounds it in Jasperino's eavesdropping (IV.ii.81–102), winding up the tension by means of a device borrowed from Digges – the introduction of Diaphanta as a substitute bride.

The dramatists did, however, introduce one crucial alteration for

6 See below, pp. xix–xx. Reynolds' text can be found at www.acblack.com/thechangeling.
7 Acts I–III occupy no more than two days, and Acts IV–V another two days, while a gap of 'some ten days' (IV.ii.7) intervenes between the end of Act III and Beatrice-Joanna's wedding to Alsemero at the beginning of Act IV.

which it is difficult to account in such straightforwardly technical ways. This involves their transformation of Beatrice-Joanna's adulterous accomplice, who – even as he is promoted from his relatively insignificant role in the original narrative to become the co-protagonist of the tragedy – is simultaneously degraded to an inferior position in the play's social hierarchy. In Reynolds he is 'a Gallant young Gentleman, of the Garrison of the Castle . . . *Seigneur Antonio de Flores*', a youth of some status, whom Beatrice-Joana chooses as her accessory, and ultimately as her lover, because she knows that he 'doth deeply honour, and dearly affect her';[8] by contrast Middleton and Rowley's Deflores is a mere household servant – a gentleman by birth, it is true, but one whose lowly rank is matched by the coarsely pock-marked 'deformity' that makes him doubly repugnant in the eyes of the spoilt young noblewoman who is the object of his obsessive desire. In the source there is no suggestion that de Flores' place as a follower of Vermandero makes him unworthy of Beatrice-Joana: and, in so far as 'service' figures significantly in Reynolds' narrative, it is only in the specialised chivalric sense, by which a courtly wooer declared himself 'servant' to his mistress. In *The Changeling*, by contrast, Deflores' reduction to literal servitude casts his affair with his lord's daughter in a completely different light, stressing the humiliations of his position and producing a complex set of verbal and gestural equivocations on the vocabulary of service.[9]

The dramatists' exploration of the ironic relationship between the two kinds of service may have been prompted by certain details in their secondary source. It was in *Gerardo* that the dramatists found the story of a bed-trick that goes awry and ends in murder: in one of its inset tales, the melancholy pilgrim Roberto tells the grim story of his bride Isdaura who, like Beatrice, sought to conceal her lost virginity by persuading her maid and confidante, Julia, to take her place on the wedding night. As in *The Changeling*, the bride's scheme was imperilled by her substitute's excessive enjoyment of Roberto's embraces. Seeking to drive Julia from the nuptial bed, Isdaura set fire to a tapestry, and then, fearful of betrayal, pushed the maid into a deep well, drowning her.[10] While *The Changeling*'s

8 Ibid, p. 127.

9 See below, pp. xxviii–xxxiii. The play's quibbling on 'service' is discussed by Christopher Ricks, 'The Moral and Poetic Structure of *The Changeling*', *E.Crit.* 10 (1960), 290–306 (296–9), and Anthony B. Dawson, 'Giving the Finger: Puns and Transgression in *The Changeling*', in A. L. Magnusson and C. E. McGee (eds.) *The Elizabethan Theatre XII* (Toronto 1993), pp. 93–112 (100–2).

10 G. de Cespedes y Meneses, *Gerardo The Unfortunate Spaniard*, trans. Leonard Digges (London 1622), pp. 105–6.

most obvious debt to *Gerardo* is to be found in this episode, a more profound one lies in its influence on the transformation of Deflores from a gallant young soldier to a lustful and treacherous lackey. In the novel, Isdaura's virginity has been taken by another member of her father's household, 'an old trusty servant, [a Biscayner,] whom he love[s] as an adopted son . . . for his good service', and upon whose 'faith and honesty' as a steward he entirely relies[11] – though he is to prove as treacherous as Deflores. Shortly before Isdaura's wedding, the Biscayner, who has fallen ill with a mysterious complaint, comes to her bedchamber and demands a reward for his 'good deeds and service' declaring that only in the possession of her body can he find 'the antidote and wholesome physician' for 'the mischief and sickness that afflicts [him]'.[12] Declaring that 'I fear no refusal, since in mine own will lies the satisfaction of my desire', he threatens her with a dagger and then rapes her, only for Isdaura to kill him as he sleeps. Deflores too, who ends the opening scene of *The Changeling* by proclaiming the ascendancy of his 'will' in the same phallic sense (I.i.230), goes on to make his mistress's virginity the price of his 'service' (III.iii.53–7, 64–7), and to insist upon the medicinal necessity of the conquest: 'I'm in pain / And must be eased of you; 'tis a charity' (III.iii.98–9). From such small details, Middleton and Rowley worked up the story of sexual insurrection and domestic betrayal that transformed the crudely moralised sensationalism of Reynolds' narrative.

There are no other generally acknowledged sources for *The Changeling*, but the tragedy – as we might predict from its authors' long careers in the theatre – is full of recollections of earlier plays, notably *A Midsummer Night's Dream, Othello* and *The Duchess of Malfi*. From *Dream* it self-consciously borrows the theme of change; from *Othello* (published in the year of its first performance) the central figure of an 'honest' servant whose fidelity masks his true role as demonic tempter; and from *Malfi* (where another embittered servant murders his mistress) the wild antics of the madhouse inmates, figurations of a world given over to vicious insanity.

The Play

DRAMATIC COHERENCE AND THE DOUBLE PLOT

As we have seen, *The Changeling* is constructed from two parallel plot-lines. In the tragic high-plot, Beatrice-Joanna, the beautiful, spoilt

11 *Gerardo*, pp. 91, 95.
12 *Gerardo*, pp. 103–4.

daughter of Vermandero, lord of the castle of Alicante, falls in love with Alsemero, a handsome young visitor to the city; desperate to be rid of the suitor (Alonzo de Piracquo) to whom she is inconveniently betrothed, Beatrice suborns her father's ill-favoured servant, Deflores, to kill him. Even as the murder clears the way for Beatrice to marry Alsemero, however, it delivers her into the power of her loathsome co-conspirator, who now insists upon possessing her. Beatrice attempts to conceal the loss of her virginity from her bridegroom by persuading her maid, Diaphanta, to take her place on the wedding night. Fearing that this new accomplice will betray them, Deflores kills her, arranging a house-fire to cover up the murder. Despite his best efforts, however, their crimes are exposed, whereupon Deflores stabs his mistress to death, before taking his own life.

In the comic low-plot, Isabella, the young, attractive wife of the elderly Alibius, keeper of the city's madhouse, is besieged by two courtly admirers, Antonio and Franciscus, who have disguised themselves as inmates of the asylum in the hope of seducing her. Alibius' subordinate, Lollio, becomes aware of their attentions, and seeks to blackmail his mistress into an adulterous affair; but Isabella successfully resists all of their importunities, and by virtue of her constancy is able to shame her lustful suitors into confession and her jealous husband into rueful vows of reform.

Double plots are, of course, common enough in the drama of the period, but few plays treat them quite as cavalierly as *The Changeling* with its bald juxtaposition of two almost unrelated stories. Only two rather offhand details pretend to join the two: Antonio and Franciscus come briefly into suspicion for Alonzo's murder when they are found to have absconded from Vermandero's household, and Alibius' patients are hired to perform a masque at Beatrice's wedding; but the masque never takes place, and the absconders are almost immediately cleared by the incrimination of Beatrice and Deflores. The broadly farcical treatment of the madhouse world makes the two plots seem even more ill-assorted.

However, as the play's critical and performance histories have amply demonstrated,[13] what the two plots lack in superficial connectedness, the

13 Critical readings that stress the thematic connections between the two plots include M. C. Bradbrook, *Themes and Conventions of Elizabethan Tragedy* (Cambridge 1980), pp. 206–17; Richard Levin, *The Multiple Plot in English Renaissance Drama* (Chicago 1971), pp. 34–48; Nicholas Brooke, *Horrid Laughter in Jacobean Tragedy* (London 1979) pp. 70–88; for productions that have similarly emphasized the work's 'organic' unity, see below pp. xxxiv–ix. More sceptical accounts of the play's structure are given by Leo Salingar, *Dramatic Form in Shakespeare and the Jacobeans* (Cambridge 1986), pp. 222–35; T. McAlindon, *English Renaissance Tragedy* (Basingstoke 1986), pp. 207–9; Robert Ornstein, *The Moral Vision of Jacobean Tragedy* (Madison 1960), pp. 179–90.

overall design makes up in thematic and poetic coherence. At the most obvious level, the aristocratic Beatrice's surrender to vice is contrasted with the bourgeois Isabella's resolute adherence to her wedding vows; the conniving, lecherous Lollio emerges as a burlesque version of the false servant Deflores, while Diaphanta and Jasperino provide exemplars of less ruthless, but still self-interested modes of subordination. But the connections go far beyond such simple parallels, and the more closely one looks at the text, the more one is struck by how intimately the two dramatists must have co-operated in order to stitch together the disparate parts of their design. Thus, for example, Deflores' obscene mime with Beatrice's glove at the end of I.i – 'I know / She had rather wear my pelt tanned in a pair / Of dancing pumps than I should thrust my fingers / Into her sockets here' (ll. 224–7) – is echoed and partly glossed by the bawdy exchange between Alibius and Lollio in the following scene:

[ALIBIUS]
I would wear my ring on my own finger;
Whilst it is borrowed it is none of mine,
But his that useth it.

LOLLIO
You must keep it on still, then; if it but lie by, one or other will be thrusting into't

(I.ii.27–31)

Rowley was responsible for both these episodes, but their full resonance ultimately depends on a climactic moment in Middleton's portion of the play, where the phallic suggestiveness of fingers and rings is given a shocking new twist by the bloody 'token' that verifies the demise of Alonzo: 'I could not get the ring without the finger' (III.iii.28). Originally an engagement gift from Beatrice herself, the ring 'stuck', Deflores explains, 'As if the flesh and it were both one substance' (l. 38): standing for the unbreakable ties between a betrothed couple – to which early modern custom granted all the moral force of the wedding bond itself – the ring declares that Piracquo and Beatrice are as much 'one flesh' as any husband and wife; but it also stands – as the language of this scene repeatedly insinuates – for the new bond between the murderess and her accomplice that will be sealed by their sexual union: 'we should *stick* together . . . Nor is it fit we two, engaged so *jointly*, / Should part and live asunder . . . peace and innocency has turned you out / And made you *one with me*' (ll. 84, 88–9, 139–140).

The play's densely worked linguistic surface is full of such details: the recurrent imagery of eyesight, for example, draws attention to the way in which the characters in both plots are blinded by folly or desire, while numerous variations on the title-motif of change highlight the extraordinary transformations that seem to confound all that these deluded creatures have believed about one another. Most strikingly, perhaps, *The Changeling* repeatedly figures erotic passion as a disease of the mind, compared to whose destructive frenzies the crazy antics of Alibius' lunatics seem almost harmless. Love turns out to be the 'hidden malady' of which the apprehensive Alsmero speaks in the opening scene (I.i.24) and that breaks out in the corrupted 'ulcer' of Beatrice's infidelity (V.iii.7–9, 16); it is the sickness that taints the 'maddest blood' of Jasperino's desire for Diaphanta (I.i.138–9), that manifests itself in the 'mad qualm' that 'ails' Deflores at the mere thought of Beatrice-Joanna (II.i.27, 79), and that takes an especially perverse form in the mysterious 'infirmity' that afflicts Beatrice at the very sight of Deflores, leaving her 'trembling an hour after' (I.i.104; II.i.91). The relationship between love and madness is more than simply metaphorical, for early modern medicine tended to regard sexual passion as a literal madness. Thus Robert Burton in his *Anatomy of Melancholy* (1621) devotes one third of his compendious psychological treatise to cataloguing and describing the various kinds of insanity that constitute 'Love Melancholy': 'That lovers are mad,' avers Burton, 'I think no man will deny', and the passion that devours them is 'a disease, frenzy, madness, hell . . . It subverts kingdoms, overthrows cities, towns, families, mars and corrupts, and makes a massacre of men; thunder and lightning, wars, fires, plagues, have not done that mischief to mankind, as this burning lust, this brutish passion.'[14]

Burton's 'hell' of madness is precisely where Middleton and Rowley's characters find themselves in the final moments of the play as they contemplate the massacre wrought by the 'brutish passion' that has subverted Vermandero's domestic kingdom and overthrown his family: here Deflores gives a defiant account of his liaison with Beatrice-Joanna, triumphantly informing his rival that, even as he was consummating his wedding upon the substitute body of Diaphanta, 'I coupled with your mate / At barley-break – now we are left in hell' (V.iii.162–3). This wry acknowledgement of his own damnability, with its quibbling allusion to a popular children's game, uncannily echoes the madman's offstage cry

14 Robert Burton, 'Democritus to the Reader', in *The Anatomy of Melancholy*, intro. Holbrook Jackson, 3 vols. (London 1932), I, p. 114, III, p. 49; and cf. Francis Bacon, 'Of Love', in *Essays*, intro. Oliphant Smeaton (London 1906), p. 29.

from III.ii. 'Catch there, catch the last couple in hell' (l. 160);[15] and when Vermandero responds 'We are all there, it circumscribes us here' (l. 164), it is as if the entire company have been caught up in a bloody reprise of the madmen's game. In retrospect, the offstage cries and howls that punctuate the action of the sub-plot become the voice of repressed appetites working away beneath the veneer of courtly civility in Vermandero's citadel and demanding to 'be fed' (I.ii.192); while the violent eruption of the madmen onto the stage in III.ii, 'some as birds, others as beasts' (l. 183 s.d.) resembles a Breughelian allegory, bodying forth the animality of those hidden desires, and revealing Alibius' madhouse as the parodic double of Vermandero's castle:[16]

> [They] act their fantasies in any shapes . . .
> Sometimes they imitate the beasts and birds,
> Singing, or howling, braying, barking; all
> As their wild fancies prompt 'em.
>
> (III.ii.186, 189–91)

'CHANGED SO SOON': MAGIC AND METAMORPHOSIS

When Lollio is made to declare – with a sideways glance at the playhouse audience – 'We have but two sorts of people in the house . . . that's fools and madmen' (I.ii.42–3) he invokes a world of universal madness like that imagined in Burton's *Anatomy*: 'We accuse others of madness, of folly,' wrote Burton 'and are the veriest dizzards ourselves . . . giddy, vertiginous and lunatic within this sublunary maze . . . all the world is melancholy, or mad, dotes, and every member of it.'[17] Lunacy, Burton's reference to the 'sublunary maze' reminds us, was often attributed to the unstable influence of the moon (*luna*); and it is upon this the planet of change, responsible for the mutability of all earthly things, that Alsemero blames the catastrophe that has engulfed Vermandero's castle: 'What an opacous body had that moon / That last changed on us' (V.iii.196–7).[18] There is thus a direct connection between *The Changeling*'s treatment of

15 See Commentary, III.ii.170.
16 On this point, see also Mohammed Kowsar, 'Middleton and Rowley's *The Changeling*: the Besieged Temple', *Criticism*, 28 (1986), 145–64 (160–1).
17 *Anatomy*, I, pp. 71, 78, 120.
18 In *The Changeling* it is possible to see the twists and turns of Burton's 'sublunary maze' reflected in the winding progress of the doomed Alonzo, as Deflores leads him down through the narrow passages of the castle to the hellish secret at its heart (III.i); and they have their rhetorical counterparts in the 'labyrinth' of Beatrice's confusion after the murder (III.iii.71), in the obscene 'lower labyrinth' of Isabella's imagination (IV.iii.99), and the baffled 'amaze' of Vermandero in the final scene (V.iii.148).

madness and the preoccupations announced by its title – a connection highlighted by Rowley's schematic conclusion in which, as one character after another is identified as a changeling of sorts, Franciscus confesses himself 'changed from a little wit to be stark mad' (l. 207) – a 'transformation' mirroring that which has overcome Beatrice herself.

'Changeling', in seventeenth-century parlance, had a number of possible senses: slightingly used to designate an idiot, it could also refer to a faithless, inconstant person, or to someone illegitimately substituting for another. Each of these senses has an obvious literal relevance to the play,[19] but the word's most resonant meaning is one that is employed metaphorically: a stupid or deformed child left in place of one stolen by malevolent fairies. While *The Changeling* is a play largely free of supernatural intervention, the metamorphosis of Vermandero's adored daughter from 'beauty . . . To ugly whoredom' (V.iii.78, 197–8) resembles just such an uncanny substitution – one parallelled in the equally baffling transformation of Deflores from the incarnation of 'servant obedience' to its rebellious opposite, the 'master sin, imperious murder' (ll. 198–9).

For Middleton and Rowley's audience (as for most playgoers today) the most familiar example of such a changeling will have been the mortal child who so infatuates the fairy queen, Titania, and provokes the jealousy of her husband, Oberon, in *A Midsummer Night's Dream*; and in choosing a title for their play, the dramatists must surely have had in mind the 'little changeling boy' (*MSND*, II.i.120) who serves as an emblematic figure for the dizzying sequence of physical and psychological transformations that make up Shakespeare's plot. Not only does Franciscus greet Isabella as 'bright Titania' and refer to Alibius as 'Oberon' (III.ii.47–9), but Isabella's invocation of 'the waxing moon' under whose influence love 'turn[s] fool, run[s] mad, and all at once' (IV.iii.1–2), recalls the repeated references to the moon's maddening influence upon Shakespeare's mortal fools; and Alsemero's meditation on the malign power of the 'opacous moon', as he stands over the corpses of Beatrice and Deflores, rewrites the ending of the mechanicals' play – where Moonshine presides over the deaths of Piramus and Thisby – turning travesty back to tragedy.

The recollections of *A Midsummer Night's Dream* extend further than this, however, for the main plot of *The Changeling* can be read as a grotesque riff on the theme announced by Helena at the end of Shakespeare's opening scene – 'Things base and vile, holding no quantity, /

19 See note on p. liv.

Love can transpose to form and dignity' (*MSND*, I.i.233–4): 'hunger and pleasure,' as Deflores' sardonic paraphrase expresses it, will 'commend sometimes / Slovenly dishes' (II.ii.150–1). Just as the ass-headed 'monster', Bottom, is transformed by Oberon's magic into Titania's 'gentle joy' (*MSND*, II.ii.6, IV.i.4), so Deflores' loving 'service' renders this hideous 'basilisk' miraculously 'beauteous' to Beatrice (I.i.110; II.ii.135; V.i.72); and just as Helena and Hermia are 'transfigured' by the same love-juice that works its change on Bottom, so in *The Changeling*'s other plot, Antonio pretends to be transformed by the 'magic' of Isabella's 'powerful beauties' (III.ii.117–18, 179–81).[20] In the last analysis, of course, Shakespeare's fairy love-juice is no more than an allegory for the delusive effects of desire, yet *A Midsummer Night's Dream* preserves a place for magic, if only as an effect of the transformative power of poetry. In the materialist world of *The Changeling*, by contrast, the notion of change and metamorphosis is subjected to a ruthless scrutiny that exposes it as a self-justifying coinage of the characters' fatal delusions.

'CONSPICUOUS TO OUTWARD VIEW': THE CASTELLATED BODY AND THE SECRET SELF

The Changeling is obsessed by the disjunction between what is hidden and what is seen: the offstage howling of Alibius' madmen functions as a dramatic metaphor for the invisible threat of what lies 'within'; and the same theme is reflected in recurrent images of eyesight and blindness. Middleton and Rowley's characters frequently congratulate themselves on the special insight given them by love: 'Love,' declares the disguised Antonio, 'has an intellect that runs through all / The scrutinous sciences . . . Into one mystery . . . one secret that he proceeds in' (III.ii.120–5). Beatrice professes to love Alsemero with the 'eyes of judgement' (II.i.13, 19), just as he himself insists that his infatuation with Beatrice's outward appearance is warranted by his penetrating 'judgement' (I.i.73–5); yet later we will see this professed 'master of the mystery' (IV.i.38) calling on Antonio's 'scrutinous sciences' in an absurd effort to expose the 'secret' of her real nature.

In the early scenes it is, ironically enough, Beatrice who warns of the difference between the 'mistaken' perception that drew her to Piracquo (I.i.80), and her clear vision of Alsemero

> Our eyes are sentinels unto our judgements,
> And should give certain judgement what they see;

20 Further parallels with *A Midsummer Night's Dream* are noted by McAlindon (pp. 196–8).

> But they are rash sometimes, and tell us wonders
> Of common things, which when our judgements find,
> They can then check the eyes, and call them blind.
>
> (I.i.68–72)

In the allegorical tradition, however, while the eyes might be watchmen to the soul, they were more likely to be figured as its windows – dangerous apertures that could betray it to the enemy: thus for Samuel Purchas the eye is 'a window for Hell, a loop-hole for Lust to shoot at, a look-hole for the Devil to shoot in himself and his fiery darts' (cf. Fig. 1).[21] As for Beatrice's 'intellectual eyesight' (II.i.19), its true nature is indicated by Lollio's obscene gibe to the love-blind Franciscus: 'a woman, they say, has an eye more than a man' (III.ii.73–4). Unable to recognise the promptings of this third eye for what they are, Beatrice-Joanna, like Alsemero himself, is in thrall to a dilute platonism that persuades her of the perfect correspondence of outward appearance and inward truth. There is thus a telling symmetry between the desire inspired in her by the handsome Alsemero, and the disgust with which she responds to Deflores' ugliness – an ugliness which, she persuades herself, suits him rather than Alsemero to the act of murder: 'Blood-guiltiness becomes a fouler visage, / And now I think on one . . . The ugliest creature / Creation framed for some use' (II.ii.40–44). Until she finds a use for him, it is as though Deflores exists for the Beatrice only as an affront to her eyesight, a thing she might readily eliminate from view simply by exploiting her father's 'next good mood' to have him 'quite discarded' (II.i.59, 73, 92–3); and it is Deflores' recognition of this ocular solipsism that inspires the brilliantly directed euphemism of his promise to murder Alonzo: 'He shall be *seen* no more' (II.ii.135).

The spoilt petulance of Beatrice's behaviour is marvellously realised; but there is also something about the visceral intensity of her response to Deflores – epitomised in her identification of him with the basilisk, a creature whose mere look could kill (I.i.109–10) – that suggests a more significant resemblance between her loathing and the equally compulsive emotion that forces her subordinate 'some twenty times a day' to 'frame ways and excuses / To come into her *sight*' (II.i.27–31), courting her abuse only because he 'must *see* her' (II.i.77–8; II.ii.65–6). Accordingly modern criticism has tended to discover in Beatrice's obsessiveness the sign of 'unconscious sexual interest in Deflores'.[22] In a probing feminist

21 Samuel Purchas, *Microcosmus; or the Historie of Man* (1619), p. 231.
22 Daalder, p. xxvi.

Figure 1. Death entering the windows of the soul; engraving by Theodore Galle from a chapter devoted to the temptations of eyesight in Jean David, *Veridicus Christianus* (Antwerp 1601). Courtesy of the Folger Shakespeare Library.

account of the play's recent performance history, such approaches have been severely criticised by Roberta Barker and David Nicol as amounting to an a-historical 'post-Freudian appropriation of an early modern text'.[23] These critics insist that Middleton and Rowley present Beatrice as a rape-victim who 'never . . . takes any pleasure in her brutalisation', and argue that the true irony of the play is that, far from Beatrice's being ignorant of her own will, 'by pursuing it too vehemently, she loses it'; for them *The Changeling* is a straightforward fable of 'a sinner who strays from the path of righteousness and . . . is appropriately punished when her appointed scourge takes from her precisely [what] she so wanted to save for the lover of her choice.'[24] But the play's rhetorical stress upon the 'secrets' and 'mysteries' resists such simple moralising – even if Beatrice's acknowledgement of Deflores as the embodiment of a mysterious fatality and of her former loathing as 'prophet' to all that followed (V.iii.154–7) is as close as she comes to an explicit recognition of unconscious motives.

In fact Middleton and Rowley's contemporaries had their own ways of describing the obscure promptings of the hidden self; and John Stachniewski has shown how seventeenth-century Calvinism, in particular, encouraged an interest 'in the logic of an inner, unknown self', resulting in 'a conception of character as strung between conscious purposes and unconscious identity.'[25] A person's buried thoughts and desires, according to Levin Lemmins in *The Touchstone of Complexions* (1581) are to be discovered in the 'most secret corners and innermost places . . . conveyed by many crooked by-ways and windings';[26] and it is in such privy corners, according to the poet and divine, John Donne, that the devil 'works upon us in secret . . . to make us so like himself as to sin in secret that others may not see us; but *his masterpiece is to make us sin in secret so as we may not see ourselves sin*.'[27] The repressed appetites that, in Deflores' hyperbolical obscenity, promise to make Beatrice 'sutler to an army royal' (II.ii.64), belong to this mode of sinning – a vice so privately closeted that even the sinner cannot recognise it. Thus, as Stachniewski argues, not only does Beatrice's 'reprobate character, though unperceived, inhere . . .

23 Roberta Barker and David Nicol, 'Does Beatrice Joanna Have a Subtext?: *The Changeling* on the London Stage', *Early Modern Literary* Studies 10.1 (May 2004), 3.1–113(3).

24 Ibid, 43.

25 John Stachniewski, 'Calvinist Psychology in Middleton's Tragedies', in Roger Holdsworth (ed.), *Three Jacobean Revenge Tragedies: A Casebook* (Basingstoke 1990), 226–47 (228).

26 Cited in Anne Ferry, *The 'Inward' Language: Sonnets of Wyatt, Sidney, Donne and Shakespeare* (Chicago 1983), p. 59.

27 John Donne, *Devotions Upon Emergent Occasions*, 1624 (Ann Arbor 1959), p. 65.

in her from the very start,' but 'discovery of the hidden logic of character [turns out to be] the unifying purpose linking the play's disparate episodes and propelling its action.'[28]

We are first alerted to this scheme by Alsemero's half-serious reference to some 'hidden malady' within him that lies beyond the reach of his comprehension (I.i.24–5); but it is even more conspicuously signposted by Vermandero's description of the castle that Alsemero so desires to enter:

> We use not to give survey
> Of our chief strengths to strangers; our citadels
> Are placed conspicuous to outward view
> On promonts' tops, but *within are secrets.*
>
> (I.i.156–9)

Vermandero is speaking in military terms, but the larger resonances of the passage depend on the tradition of figuring the human body as the fortress of the soul, subject to the assaults of sickness, sin, and death.[29] Inherited from medieval allegory, the device is perhaps best known from the Castle of Alma episode in Spenser's *Faerie Queen* (Book II, Canto ix), but allegory of this sort is common to a whole range of early modern texts from medical manuals to sermons and popular tracts. Significantly for *The Changeling*, it was often given a gendered inflection as a figure for female chastity: in the misogynistic tract *Hic Mulier* (1615), for example, women, 'armed with the infinite power of virtue, are castles impregnable'. In order to avoid 'immodest discoveries', however, it is necessary to keep 'every window closed with a strong casement, and every loophole furnished with such strong ordnance that no unchaste eye may come to assail them; no lascivious tongue woo a forbidden passage' (sig. A3v-B4); after all, as Bacon warned, 'love can find entrance not only into an open heart, but to a heart well fortified, if watch be not kept.'[30]

The Changeling exploits this tradition to establish an imaginative equivalence between the two repositories of Vermandero's honour and patriarchal authority – his castle and the person of his daughter.

28 Ibid, 228–9.

29 For varying accounts of the play's use of architectural allegory, see Thomas L. Berger, 'The Petrarchan Fortress of *The Changeling*', *Renaissance Papers* (1969), 37–46; Anne Lancashire, 'The Emblematic Castle in Shakespeare and Middleton', in J. C. Gray (ed.), *Mirror up to Shakespeare: Essays in Honour of G. R. Hibbard* (Toronto 1984), pp. 223–41; Kowsar, 'The Besieged Temple'; and Neill, *Issues of Death*, pp. 175–80.

30 Bacon, 'Of Love', p. 29.

Capitalising on the enclosed intimacy of the Cockpit theatre, Middleton and Rowley evoke the interior spaces of the citadel with unusual fullness, equipping it with a gatehouse, postern, sconces, stores of munition, corridors, closet, bedchambers, chimneys, and locked doors, as well as a spacious park, a small-pleasure garden, and an adjacent church; but this naturalistic detail proves to be charged with rich metaphoric suggestiveness.

In broad terms it is possible to trace an imaginative movement beginning at the temple-church where Beatrice and Alsemero first meet, on through the castle gateway into the labyrinthine passageways where Alonzo meets his end, continuing into the secret regions of Alsemero's privy closet and Beatrice's bedchamber, and ending in the 'common sewer' of Beatrice's self-excoriating apology to Vermandero. This is a movement that corresponds to the allegorical journey described in Samuel Purchas' physiological treatise *Microcosmus* which, beginning at the eyes, moves through the seat of reason and 'judgement', and descends through the intestines (where 'all wheyish and liquid superfluities' are sluiced away 'to the *grates*, that is the *kidneys*') into the typically female domain of animality, passion and sin, the 'chamber of generation [where] there is nothing to be seen but secrets', to end in 'the privy lodging, betwixt and among variety of excrements' where humankind are conceived – the place where 'the *ureters*, as two *common sewers*, convey the [body's wastes] to the *sink*, or greater vault the *bladder*, thence to be exonerated (as by sweat and menstrous purgations . . .) from the body's community'.[31]

For Vermandero, his castle's strength is dependent less on its imposing exterior than on the military secrets concealed within, much as his daughter's value depends less on her outward beauty than on her invisible virtue – the virginity which the bawdy Lollio will characterise as a woman's 'secret' (I.ii.8). Ironically, however, the real secrets behind these 'conspicuous' facades prove to be a source of weakness rather than strength, as Vermandero implicitly confesses when confronted by his dying child: 'An host of enemies entered my citadel / Could not amaze like this' (V.iii.147–8). No surprise assault was needed; for the enemy, it turns out, has always been within. On the literal level, this is the revelation brutally acted out when Deflores fulfils his promise to show Alonzo

31 Purchas, *Microcosmus*, pp. 34, 44, 177–8, 42–3. Noting the play's use of the medieval castle/body allegory, Nicholas Brooke writes that 'the peculiar imaginative power of De Flores' leading Alonso through the dark passages [depends on the suggestion that] it is also a journey through the organs of the female body to an anal death, *and* a descent into hell' (*Horrid Laughter*, p. 85).

'the full strength of all the castle': as his unsuspecting victim 'spend[s] his eye' upon its defensive ordnance, Deflores performs his 'work of secrecy' and stabs him from behind (III.i.17–18, 27). More than one kind of secrecy is involved here: carried out in secret, the murder is also designed to block Alonzo's access to a very different secret – one identical to the 'knowledge . . . dearer, / Deeper and sweeter' (I.ii.1–13) that Alibius vainly seeks to lock away in the 'cage' or 'pinfold' of his wife's domestic prison (III.ii.2–8). This is the privy knowledge that Deflores will claim for himself, and that the self-deluding 'master of the mystery', Alsemero, will seek to unlock with the aid of a manual suitably entitled '*Secrets in Nature*' (IV.i.25, 38; ii.111; Fig. 2). Ironically, however, Beatrice's secret viciousness will be exposed not by any 'pretty secret' of Alsemero's closet, but by the fatal indiscretion of Diaphanta – a woman he identified as a repository of secrets – one of those 'ladies' cabinets [into which] / Things of most precious trust are lock[ed]' (II.ii.6–7) – but who proves so unsecret that she 'cannot rule her own blood to keep her promise' (V.i.6–7).

The language of the final scene is especially striking for the way in which it relates the motif of secrets and discovery to the great unifying symbol of the play, the castle. Stung by Alsemero's denunciation of her as a whore, Beatrice accuses her husband of having 'ruined / What you can ne'er repair again' (V.iii.35–6); his riposte picks up and elaborates her subdued architectural metaphor, figuring her body as a castle to be pillaged and slighted

> I'll all demolish and seek out truth within you,
> If there be any left. Let your sweet tongue
> Prevent your heart's rifling – there I'll ransack
> And tear out my suspicion.
>
> (V.iii.37–40)

'You may, sir – 'tis an easy passage' she responds, recalling the narrow 'passages' through which Deflores led Alonzo to his secret death, and looking forward to the final purge of the castle's hidden corruption announced in her death-speech

> O come not near me, sir, I shall defile you:
> I am that of your blood was taken from you
> For your better health; look no more upon't,
> But cast it to the ground regardlessly,
> Let the common sewer take it from distinction.
>
> (V.iii.149–53)

Figure 2. Beatrice (Mary Ure) pores over Alsemero's book of *Secrets in Nature*, Royal Court, 1961. Photograph by Sandra Lousada.

Here is disclosed the final secret of the castle/body – the death which John Donne imagined as a grotesque evacuation through the 'sordid *postern*, by which I must be thrown out of this world.'[32]

32 *The Sermons of John Donne*, ed. Evelyn M. Simpson and George R. Potter, 10 vols. (Berkeley 1954), vii, 14, p. 359.

MASTERS AND SERVANTS

Deflores' privileged access to the castle's secrets is symbolised by the bunch of keys he carries at his belt. Among the play's more conspicuous properties, they are visually and imaginatively linked to the key that opens up the secrets of Alsemero's closet – and which is subsequently used to lock away Deflores and Beatrice in that same space (IV.i.18; IV.ii.111; V.iii.87, 114) – as well as to the wardrobe key that Isabella will use in her plan to penetrate the 'labyrinth' of her wooers' pretences (IV.iii.45). On the literal level, Deflores' keys are the badge of his servantly office, but they become the sign of a mastery so absolute that, in a neat metatheatrical joke, it even enables him to hide a naked rapier in the conventionally inaccessible space/time between the acts.[33] The keys represent not merely his physical management of the castle's interior spaces, however, but the growing psychological and sexual control that reveals him as him the true 'master of the mystery', including the forbidden zone of sexuality and death where 'servant obedience' metamorphoses into the 'master sin, imperious murder.'

As we have seen, the transformation of Beatrice's lover from a 'Gallant young Gentleman, of the Garrison of the Castle' into an ill-favoured and detested manservant was the dramatists' most prominent alteration to their source material; and this degradation appears even more significant because of the paradoxical way in which it was combined with the elevation of Reynolds' mere accessory to become joint protagonist of the tragedy. Conscious of being 'out of his place' in more than the dismissive sense employed by Alsemero (I.i.131), and consumed by acrimony at the 'hard fate [that] thrust [him] out to servitude' (II.i.48), Middleton and Rowley's Deflores joins the ranks of treacherous servants who abound in the drama of the time – creatures whose egotistical resentment at the 'obsequious bondage' that constitutes 'the curse of service' (*Othello*, I.i.45, 34) renders them by turns conniving, deceitful, subversive, or openly rebellious.

There were, of course, good material reasons why such figures should have exercised so compelling a grip upon the early modern imagination.[34]

33 See Commentary, III.i.0 s.d.

34 See e.g. Mark Thornton Burnett, *Masters and Servants in English Renaissance Drama and Culture* (Basingstoke 1997); David Evett, *Discourses of Service in Shakespeare's England* (Basingstoke 2005); Judith Weil, *Service and Dependency in Shakespeare's Plays* (Cambridge 2005); Linda Anderson, *A Place in the Story: Servants and Service in Shakespeare's Plays* (Newark, Del. 2005); Michael Neill (ed.) 'Shakespeare and the Bonds of Service', special section in Graham Bradshaw and Tom Bishop (eds.) *Shakespearean International Yearbook* 5 (Aldershot, Hants. 2005).

The feudal idea of master-servant relationships continued to provide the paradigm for virtually all structures of authority in the period, so that even the most powerful noblemen owed service to a royal 'master', who was himself imagined as the servant of God. At the same time, however, the structures of mutual obligation on which this ideal rested were widely perceived to be in decay; and the resulting tensions are apparent not merely in imaginative literature, but in the numerous tracts and manuals that address the conduct of household government. These latter chart a widening disparity between loftier forms of service and the role performed by domestic servants, which was increasingly seen as degrading drudgery, governed not by traditional love and fidelity but by the base demands of contract and wages. From the perspective of commentators like 'I.M.', the corrupting effect of substituting mere pecuniary obligation for the supposedly 'undissoluable bond of assured friendship' between masters and servants was to render what he called '*the Gentlemanly profession of Servingmen*' no longer suitable to a gentleman's ambition, since it threatened to reduce him to 'the degree of a servile drudge'.[35]

The false servants of the drama are nightmare embodiments of such anxieties, figurations of the fear that, once the bonds of heaven are slipped, society's greatest enemies may appear not from without, but from deep within the social order – from the bosom of the family itself. Because their rebellion mimics that of Lucifer, who thought it 'Better to reign in hell, than serve in heaven' (*Paradise Lost*, i.263), they are often demonic figures, like Mephistophilis, in Marlowe's *Dr Faustus*, the diabolic servant whose sole desire is to encompass his master's destruction. As the archetype of false service, Mephistophilis became the progenitor of a whole line of treacherous subordinates – among them Iago, Edmund, Malvolio, and Caliban, as well as Bosola in Webster's *Duchess of Malfi*, Mosca in Jonson's *Volpone*, the diabolically named D'Avolos is Ford's *Love's Sacrifice*, and (not least) Deflores himself.[36] Because of his psychological complexity, Deflores is among the most compellingly depicted of these figures: eaten up by the same social resentment that gnaws at Iago, he is seen as the 'serpent' of a new Temptation (II.i.218, V.iii.67), responsible for the loss of that 'blest' Garden of 'man's first creation' to which Alsemero naively dreamed that love would return him (I.i.6–12); yet, by virtue of his tortured infatuation with Beatrice, he is

35 'I.M.', *A Health to the Gentlemanly profession of Servingmen: or, the Servingman's Comfort* (1598) in *Inedited Tracts* (London 1868), pp. 114–15, 134.

36 Helen Gardner makes the connection between *The Changeling* and *Dr Faustus* in 'The Tragedy of Damnation' – see R. J. Kaufmann (ed.), *Elizabethan Drama; Modern Essays in Criticism* (New York 1961), pp. 320–41.

Figure 3. Bob Hoskins as Deflores, BBC Television 1993.

able to attract something of the dark pathos that Webster discovers in Bosola.[37] Having 'tumbled into th' world a gentleman' (II.i.49), he is now humiliatingly consigned to the performance of a lackey's trivial 'errands' (II.i.30, 59): his master can order him to retrieve a fallen glove – only to expose him to the gall of his mistress's disdain for this display of 'officious forwardness' (I.i.219–20). The tormenting irony of Deflores' situation is that his desire for Beatrice is exactly proportionate to her power to humble him: this, surely, is what underlies his ironic description of the glove she throws at him as 'a favour come – with a mischief' (I.i.224). His sickness lies not simply in his need to see her, but in his desperation 'to come into [the] sight' of 'her blessed eye' (II.i.31, 50) – to expose himself to the very gaze that has taught him to scan ugliness in such self-lacerating detail:

37 For further analyses of the motif of service in *The Changeling*, see Mark Thornton Burnett, '*The Changeling* and Masters and Servants', in Garrett A. Sullivan, Patrick Cheney, and Andrew Hadfield (eds.), *Early Modern English Drama: A Critical Companion* (New York 2006), pp. 298–308; Swapan Chakravorty, *Society and Politics in the Plays of Thomas Middleton* (Oxford 1996), Chap 7 'Servants and Masters: *The Changeling*', pp. 145–65; Neill ' "Servant Obedience and Master Sins": Shakespeare and the Bonds of Service', in *Putting History to the Question: Power, Politics and Society in English Renaissance Drama* (New York 2000), pp. 13–48, and ' "A woman's service": Gender, Subordination, and the Erotics of Rank in the Drama of Shakespeare and his Contemporaries', *Shakespearean International Yearbook*, 2005, 127–144; and Leo Salingar, '*The Changeling* and the Drama of Domestic Life', *Essays and Studies* 33 (1979), 92–3.

she baits me still
Every time worse than other, does profess herself
The cruellest enemy to my face in town,
At no hand can abide the sight of me . . .
I must confess my face is bad enough,
But I know far worse has had better fortune . . .
And yet such pick-hatched faces, chins like witches,
Here and there five hairs, whispering in a corner
As if they grew in fear one of another,
Wrinkles like troughs, where swine-deformity swills
The tears of perjury that lie there like wash
Fallen from the slimy and dishonest eye.

(II.i.32–45)

In the case of Deflores, social resentment and ambition on the one hand, and sexual desire on the other, do not constitute discrete motives (as moderns might easily suppose), but are simply different aspects of the same nexus of emotions – a point beautifully underlined in the servant's ecstatic physical response when his mistress condescends to inspect his 'scurvy' complexion – 'Her fingers touched me – / She smells all amber!' (II.ii.81–2) – where the sexual arousal produced by Beatrice's perfume is inseparable from his ability to sniff out its costly ingredients. Yet, of course, this decayed gentleman would never wish to construe his relationship to a mistress in crassly material terms, and one advantage of the abject position in which he is placed by her disdain is that it enables Deflores to reinvent his drudgery as a mode of courtship. The rhetoric of courtly love which the Renaissance inherited from the medieval chivalric code, imagined love as a kind of sublime 'service' offered by a knight to his lady; and the paradigm of such relationships was one in which the wooer abased himself before a woman of higher rank – typically the chatelaine of his lord's castle. When Deflores reacts to Beatrice's tongue-lashing in II.i with the reminder that 'True service merits mercy' (II.i.63), he makes adroit use of the knightly servitor's plea to his conventionally cruel mistress, implicitly transforming his despised 'errand' (ll. 59, 74) into a piece of chivalric errantry for which amatory reward is due. Ironically the expected earnest of a lady's 'mercy' would have been precisely such a 'favour' as Deflores pretends to have received from Beatrice at the end of the opening scene – the glove or sleeve that a knight could wear on his helm as proof of his lady's acceptance.

The connection that this would-be suitor forges between the two forms of service has its effect on Beatrice's own language; for, in the following scene, having dismissed Alsemero's offer to challenge Alonzo to a duel by way of gallant 'service' (II.ii.21, 26), she proceeds to 'serve [her] turn' (l. 68) upon Deflores by herself equivocating on the two meanings of 'service', luring him into a murderous undertaking that he in turn chooses to accept as though it were some quest of pure chivalry:[38]

BEATRICE

Hardness becomes the visage of a man well,
It argues *service*, resolution, manhood,
If cause were of *employment* . . .

[DEFLORES]

I would but wish the *honour of a service*
So happy as that *mounts* to . . .
It's a *service* that I kneel for to you.

(II.ii.92–117)

The final irony of this exchange lies in the way that Beatrice's complicity in equivocation draws Deflores so deeply into his own courtly charade that he begins to take it as reality: for when he returns to announce the fulfilment of the 'service' that he 'sued and kneel'd for' (III.iii.23, 54, 110), he appears genuinely outraged at her offer of mere financial recompense, responding with the indignation appropriate to a deliberate violation of social decorum:

What, *salary*? Now you move me . . .
Do you place me in the *rank* of *verminous fellows*,
To destroy things for *wages*? Offer *gold*? . . .
I could ha' *hir'd*
A *journeyman* in murder at this rate,
And mine own conscience might have slept at ease,
And have had the work brought home.

(III.iii. 63–71)

'Salary', 'wages', 'hire': to soil oneself with such considerations is to be reduced from the stately rank of a gentleman to the rank state of a menial, some louse-ridden peasant, or mercenary tradesman. If she chooses to disparage him in this fashion – instead of raising him to her

38 For further discussion of Deflores' systematic confusion of chivalric and domestic service, see Swapan Chakravorty, *Society and Politics in the Plays of Thomas Middleton* (Oxford 1996), pp. 147–52.

level with the reward that courtly convention dictates – then he will debase her in the act of revolutionary levelling that becomes the ground of his sexual conquest:

Look but into your conscience, read me there –
'Tis a true book, you'll find me there your equal.
Push! fly not to your birth, but settle you
In what the act has made you, you're no more now –
You must forget your parentage to me.

(III.iii.132–6)

Playing on Beatrice's appeal to 'the distance that *creation* / Set 'twixt thy blood and mine' (ll. 130–1) he disparages her with a contemptuous term for the most servile kind of lackey ('You're the deed's *creature*', l. 137), consigning her to a moral enslavement that matches his own social abjection:

by that name
You lost your first condition; and I challenge you,
As peace and innocency has turn'd you out;
And made you one with me.

(III.iii.137–40)

Like husband and wife they have become 'one flesh', joined – as we are reminded by the play's recurrent punning on the 'blood' that once stood for noble birth, but that now represents only the imperatives of desire and the brute fact of murder – by the very thing that once divided them; 'Justice invites your *blood* to understand me' (l. 100). Confronting his accusers in the final scene, Deflores makes it clear that his conquest of Beatrice-Joanna is the delicious extreme of a servingman's revenge: where his mistress once rebuked him for seeking to make Alonzo's death 'the murderer of my honour' (III.iii.122), he now proclaims possession of a 'reward' that consists less in the enjoyment of her body, than in his capture of 'her *honour*'s prize' – his triumphant assault on the very attribute of rank that set her so humiliatingly above him. Standing possessed of this deeply sexualised object of the hatred and desire that made him 'as greedy . . . As the parched earth of moisture' (III.iii.107–8), Deflores exults in a usurpation so absolute that it amounts to an act of revolutionary annihilation:

I thank life for nothing
But that pleasure; it was so sweet to me

That I have drunk up all, left none behind
For any man to pledge me.

(V.iii.168–71)

Performance History

The Changeling was licensed by Sir Henry Herbert, Master of the Revels, on 7 May 1622 for performance by the Lady Elizabeth's Men at the Phoenix, an indoor playhouse belonging to Christopher Beeston and situated in Drury Lane, close to the most fashionable part of London. Although surviving records are sparse, it seems to have enjoyed immediate and continuing success, being chosen for a court performance on 4 January 1623/4, and remaining in the Phoenix repertory until 1636, when Beeston thought it valuable enough to appeal to the Lord Chamberlain after a breakaway company took it to the Salisbury Court. Following Beeston's death in 1638, his son William was careful to have his own rights to the play confirmed by the Chamberlain's office, and it stayed in his possession until the outbreak of civil war closed the theatres in 1642. After the Restoration, *The Changeling* was among the first plays to be revived at the re-opened Salisbury Court, where Pepys saw the Duke of York's Company perform it on 23 February, 1660/1, reporting that 'it takes exceedingly'.[39] His claim is borne out by the fact that it was again staged at Court on 30 November 1668. Evidently it continued in the company's repertory well after their move to their new scenic theatre in Lincoln's Inn Fields in 1661. By the 1670s, however, the tragedy must have begun to seem old-fashioned; and in the high Restoration theatre, with its self-consciously neo-classical aesthetic, it descended into the oblivion shared by most pre-war plays: apart from an adaptation by William Hayley, entitled *Marcella*, which had three performances in November 1789, there are no records of any further revivals before the mid-twentieth century.

Oddly enough, much of the play's early reputation seems to have depended on what is sometimes dismissed as an inferior sub-plot. Seventeenth-century allusions typically single out 'the changeling', Antonio, as the centre of dramatic interest;[40] and a series of comic actors, including William Robbins and Timothy Reade, achieved fame in the role. Even after the Restoration, John Downes placed Thomas Sheppey's Antonio

39 Cited from Sara Jayne Steen, *Ambrosia in an Earthen Vessel: Three Centuries of Audience and Reader Response to the Works of Thomas Middleton* (NY: AMS, 1993), p. 61.
40 These allusions are discussed in detail by Bawcutt (1958), pp. xxvi–viii.

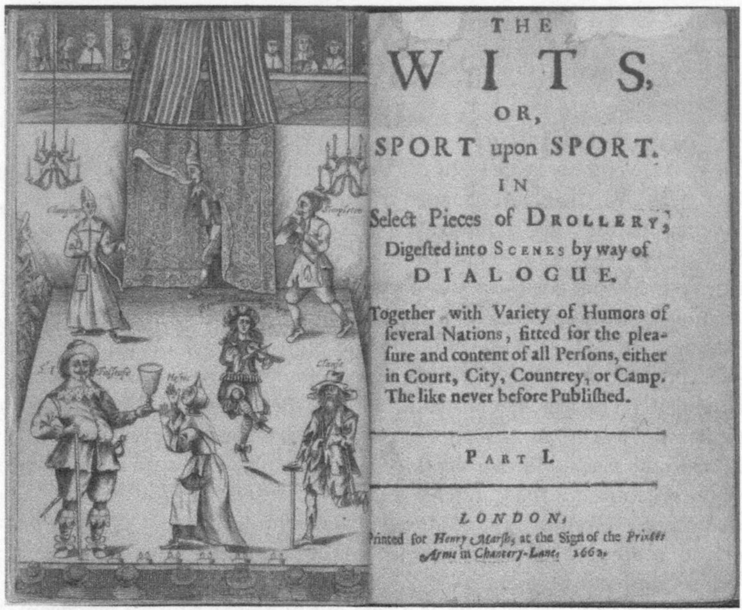

THE
WITS,
OR,
SPORT upon SPORT.
IN
Select Pieces of DROLLERY,
Digested into SCENES by way of
DIALOGUE.
Together with Variety of Humors of
several Nations, fitted for the plea-
sure and content of all Persons, either
in Court, City, Countrey, or Camp.
The like never before Published.

PART I.

LONDON,
Printed for Henry Marsh, at the Sign of the Princes
Arms in Chancery-Lane, 1662.

Figure 4. Frontispiece to Francis Kirkman, *The Wits* (1672). Courtesy of the Folger Shakespeare Library.

on a par with the great Betterton's early triumph as Deflores.[41] Only the great popularity of the part can account for the inclusion of 'The Changeling' among the gallery of characters displayed in the frontispiece of Francis Kirkman's *The Wits* (1672) – even though no such personage actually appears in this collection of 'drolls' (Fig. 4). In the twentieth century, by contrast, the revival of critical interest fostered by T. S. Eliot, William Empson, Una Ellis-Fermor and others decisively shifted the focus of attention away from the comic world of Antonio to the tragic story of Beatrice-Joanna and Deflores. However, just as more recent criticism has tended to emphasise the coherence of the whole design, so the most successful stage versions have invariably been those that have sought to realise the close integration of the sub-plot, without which the tragic action can feel crowded and improbably hasty.

The lead here was given by Tony Richardson's landmark production for the English Stage Company at the Royal Court in 1961. Although this

41 See Bawcutt (1958), pp. xxvii–viii.

was promoted as the first revival since Pepys, there had in fact been scattered amateur productions in London (1950, 1954) and Oxford (1956), as well as radio versions in 1950 and 1960. But it was the Royal Court that successfully advertised *The Changeling*'s claims to a permanent place in the classical repertoire. Richardson admired the play for the modernity he recognised in the 'almost Strindbergian love-hate relationship' between Beatrice and Deflores, in its 'existentialist' approach to individual responsibility, and in the boldness of its generic mixtures;[42] and, although some reviewers were disconcerted by his emphasis on 'abrupt switches from farce to thriller, and from thriller to tragedy,'[43] others were surprised to discover a tragedy that resembled *Macbeth* in its unblinking analysis of characters who become trapped in the consequences of their own crimes.[44]

The success of the Royal Court's initiative helped to ensure a steady trickle of revivals over the next fifteen years, including productions by the Oxford Stage Company (Jeanette Cochrane Theatre, 1966), the Birmingham Repertory Theatre (1973), and the Glasgow Citizens' Theatre (1976), as well as television adaptations by Granada (4 January 1965), and the BBC (20 January 1974), while across the Atlantic it began its American stage life with a production by Elia Kazan for the Lincoln Center Repertory Company in 1964. *The Changeling*'s popularity reached a new peak between September 1978 and June 1979, when there were no fewer than six professional productions on the British stage, with notable versions by Peter Gill at the Riverside Studios and Terry Hands at the Royal Shakespeare Company's Aldwych Theatre.

Like Richardson, both Gill and Hands stressed the close thematic relationship between the two plots. Hands, in particular, made their juxtaposition seem less discordant by emphasising the savage verbal wit and

42 Interview in *Plays and Players* (April 1961), cited in Michael Scott, *The Changeling*, Penguin Critical Studies (London 1989), p. 56.

43 Ibid.

44 See e.g. Philip Hope-Wallace, *Manchester Guardian*, 23 Feb 1961; Anon, *Times* 22 Feb 1961. Resemblances to *Macbeth* (which Middleton is now thought to have revised at some point before its appearance in the 1623 Folio) were also noticed by reviewers of Michael Attenborough's Royal Shakespeare Company production 1993: *The Times'* Benedict Nightingale (27 May 1993) saw *The Changeling* as 'an Iberian Macbeth', while in the *Daily Mail* (6 May 1993), Jack Tinker identified Beatrice as 'The closest blood relation . . . to Lady Macbeth in all literature. . . . Like her more infamous Scottish counterpart, this Spanish beauty also becomes "the deed's creature".' Both reviewers may have been influenced by Helen Gardner's, 'The Tragedy of Damnation' (see esp. pp. 328–31).

elements of black comedy in the main plot – though some reviewers were troubled by a 'note of exultant farce' that seemed to compromise the tragic catastrophe.[45] Both directors made imaginative use of the madhouse scenes: Gill's capering madmen 'congregate[d] beneath the audience, howling and banging instruments before spilling out on to the stage' where their postures echoed the Dance of Death murals of Elizabeth Da Costa's set;[46] between scenes they were used to move furniture and props 'as if to evoke the way insanity suddenly invades the main plot.'[47] Hands' lunatics remained on stage throughout the final movement of the play, providing a silent commentary on the madness consuming Alsemero's household, while lighting that fell in parallel bars across the stage suggested that castle and madhouse alike were simply different kinds of prison.[48] In each case, parallels in characterisation and plot were underlined by the staging: at the Riverside, Beatrice and Isabella were made to 'pass each other in opposite directions like two mirror images, each invisible to the other'; at the Aldwych, Lollio spied on Antonio's wooing of Isabella in III.ii from the same concealed position that Deflores had used to observe Alsemero's wooing of Beatrice in II.ii.[49] Both productions implied 'that uncontrolled sexuality is madness', but Hands' relatively restrained treatment of Isabella's wooing scenes seemed to indicate 'that the mad are more controlled in their desires than the sane.'[50]

Such was the interest generated by these productions that the following decade alone witnessed a further twenty-six professional revivals.[51] Television adaptations were mounted by the BBC in 1974 and 1993, and by the 1990s *The Changeling*'s reputation was sufficiently established to generate a series of experimental re-visionings evidently intended to

45 Milton Shulman, *Evening Standard*, 17 Oct 1978; Robert Cushman, *Observer*, 22 Oct 1978; Wardle, *op. cit.*; Michael Billington, *Guardian*, 6 Sept 1978; and cf. Bernard Levin, *Sunday Times*, 22 Oct 1978; Sheridan Morley, *Punch*, 25 Oct 1978.

46 Scott, p. 59.

47 Billington, *op.cit.*

48 Cushman, *Observer*, 22 Oct 1978; Irving Wardle, *Times*, 17 Oct 1978; Billington, *Guardian*, 17 Oct 1978.

49 Wardle, *op. cit.*

50 John Elsom, *Listener*, 26 Oct 1978. Richard Eyre's 1988 National Theatre production similarly used the parallels between the plots to convey 'a powerful impression that the structured insanities inherent in the social order are more dangerous and less containable than the disorders of the mind which cause individual sufferers to be condemned to exclusion from the world' (Janet Clare, *Renaissance Drama Newsletter*, Autumn 1988 – cited in Scott, p. 62).

51 Scott, p. 58.

Figure 5. Set for the 1988 National Theatre Production. Photograph by Jock McDougall.

breathe new life into an all-too-familiar classic.[52] Many of these productions, including the television versions, dispensed with the sub-plot; but the best work generally followed the pattern set by Richardson, Gill,

52 These included Mark Rylance's modern-dress production for the British Chinese Theatre in which Vermandero's fortress became the Golden Castle Restaurant in Earl's Court, and Deflores was a greasy kitchen-hand who cut off Piracquo's finger 'with the same knife he ha[d] been using for slicing the vegetables' (Malcolm Rutherford, *Financial Times*, 19 Jan 1991); John Wright's much cut and rewritten version for BAC/Third Party (2001); Jenny Sealey's modern dress production for Graeae at the Phoenix, Exeter, which transposed the action to 1960s Merseyside, where Beatrice became 'a young swinger in a psychedelic miniskirt and a fast-changing world of sex, drugs, and rock and roll' (Lyn Gardner, *Guardian*, 16 Oct 2002); Manamassi Productions' similarly revamped version at the Southwark playhouse, which 'whipped [the play] into a multicultural twenty-first century world where slippery dealers and street boys rule the day' (Rachel Haliburton, *Evening Standard*, 15 Oct 2002); and an unusually gory dance-drama directed by Robert Woodruff for the Theater for New Audience at St Clements Church in New York, in which the sexualised violence of the main plot was matched by the spectacle of women strapped to gurneys undergoing cliterectomies in Alibius' hospital. In addition to these reworkings, the play has also been made into a feature film, Marcus Thompson's bizarrely misconceived *Middleton's Changeling* (1997), starring the Scottish comedian Billy Connolly as Alibius, and the punk-rocker Ian Dury as an

and Hands, treating Isabella's story as a satiric meta-commentary on Beatrice-Joanna's tragedy. Thus, for example, Richard Eyre's 1988 National Theatre production opened with a dumb-show featuring a pile of bodies representing the denizens of an asylum; as the bodies began to stir, '[o]ut of the pile emerge[d] the figure of Beatrice-Joanna' who was placed 'puppet-like, on the stage', to be followed by the equally puppet-like figure of Alsemero. At the end of the play the lunatics reappeared as Alsemero stepped forward to speak his epilogue; grouping themselves 'as in the opening dumb-show,' they surrounded him at the conclusion of his speech and took him back to the pile of bodies.[53] Other details of the staging further underlined the connections between the play's two worlds: 'the asylum's inmates, dressed in grey, [resembled] shadows of the castle's inmates', whose lives 'they mirrored only a little distortedly'; while, 'in a witty piece of grouping . . . De Flores and his madhouse counterpart, Lollio, literally look[ed] down on this world of tormented . . . lust from a curved balcony high up in the roof.'[54] In William Dudley's set, church, castle, and madhouse were indiscriminately 'dominated by a great iron grill', once again emphasising the 'concern with imprisonment' in both plots;[55] and, in a particularly effective touch, the Lyttelton stage was fitted with a false proscenium, supported on either side by two zig-zagging staircases over which Alibius' madmen swarmed in contorted postures, framing the entire action of the play (Fig. 5).

The idea of madness as a unifying theme was continued in Michael Attenborough's 1993 Royal Shakespeare production, whose programme was decorated with a collage of quotations on the subject, including a passage from *As You Like It*: 'Love is merely a madness; and . . . deserves a

oddly expressionless cockney Deflores; shot on location in Spain, it mixed Jacobean costumes with sports trainers, nineteenth-century carriages with Mercedes limousines and police motorbikes, and mangled original dialogue with contemporary slang. Rather more promising – though never brought to fruition – was the American dramatist Sam Shepherd's wholesale rewriting of Middleton and Rowley's story as *The Bodyguard* (1973/78), a film script commissioned by none other than Tony Richardson – see Johan Callens, *From Middleton and Rowley's 'Changeling' to Sam Shepherd's 'Bodyguard'* (Leiston, 1997).

53 National Theatre prompt-book, 1988. This device was echoed in Declan Donnelan's 2006 production for Cheek by Jowl at the Barbican which underlined the relationship between the two plots by 'turning the actors in the main story into the asylum inmates'; the theatrical climax of the production came 'when the inhabitants of both worlds join[ed] forces in a wild wedding dance that link[ed] love and madness, and suggest[ed] there is scarcely a cigarette paper between them' (Billington, *Guardian*, 16 May 2006).

54 David Browne, *What's On in London*, 29 June 1988; Jim Hiley, *Listener*, 7 July 1988; Billington, *Guardian* 25 June 1988.

55 Peter Kemp, *Independent*, 25 June 1988.

dark house and a whip as madmen do.' This was an explanatory strategy borrowed from Terry Hands' programme for the same company, which contained information about various forms of mental illness – as did those for the Contact Theatre Company (1978) and the Crucible Theatre Company (1984), both of which cited R. D. Laing's then fashionable study of schizophrenia, *The Divided Self.* The idea of psychological splitting has been mirrored in a succession of programme covers – beginning with the Riverside production – where a female portrait is either split like a mask to reveal another face beneath, or divided into a light and dark side.[56] In the text itself it is Beatrice-Joanna whom Alsemero accuses of having worn a 'black mask' or 'visor / O'er [her] cunning face' (V.iii.3, 47–8), but in production the idea has more often been projected onto Deflores: at the Aldwych, for example, Emrys James wore a half-mask[57] – ostensibly to conceal his deformity, but also suggesting a split personality, like that figured in the red birthmark covering half of Bob Hoskins' face in the 1993 television adaptation (Fig. 3).[58] It was Beatrice's divided self that was represented, however, in the more elaborately theatrical version of this conceit that Hands added to the wedding masque in Act IV: here, while Beatrice was 'married in effigy to her beloved Alsemero . . . at the back of the stage her actual body [was] enthusiastically humped by De Flores.'[59]

Whilst the theme of universal madness has provided a number of directors with the key to establishing a proper relationship between the tragic and comic halves of the play, few have been as successful in developing a satisfactory balance between its twin protagonists. Reviewers have typically blamed this on the shortcomings of individual performances, but its root cause may lie in directorial failure to completely grasp the social parameters on which the psychology of Middleton and Rowley's characters depends. Actors who stress the passive, child-like side of

56 Thus the 1978 Royal Shakespeare Company programme showed Botticelli's Venus pulling back her face-mask to show a death's head beneath, while that for the 1988 National Theatre production featured Beatrice-Joanna's face in heavy chiaroscuro, her cheeks marked by the same scars worn in performance by George Harris's Deflores (Fig. 8), those on her right cheek oozing blood – a cover-design echoed by that for 2001 BAC/ Third Party production.

57 Scott, p. 60.

58 This device was replicated in the 2004 Bristol Tobacco Factory production (subsequently transferred to The Pit at the Barbican Centre), where the true nature of Matthew Thomas' decent-seeming and sympathetic Deflores was conveyed by the 'symbolically two-faced make-up' that prepared for his transformation into Beatrice's murderous accomplice – see Roderick Swanston, *Times Literary Supplement*, on-line review, September 2004.

59 Cushman, *Observer*, 22 Oct 1978.

Figure 6. Deflores as sympathetic villain: Brian Cox (Deflores) and Emma Piper (Beatrice-Joanna) at the Riverside Studios, 1978. Photograph by Douglas H. Jeffery, courtesy of Riverside Studios.

Beatrice, easily fall in the shadow of Deflores; those who emphasize her wilfullness and aggressive sexuality, tend to diminish the terrifying force of his personality. In Richardson's production, for example, Mary Ure seemed a mere puppet in the hands of Robert Shaw's Deflores, who impressed reviewers with the 'dark fire' of an 'artist in hatred', driven to extremes of villainy by the irresistible force of 'obsessive desires';[60] and at the Riverside, Emma Piper was generally upstaged by Brian Cox's powerful but surprisingly sympathetic villain (Fig. 6), whose 'pain . . . [and] self-hatred . . . offset by . . . brutal intelligence and terrifying bursts of speech' almost persuaded Robert Cushman that he was the real victim of the play.[61]

By contrast, the 'voluptuous magnetism' of Diana Quick's Aldwych Beatrice (Fig. 7), with her 'see-nipples-and-die costume', not only eclipsed Emrys James' abstract, intellectualised, and rather 'avuncular' Deflores, but seemed hard to reconcile with the naivety apparent in her response to the murder (' 'tis impossible thou canst be so wicked . . . To

60 Anon, *Times*, 22 Feb 1961; Philip Hope-Wallace, *Manchester Guardian*, 23 Feb 1961.
61 Billington, *Guardian*, 6 Sept 1978; Wardle, *Times*, 7 Sept 1978; Cushman, *Observer*, 10 Sept 1978.

Figure 7. Beatrice as sensual temptress: Diana Quick as Beatrice-Joanna and Emrys James as Deflores, Royal Shakespeare Company, 1978. Photograph by Reg Wilson, courtesy of the Royal Shakespeare Company.

make his death the murderer of my honour' III.iii.120–3); as a result, the panic that overwhelms the heroine after her marriage ('This fellow has undone me endlessly' IV.i.1) was shorn of pathos, provoking only incredulous laughter from the audience.[62] Similar problems beset Elizabeth McGovern's otherwise fascinating performance in the second BBC adaptation (11 December 1993). McGovern made Beatrice's peculiar combination of naivety, sensuality, and solipsistic wilfulness seem entirely plausible: from the beginning she was able to suggest an undercurrent of sick fascination in her aversion to Deflores; but by overplaying the element of deliberate erotic temptation in the scene where she engages him as Alonzo's murderer, she made Beatrice's shocked reaction to the servant's demand for sexual reward appear comically improbable. It was perhaps because her surrender seemed prompted as much by her own secret desires as by Deflores' threats and importunities, that her degradation from virgin to whore was registered with such crudity in the final scene: Alsemero (Hugh Grant) came upon his wife at her dressing-table, decked out in a scarlet petticoat and low-cut corset that contrasted

62 Shulman, *Evening Standard*, 17 Oct 1978; Cushman, *Observer*, 22 Oct 1978; Kenneth Hurren, *What's on in London*, 9 Nov 1978; Wardle, *Times*, 17 Oct 1978.

with the severe black of the other costumes, her cheeks daubed with heavy rouge and a conspicuous beauty-spot, and a goblet of red wine clutched in her unsteady hand. The completeness of this transformation was registered by the way in which her ostensibly penitent speech of farewell was spoken as she caressed Deflores' face, before he died with his head cradled in her lap.

A better balance was achieved by the Royal Shakespeare Company's pairing of Malcolm Storry and Cheryl Campbell in the 1993 RSC version: less ugly than usual, this Deflores exhibited a 'charm, wit, and intelligence' that made him a plausible partner for Campbell's selfish aristocrat, so that they became true 'partners in evil: she ... no less infatuated than he'.[63] This production was more explicit than any of its predecessors about the admixture of sick attraction tainting Beatrice's obsessive aversion to Deflores from the beginning: just as he could not be in the same room 'without digesting her from top to toe', so 'she [could not] be near him without enjoying his cannibalism;'[64] and what began as duel 'between coquettish freedom and insane devotion' emerged as 'a warped [and surprisingly moving] love-story' whose dying protagonists 'are in a way as striking as Antony and Cleopatra or Romeo and Juliet. Only their world is different.'[65]

The main weakness of this conspicuously post-Freudian version was that it seemed to leave the central love affair unanchored in any readily comprehensible social context. This was something that Richard Eyre had consciously sought to address at the National Theatre in 1988. Searching for a way 'to make more visibly apparent the Jacobean interdependence of rank and money'[66] and to reanimate the tensions generated by the social gap between the protagonists, Eyre settled on race as a substitute for rank and set his production in a nineteenth-century Spanish slave colony. George Harris' Deflores, a freed man appointed as steward to Vermandero's household, was 'no Jacobean cutpurse, but a lordly black in white livery who clearly awakes fierce sexual longings in his mistress'.[67] 'Tall [and] dignified,' with conspicuous tribal scars replacing the pock-marks of the script (Fig. 8), Harris was 'an engaging, simple

63 Peter Cromer, *What's On*, 2 June 1993; Malcolm Rutherford, *Financial Times*, 27 May 1993.

64 Benedict Nightingale, *Times*, 27 May 1993.

65 Irving Wardle, *Independent on Sunday*, 30 May 1993; Rutherford, *op. cit.* Wardle too was reminded of a deformed version of Shakespearean love-tragedy: 'like Anthony and Cleopatra they are made for each other.'

66 Eyre quoted by Christopher Edwards, *Spectator*, 2 July 1988.

67 Edwards *op. cit*; Hiley, *op. cit*; Billington, *Guardian*, 25 June 1988.

Figure 8. The death scene: George Harris as Deflores and Miranda Richardson as Beatrice-Joanna, National Theatre, 1988. Photograph by John Haynes.

villain', who gave 'a performance of remarkable containment,' marked by 'a cool, sometimes chilling nonchalance'. The introduction of colour as a motivating factor in the central relationship had a complex effect: it made unexpected capital out of the play's debt to *Othello* by creating a Deflores who was not merely a reworking of Iago, but who attracted some of the pathos of Shakespeare's Moor by virtue of his status as a racial outsider – thereby inviting further sympathy for his transgressive relationship with Beatrice.[68] However, Harris' 'limited ability to explore the rhythms of the verse' meant that he was unable to exploit the ferocious ironies of Deflores' language, and his emotional restraint made for a certain lack of electricity between the lovers, so that in the end 'the promised evocation of passion fail[ed] to materialise.'[69]

Different problems beset Simon Curtis' attempt to evoke a social context for his 1993 television adaptation. Making creative use of the small screen to build up the claustrophobic feel of the castle's interior spaces, Curtis gives peculiar intensity to the exchanges between Beatrice and her rival lovers: the wooing scene between Alsemero and Beatrice, dominated by heavily barred windows, from behind which the camera itself first observes the scene – rather as Deflores spies on the lovers from a gallery above – becomes particularly oppressive. However, despite its meticulously rendered Jacobean costumes and set designs that carefully mimic seventeenth-century Dutch interiors, this is a production that seems oddly insensitive to the play's historical dimensions, not just in its strenuously naturalistic acting style, which often obscures the nuances of the verse, but in its treatment of Deflores and Diaphanta as servants who belong to a completely different regime of service from the one imagined by Middleton and Rowley. While the play is careful to specify that both servants are of gentle birth, Bob Hoskins and Adie Allen speak in accents that clearly set them apart from the castle's elite. As a result the erotic tension between Deflores and Beatrice seems to derive more from the nineteenth-century class hostility that animates a play like *Miss Julie*, than from the specifically early modern anxieties about 'rank' and 'place' that give Middleton and Rowley's dialogue its vicious cutting edge. A contemporary audience need not be expected to understand the historical particularity of the emotions that drive the protagonists of this

68 The *Othello* connection was noticed by several reviewers, including Edwards and Betty Caplan (*New Statesman*, 8 July 1988). Barker and Nicol suggest that '[p]laying to a liberal London audience in the dying days of Apartheid, this staging could be seen as encouraging its spectators to formulate an ideologically sympathetic reading of [the central relationship]' (18).

69 Edwards, *op. cit.*; Maureen Paton, *Daily Express*, 27 June 1988; Hiley, *op. cit.*

tragedy to their doom, but it is, I believe, essential for directors and actors to do so, if they are bring this five hundred year-old masterpiece alive.

A Note on the Text

The Changeling survives in a single seventeenth-century edition whose nature and textual source are discussed in the Appendix. The present edition has been prepared using N. W. Bawcutt's facsimile of the British Library copy (shelfmark 162.k.10), collated with copies from the library of Trinity College, Cambridge, and the Folger Shakespeare Library (including a copy of the 1668 issue). The text has been thoroughly modernised; and since the punctuation of Q is often careless, bearing little relation to what we know of the dramatists' own practice, I have altered it freely, while being as attentive as possible to whatever clues it may have to offer about meaning; spelling conforms as much as possible to modern practice, and (where it does not affect the metre) I have amended some of Q's contracted forms to their modern equivalents – so that 'y'are', for example, becomes 'you're' – in a fashion that seems to me in accord with the colloquial feel of the play's style.

The five act divisions are those of Q, and correspond to the staging practice of the indoor theatres, where the dramatic action was habitually punctuated by four entractes, which provided the occasion for musical interludes. The scene divisions, by contrast, follow those proposed by Dyce and adopted by nearly all subsequent editors – except that I have amalgamated Dyce's III.i and III.ii, on the grounds that, although the stage is technically empty for a brief period, the action – as indicated by the s.d. '*Exeunt at one door and enter at the other*' – is imagined as continuous.

FURTHER READING

Editions

N. W. Bawcutt, ed., *The Changeling*, Revels Plays (London 1958). A reliable text with a comprehensive and lively introduction.

N. W. Bawcutt, ed., *The Changeling*, Revels Student Edition (Manchester 1998). An updated and simplified version of the original Revels edition, aimed at A-level students and junior undergraduates.

Joost Daalder, ed., *The Changeling*, New Mermaids (London 1990)

G. W. Williams, ed., *The Changeling*, Regents Renaissance Drama (London 1967). Reliable student edition, beginning to show its age.

Reception and Performance History

Roberta Barker and David Nicol, 'Does Beatrice Joanna Have a Subtext?: *The Changeling* on the London Stage,' *Early Modern Literary Studies* 10.1 (May, 2004): 3.1–43 (18). Feminist essay which uses recent performance history to critique the notion of Beatrice's unconscious infatuation with Deflores.

Sara Jayne Steen, *Ambrosia in an Earthen Vessel: Three Centuries of Audience and Reader Response to the Works of Thomas Middleton* (New York 1993). Useful guide to the play's reception on stage and in the study.

Authorship

Cyrus Hoy, 'The Shares of Fletcher and his Collaborators in the Beaumont and Fletcher Canon (V),' *Studies in Bibliography* 13 (1960), 77–108. The first systematic attempt to assign the shares of Middleton and Rowley in *The Changeling*.

MacD. P. Jackson, *Studies in Attribution in Middleton and Shakespeare* (University of Salzburg: Salzburg 1979). A key text in the establishment of the Middleton canon; Jackson was a pioneer of the contemporary scientific approach to authorship studies.

Critical Studies

Thomas L. Berger, 'The Petrarchan Fortress of *The Changeling*,' in G. W. Williams, ed., *Renaissance Papers* (1969), 185–212. Excellent account of Middleton and Rowley's quasi-allegorical use of Vermandero's castle and its relation to medieval love-allegory.

Bruce Boehrer, 'Alsemero's Closet,' *JEGP* 96 (1997) 349–68. Stimulating exploration of the motif of secrets in the play.

Muriel Bradbrook, *Themes and Conventions of Elizabethan Tragedy*, 2nd ed. (Cambridge 1980). Key text in the establishment of the play's seriousness; gives a rather negative account of the sub-plot.

Norman A. Brittin, *Thomas Middleton* (New York 1971). Useful general introduction to Middleton's writing.

Lois E. Bueler, 'The Rhetoric of Change in *The Changeling*,' *ELR* 14 (1984), 95–113. Explores the significance of the play's title.

Mark Thornton Burnett, '*The Changeling* and Masters and Servants,' in Garrett A. Sullivan, Patrick Cheney, and Andrew Hadfield, eds., *Early Modern English Drama: A Critical Companion* (New York 2006), pp. 298–308. Sound essay on the play's social parameters.

Swapan Chakravorty, *Society and Politics in the Plays of Thomas Middleton*, (Oxford 1996). Historicist monograph which includes an excellent chapter on *The Changeling*.

Anthony B. Dawson, 'Giving the Finger: Puns and Transgression in *The Changeling*,' in A. L. Magnusson and C. E. McGee, eds., *The Elizabethan Theatre* XII (Toronto 1993), pp. 93–112. Outstanding essay on Middleton and Rowley's word-play.

Dorothy M. Farr, *Thomas Middleton and the Drama of Realism* (New York 1973). Sensible introductory study.

T. S. Eliot, 'Thomas Middleton', in *Elizabethan Dramatists* (London 1927). Eliot's essay, with its sensitive response to the play's verse, played an important part in the early twentieth-century rehabilitation of Middleton.

Roger Holdsworth, ed., *Three Jacobean Revenge Tragedies* (London 1990). Casebook which includes an excellent selection of essays on *The Changeling*, representing a variety of more recent approaches.

David M. Holmes, *The Art of Thomas Middleton* (Oxford 1970). Another sound introductory study.

Lisa Hopkins, 'Beguiling the Master of the Mystery,' *MRDE* 9 (1997) 149–61. A feminist account of the play's symbolic topography which complements Boehrer's study of secrets.

Robert Jordan, 'Myth and Psychology in *The Changeling*,' *RenD* ns.2 (1970), 157–65. Explores the play's use of mythic material to illuminate the psychology of its characters.

Mohammed Kowsar, 'Middleton and Rowley's *The Changeling*: The Besieged Temple,' *Criticism* 28 (1986), 145–66. The castle as a bastion of patriarchal law and authority.

Anne Lancashire, 'The Emblematic Castle in Shakespeare and Middleton,' in J. C. Gray, ed., *Mirror up to Shakespeare: Essays in Honour of G. R. Hibbard* (Toronto 1984), pp. 223–41. Beginning as an emblem of female chastity, Vermandero's castle ends as a version of Macbeth's hell-castle.

Richard Levin, *The Multiple Plot in English Renaissance Drama* (Chicago 1971). Places *The Changeling* in the context of other plays making use of double-plot designs.

T. McAlindon, *English Renaissance Tragedy* (London 1986) Introductory study with a good essay on *The Changeling.*

Cristina Malcolmson, ' "As Tame as the Ladies": Politics and Gender in *The Changeling,*' *ELR* 20 (1990), 320–39. Lively feminist reading.

Michael Neill, ' "Hidden Malady": Death, Discovery, and Indistinction in *The Changeling,*' in *Issues of Death: Mortality and Identity in English Renaissance Tragedy* (Oxford 1997). Links the play's symbolic topography with the motif of secrets.

—— 'Servant Obedience & Master Sins: Shakespeare and the Bonds of Service,' in *Putting History to the Question: Power, Politics and Society in English Renaissance Drama* (New York 2000). A wide-ranging essay which complements Burnett's account of the motif of service in *The Changeling.*

—— ' "A woman's service": Gender, Subordination, and the Erotics of Rank in the Drama of Shakespeare and his Contemporaries,' *Shakespearean International Yearbook* 5 (2005), 127–44. Places *The Changeling* alongside *Twelfth Night* and *All's Well that Ends Well* as a study of the erotic aspects of domestic subversion.

Robert Ornstein, *The Moral Vision of Jacobean Tragedy* (Madison 1960). Old-fashioned, but still persuasive account of the play's ethical dimension.

Christopher Ricks, 'The Moral and Poetic Structure of *The Changeling,*' *E.Crit.* 10 (1960), 296–99. Classic study of Middleton's word-play.

Leo Salingar, *Dramatic Form in Shakespeare and the Jacobeans* (Cambridge 1986). Includes a solid account of the play's design and its use of the double-plot.

—— '*The Changeling* and the Drama of Domestic Life,' *E&S 33* (1979) 92–3. *The Changeling* as domestic tragedy.

Michael Scott, *The Changeling* (London 1989). Compact introductory study with a useful account of the play's performance history.

J. L. Simmons, 'Diabolical Realism in Middleton and Rowley's *The Changeling,*' *RenD* ns 11 (1980), 135–70. Links the play both to early modern demonology and to Jacobean court scandal.

Anne Pasternak Slater, 'Hypallage, Barley-brake, and *The Changeling,*'

RES 34 (1983), 429–40. Uses the rhetorical figure of hypallage (reversal) as a key to the play's design.

Roger Stilling, *Love and Death in Renaissance Tragedy* (Baton Rouge 1976). Wide-ranging study of the erotics of death and dying.

T. B. Tomlinson, *Elizabethan and Jacobean Tragedy* (Cambridge 1964). Combative Leavisite account of English Renaissance drama.

Martin Wiggins, *Journeymen in Murder: The Assassin in English Renaissance Drama* (Oxford 1991). Relates the character of Deflores to other tool-villains in the drama of the period.

Martin White, *Middleton and Tourneur* (New York 1992). Lively introductory study.

Sources

John Reynolds, *The Triumph of God's Revenge* (1621). The full text of this is available at www.acblack.com/thechangeling.

ABBREVIATIONS

Editions

Bawcutt (1958)	N. W. Bawcutt, ed., *The Changeling*, Revels Plays (London 1958)
Bawcutt (1998)	N. W. Bawcutt, ed., *The Changeling*, Revels Student Edition (Manchester 1998)
Black	M. W. Black, ed., *The Changeling* (Philadelphia 1966)
Bruster	Douglas Bruster, ed., *The Changeling*, in Gary Taylor et al., eds., *The Oxford Middleton* (Oxford – forthcoming)
Dilke	C. W. Dilke, ed., *Old English Plays* Vol. 4 (London 1815)
Dyce	Alexander Dyce, ed., *The Works of Thomas Middleton* Vol. 4 (London 1840)
Ellis	Havelock Ellis, ed., *Thomas Middleton* Vol. 1 (London 1887)
Frost	David Frost, ed., *The selected plays of Thomas Middleton* (Cambridge 1978)
Sampson	M. W. Sampson, ed., *Thomas Middleton* (London 1915)
Williams	G. W. Williams, ed., *The Changeling*, Regents Renaissance Drama (London 1967)

Other Abbreviations

Bacon	Francis Bacon, *Essays*, intro. Oliphant Smeaton (London 1906)
Barker and Nicol	Roberta Barker and David Nicol, 'Does Beatrice Joanna Have a Subtext?: *The Changeling* on the London Stage,' *Early Modern Literary Studies* 10.1 (May, 2004): 3.1–43 (18)
Chakravorty	Swapan Chakravorty, *Society and Politics in the Plays of Thomas Middleton*, (Oxford 1996)

Craik	T. W. Craik, proposed emendations in *NQ*, March–April 1977, 120–2, and August 1980, 324–7
Dent	R. W. Dent, *Shakespeare's Proverbial Language: An Index* (Berkeley, Calif., 1981)
E.Crit.	*Essays in Criticism*
ELR	*English Literary Renaissance*
Gerardo	Gonzalo de Sespedes y Menses's novel *Gerardo The Unfortunate Spaniard*, trans. Leonard Digges (London 1622)
Holdsworth	Roger Holdsworth, ed., *Three Jacobean Revenge Tragedies* (London 1990)
'I.M.'	'I.M.' in *A Health to the Gentlemanly Profession of Servingmen; or, The Servingmans Comfort* (London 1598)
N&Q	*Notes and Queries*
Neill, 'Hidden Malady'	Michael Neill, *Issues of Death* (Oxford 1997), Chapter 4, ' "Hidden Malady": Death, Discovery, and Indistinction in *The Changeling*.'
OED	*Oxford English Dictionary*
Partridge	Eric Partridge, *Shakespeare's Bawdy* (London 1947)
Q	1653 quarto of *The Changeling*
Reynolds	John Reynolds, *The Triumph of God's Revenge* (London 1621)
Shakespeare	*The Arden Shakespeare: Complete Works*, ed. Richard Proudfoot, Ann Thompson and David Scott Kastan (Walton-on-Thames 1998)
Tilley	M. P. Tilley, *A Dictionary of Proverbs in England in the Sixteenth and Seventeenth Centuries* (Ann Arbor 1950)

TLS — *Times Literary Supplement*

Williams, *Dictionary* — Gordon Williams, *A Dictionary of Sexual Language and Imagery in Shakespearean and Stuart Literature*, 3 vols. (London 1994)

Williams, *Glossary* — Gordon Williams, *A Glossary of Shakespeare's Sexual Language* (London 1997)

KEY

A GUIDE TO THE EDITED VERSION OF THE PLAY TEXT

Copy-text. This is explained in the Note on the Text.

New Mermaids preserve the words of the original copy-text, and the verse lineation, but modernise spelling and punctuation, making the plays more accessible to readers.

s.p. = speech prefix, these are in CAPITALS

s.d. = stage direction. These are printed in italic to distinguish them from the spoken text. Additional stage directions inserted by the Editor for clarification are in [square brackets]. A stage direction that is centred denotes a key moment of action in the play.

Verse lines are

Staggered when distributed between

Two or more speakers

ed. = editorial emendation: wherever the editor has made a substantial change to the copy-text this is recorded in a footnote. The footnote will give the emended reading followed in brackets by the copy-text reading. The editor may also add a note in explanation.

Title The word 'changeling' had a range of meanings, nearly all of which seem relevant: the nominal 'changeling' of the play is the pretended fool Antonio, whose disguise provides the opportunity for the 'amazing . . . change' with which he (like his rival, Franciscus) hopes to stun Beatrice into submission (III.iii.118–21); but Antonio's choice of masquerade is a reminder that 'changeling' also meant a 'half-witted person, idiot or imbecile' (*OED* n. 4). This meaning must have derived from what is probably the word's most familiar sense – one metaphorically appropriate to Beatrice's transformation from beautiful virgin to '[deformed] whore' (V.iii.31, 77) – 'a child (usually stupid or ugly) supposed to have been left by fairies in exchange for one stolen' (*OED* n. 3). More simply it referred to 'one given to change, a fickle or inconstant person' (*OED* n. 1) – a sense fitting not only Beatrice, whose 'giddy turning' leads her twice to 'change [her] saint' (I.i.153–4), but Alsemero, whose conversion from fearless traveller to abject lover fills Jasperino with incredulity ('have you changed your orisons?' I.i.34). Finally, a 'changeling' might also be 'a person . . . (surreptitiously) put in exchange for another' (*OED* n. 2) – a sense made apposite by Deflores' adulterous usurpation of Alsemero, and even more conspicuously by Diaphanta's role as Beatrice's physical surrogate on the wedding night. (For other possible applications, see Frost p. 413).

THE CHANGELING:

As it was Acted (with great Applause) at the Privat house in DRURY-LANE, and *Salisbury Court*.

Written by { *THOMAS MIDLETON*, and *WILLIAM ROWLEY*. } Gent^s^.

Never Printed before.

LONDON,
Printed for HUMPHREY MOSELEY, and are to be sold at his shop at the sign of the *Princes-Arms* in St. *Pauls* Church-yard, 1653.

DRAMATIS PERSONAE

[*In the castle*]
VERMANDERO, *father to Beatrice*
TOMAZO DE PIRACQUO, *a noble lord*
ALONZO DE PIRACQUO, *his brother, suitor to Beatrice*
ALSEMERO, *a nobleman, afterwards married to Beatrice*
JASPERINO, *his friend*
DEFLORES, *servant to Vermandero*
BEATRICE, *daughter to Vermandero*
DIAPHANTA, *her waiting woman*
[Gentlemen and Gallants
Gentlewomen]
Servants

[*In the madhouse*]
ALIBIUS, *a jealous doctor*
LOLLIO, *his man*
PEDRO, *friend to Antonio*
ANTONIO, *the changeling*
FRANCISCUS, *the counterfeit madman*

Names Daalder (following William Power, 'Middleton's Way with Names,' *NQ* 205 [1960], 26–9, 56–60, 95–8, 136–40, 175–9) suggests that the names of many of the major characters are meant to be ironically significant, and in the case of DEFLORES a homonymic play on 'deflowers' seems unavoidable. Other possibilities include: BEATRICE = 'she who makes happy', or 'blessed one'; JOANNA = 'the Lord's grace'; ALIBIUS = 'he who is elsewhere'; DIAPHANTA = 'diaphanous' or 'red hot'. TOMAZO, in his scepticism about his brother's death, may recall 'Doubting Thomas' in John 20:25. However, these names (like all those in the main plot) are directly derived from Reynolds' *Triumphs of God's Revenge* – including that of Alibius, which was borrowed from History V, the novella immediately following the story of 'Alsemero and Beatrice-Ioana'. Of course this need not exclude the possibility that Reynolds himself chose the names for their suggestiveness, nor that Middleton and Rowley might have preserved them for the same reason.

6 *friend* Q; but the respectful 'sir' with which Jasperino habitually addresses Alsemero suggests that his role is more that of a superior manservant (albeit a gentleman and confidant whom Alsemero condescends to address as 'friend' – see e.g. I.i.13, 15; and cf. II.i.2)

17 *changeling* idiot, fool (*OED* n. 4; and see below, *Title*). Despite the fact the Q *Dramatis Personae* seems to nominate Antonio as the title-character, there is no reason to suppose that the dramatists were responsible for this list; and it seems unlikely that the play would have been named for such a relatively minor figure. However, although the sub-plot is often cut in modern productions, the part of the pretended fool does appear to have been responsible for much of *The Changeling*'s popular currency in the seventeenth century (see Introduction p. xxiii), and the popular use of 'Tony' as a synonym for fool seems to have been inspired by Middleton's character (*OED* n^{1} 1).

ISABELLA, *wife to Alibius*
Madmen
[Fools]

THE SCENE: *Alicant*

22 *The Scene* The action of the main plot is entirely confined to Vermandero's castle in the Valencian port of Alicante, except for the opening scene which is imagined as taking place outside a church beside the castle gate. The subsidiary action takes place in the mad-house supervised by Alibius.

ACT I. [SCENE i.]

Enter ALSEMERO

[ALSEMERO]
'Twas in the temple where I first beheld her,
And now again the same – what omen yet
Follows of that? None but imaginary.
Why should my hopes of fate be timorous?
The place is holy, so is my intent;
I love her beauties to the holy purpose,
And that, methinks, admits comparison
With man's first creation – the place blest,
And is his right home back, if he achieve it.
The church hath first begun our interview,
And that's the place must join us into one,
So there's beginning and perfection too.

Enter JASPERINO

JASPERINO
O sir, are you here? Come, the wind's fair with you:
You're like to have a swift and pleasant passage.

I.i Author: Rowley (and Middleton?) Q marks act, but not scene divisions; the latter were added by Dyce.

1 *'Twas . . . too* With Alsemero's pseudo-pious sophistry, compare Bacon's description of falling in love: 'as if man, made for the contemplation of heaven and all noble objects, should do nothing but kneel before a little idol, and make himself subject, though not of the mouth (as beasts are), yet of the eye, which was given them for higher purposes' (*Of Love*, p. 29). *temple* church

2 *omen* The irony of the positive construction that Alsemero gives to the beginnings of his affair with Beatrice is suggested by the sour admonition which the same episode provokes in Reynolds.

3 *of* ed. (or Q); cf. l. 106

6 *holy purpose* i.e. matrimony

7–9 *that . . . it* marriage can be compared to the Garden of Eden, the blessed paradise which was intended as man's true home, and which he can regain through nuptial bliss. On the persistent Fall motif in the play, see Frost, pp. 413–14.

12 *beginning and perfection* The love which began in the church will be perfected there in matrimony; but Alsemero also plays on the idea of man's ultimate salvation as the 'perfection' of what began in Eden.

13–21 *the wind's . . . against me* In Reynolds Alsemero's departure is held up by genuinely adverse weather, here the contrary winds are merely a wilfully contrived excuse.

ALSEMERO

Sure you're deceivèd, friend – 'tis contrary
In my best judgement.

JASPERINO

What, for Malta?
If you could buy a gale amongst the witches,
They could not serve you such a lucky penn'orth
As comes a' God's name.

ALSEMERO

Even now I observed
The temple's vane to turn full in my face;
I know it is against me.

JASPERINO

Against you?
Then you know not where you are.

ALSEMERO

Not well indeed.

JASPERINO

Are you not well, sir?

ALSEMERO

Yes, Jasperino –
Unless there be some hidden malady
Within me that I understand not.

JASPERINO

And that
I begin to doubt, sir: I never knew
Your inclination to travels at a pause
With any cause to hinder it till now.
Ashore you were wont to call your servants up,

17–18 *If . . . penn'orth* For this superstition see Webster and Rowley, *A Cure for a Cuckold*, IV.ii.97, on 'The winds that Lapland witches sell to men'; and cf. *Macbeth*, I.iii.11.

18 *penn'orth* pennyworth (as Q); but the word was frequently pronounced and sometimes spelt in the contracted form required by the metre here

19 *a' God's name* in God's name – i.e. in the natural course of events, for nothing (but with an implied contrast between God's work and the devil's)
Even now The metre requires elision here (Ev'n now).

20 *temple's vane* weather-vane on the church tower

21 *it is* ed. ('tis Q). Whoever was responsible for the ms. copy from which Q was printed seems to have had a fondness for colloquial contractions, often preferring them even when the metre requires an uncontracted form.

23 *not well* The trick of repeating a word or phrase and giving it a new meaning is a standard clown's trick and one of which Rowley was particularly fond – see Bawcutt (1958) p. xl.

24 *hidden malady* On the importance of this motif in the play, see Introduction pp. xvi–xvii, xxiii–xxvi and Neill, 'Hidden Malady'.

27 *inclination* Dilke (inclinations Q). The awkward double plural, together with *it* in the following line make it likely that Q is a compositor's error. Bruster notes that Middleton was fond of the word, while it does not appear elsewhere in Rowley – one of a number of indications that the former may have been involved in the composition of this scene. In this instance the word is scanned as five syllables: depending on metrical requirements, the *-ion* ending can be treated as either one syllable (as at l. 12) or two (as at ll. 35, 66, 77, 185).

And help to trap your horses for the speed;
At sea I have seen you weigh the anchor with 'em,
Hoist sails for fear to lose the foremost breath,
Be in continual prayers for fair winds –
And have you changed your orisons?

ALSEMERO
No, friend,
I keep the same church, same devotion.

JASPERINO
Lover I'm sure you're none: the stoic
Was found in you long ago; your mother
Nor best friends, who have set snares of beauty –
Ay, and choice ones too – could never trap you that way.
What might be the cause?

ALSEMERO
Lord, how violent
Thou art! I was but meditating of
Somewhat I heard within the temple.

JASPERINO
Is this violence? 'Tis but idleness
Compared with your haste yesterday.

ALSEMERO
I'm all this while a-going, man.

Enter SERVANTS

JASPERINO
Backwards, I think, sir. Look, your servants.

1 SERVANT
The seamen call: shall we board your trunks?

ALSEMERO
No, not today.

JASPERINO
'Tis the critical day
It seems, and the sign in Aquarius.

30 *help . . . speed* help them harness your horses in order to speed up your departure
34 *orisons* prayers
35 *devotion* 'a veiled reference to Beatrice' (Daalder)
36 *stoic* Stoic moral philosophy, popular in the Renaissance, taught the need to subject all emotions to the absolute control of reason.
48 *critical* In astrology, the *crisis* was a particular conjunction of the heavenly bodies supposed to determine the outcome of a given set of events; in medicine, it referred to the turning point (for better or worse) in an illness.
49 *Aquarius* astrological sign of the Water-carrier, supposedly propitious for sea travel

2 SERVANT [*Aside*]
We must not to sea today, this smoke will bring forth fire.

ALSEMERO
Keep all on shore. I do not know the end –
Which needs I must do – of an affair in hand
Ere I can go to sea.

1 SERVANT Well, your pleasure.

2 SERVANT [*Aside*]
Let him e'en take his leisure too: we are safer on land.

Exeunt SERVANTS

Enter BEATRICE, DIAPHANTA, *and* SERVANTS
[ALSEMERO *greets* BEATRICE *with a kiss*]

JASPERINO [*Aside*]
How now! The laws of the Medes are changed, sure! Salute a woman? He kisses too – wonderful! Where learnt he this? And does it perfectly too! In my conscience, he ne'er rehearsed it before. Nay, go on: this will be stranger and better news at Valencia than if he had ransomed half Greece from the Turk.

BEATRICE
You are a scholar, sir.

ALSEMERO A weak one, lady.

BEATRICESa
Which of the sciences is this love you speak of?

ALSEMERO
From your tongue I take it to be music.

BEATRICE
You are skilful in't, can sing at first sight.

50 *this . . . fire* Proverbial cf. Tilley S569 'No smoke without fire'. The seaman's allusion to the heat of Alsemero's passion ironically anticipates the fire in which Diaphanta is burnt in V.i (Daalder).

54 s.d.2 Q adds 'Joanna' at the end of the s.d., presumably because a scribe or compositor, finding he had accidentally abbreviated 'Beatrice Joanna' (as the name appeared in his copy), assumed that 'Joanna' must refer to a separate character.

55 *laws of the Medes* On the supposedly unbreakable laws of the Medes, see Daniel 6:8.

57 *In my conscience* On my word; To my knowledge (stock phrase)

59 *Greece* Under Turkish rule since 1460.

61 *sciences* branches of knowledge (including arts and humanities). Cf. III.ii.120–5, where Antonio proclaims love's superiority to 'all the scrutinous sciences'.

63 *sing . . . sight* sight read (begins the persistent association of eyesight with sexual desire – see Introduction pp. xvi, xix–xxi).

ALSEMERO
And I have showed you all my skill at once;
I want more words to express me further,
And must be forced to repetition:
I love you dearly.

BEATRICE Be better advised, sir:
Our eyes are sentinels unto our judgements,
And should give certain judgement what they see;
But they are rash sometimes, and tell us wonders
Of common things, which when our judgements find,
They can then check the eyes, and call them blind.

ALSEMERO
But I am further, lady; yesterday
Was mine eyes' employment, and hither now
They brought my judgement, where are both agreed.
Both houses then consenting, 'tis agreed;
Only there wants the confirmation
By the hand royal – that is your part, lady.

BEATRICE
Oh, there's one above me, sir. [*Aside*] For five days past
To be recalled! Sure mine eyes were mistaken:
This was the man was meant me – that he should come
So near his time, and miss it!

JASPERINO
We might have come by the carriers from Valencia, I see, and saved all our sea-provision; we are at farthest, sure. Methinks I

68–72 *eyes . . . blind* Cf. III.ii.72–5.
68 *sentinels* Cf. Bacon, 'Of Love', p. 29: 'love can find entrance not only into an open heart, but also into a heart well fortified, if watch be not kept.' The figuration of the human body as a castle was a popular Renaissance trope deriving from medieval allegory – see Introduction pp. xix–xxvi, and Neill, 'Hidden Malady'.
74 *employment* Alsemero's pretense of reason is ironically undermined by the unconscious play on 'employ' = copulate.
76–8 *houses . . . royal* Alsemero's conceit imagines his suit as a bill which has been passed by the two houses of parliament, eyesight and judgement, and now awaits the royal signature (i.e. the grant of Beatrice's hand in marriage).
78 *that is* ed. (that's Q)
79 *one above me* A standard formula for God – but in this case referring to her father. Patriarchal theory construed fathers as God's deputies in the domestic realm, just as monarchs were his vice-regents in the larger kingdom.
79–80 *For . . . recalled* If only I could recall the last five days (i.e. the period of her betrothal to Alonzo de Piracquo)
83 *come . . . carriers* used land-transport
84 *we . . . sure* it's clear we're not going to travel any further now

should do something too: I meant to be a venturer in this voyage. Yonder's another vessel, I'll board her – if she be lawful prize, down goes her top-sail.

Enter DEFLORES

DEFLORES
Lady, your father –

BEATRICE
Is in health, I hope.

DEFLORES
Your eye shall instantly instruct you, lady:
He's coming hitherward.

BEATRICE
What needed then
Your duteous preface? I had rather
He had come unexpected. You must stall
A good presence with unnecessary blabbing;
And how welcome for your part you are,
I'm sure you know.

DEFLORES
Wilt never mend this scorn,
One side nor other? Must I be enjoined
To follow still whilst she flies from me? Well,
Fates do your worst, I'll please my self with sight
Of her, at all opportunities,
If but to spite her anger. I know she had
Rather see me dead than living, and yet
She knows no cause for't but a peevish will.

ALSEMERO
You seemed displeasèd, lady, on the sudden.

85–7 *venturer . . . sail* Standard tropes of sexual predation. Merchant-venturing and piracy were often closely linked in early modern voyaging; lowering one's topsail was a sign of surrender.

92 *stall* forestall (i.e. prejudice, damage in advance – *OED* 'forestall' v. 5). It remains possible that Dilke's emendation to *stale* is correct: neither Middleton nor Rowley elsewhere employs *stall* as a verb, but Middleton has 'stale your friend' in *Wit at Several Weapons* (I.i.139).

93 *A good presence* i.e. her father's impressive demeanour. A lord's 'presence' or 'countenance' included his retinue of servants.

96 *One . . . other* In any way at all

102 *peevish* A variety of senses are probably involved: foolish, mad; spiteful, malignant; perverse, headstrong, capricious; ill-tempered, childishly querulous (*OED* n. 1–5).
will In addition to the modern sense, its meanings included 'desire' and 'sexual appetite'; sometimes used to refer to the sexual organs themselves.

103 *displeasèd* ed. (displeas'd Q)

BEATRICE

Your pardon, sir, 'tis my infirmity;
Nor can I other reason render you
Than his or hers of some particular thing
They must abandon as a deadly poison,
Which to a thousand other tastes were wholesome:
Such to mine eyes is that same fellow there,
The same that report speaks of the basilisk.

ALSEMERO

This is a frequent frailty in our nature;
There's scarce a man amongst a thousand sound,
But hath his imperfection: one distastes
The scent of roses, which to infinites
Most pleasing is, and odoriferous;
One oil, the enemy of poison;
Another wine, the cheerer of the heart
And lively refresher of the countenance.
Indeed this fault – if so it be – is general:
There's scarce a thing but is both loved and loathed;
Myself, I must confess, have the same frailty.

BEATRICE

And what may be your poison, sir? I'm bold with you.

104 *infirmity* 'weakness', but also 'sickness' – cf. Alsemero's identification of love as a disease at l. 24

106 *his or hers* this or that person's
of Dilke (or Q)
particular personal; peculiar (*OED* a. 31, 7a-b)

106–8 *some . . . wholesome* Cf. 'one man's meat is another man's poison' (*Oxford Dictionary of English Proverbs*, p. 522 – though not in Tilley).

109 *fellow* person of low esteem (frequently applied to servants) (*OED* n. 10a, c)

110 *basilisk* fabulous monster, reputedly able to kill with a single glance. Beatrice's instinctive aversion to Deflores – like his ugliness (II.i.37 ff.) and his servile position (II.i.48–9) – is an addition to Reynolds' story (see Introduction, p. xii).

112 *a thousand sound* a thousand men with [otherwise] perfectly sound constitutions. However, since *f* and long *s* (as in Q) were easily confused, it may be that Dilke was correct in emending to *found.* Bruster cites Laurentius, quoted in Burton's treatise on madness, *The Anatomy of Melancholy* (1621): 'for scarce is there one of a thousand that dotes alike' (1.3.2).

113 *distastes* dislikes

114 *infinites* an infinite number of people

115 *odoriferous* fragrant

116–18 *One . . . countenance* Cf. Psalm 104:15: 'wine that maketh glad the heart of man, and oil to make his face to shine, and bread which strengtheneth man's heart'.

116 *oil* probably castor oil, a powerful purgative often used in cases of poisoning

118 *lively* invigorating (*OED* adj. 4d)

122 *I'm* ed. (I am Q)

ALSEMERO

What might be your desire perhaps – a cherry.

BEATRICE

I am no enemy to any creature
My memory has, but yon gentleman.

ALSEMERO

He does ill to tempt your sight, if he knew it.

BEATRICE

He cannot be ignorant of that, sir:
I have not spared to tell him so; and I want
To help my self, since he's a gentleman
In good respect with my father, and follows him.

ALSEMERO

He's out of his place then, now. [*They talk apart*]

JASPERINO

I am a mad wag, wench.

DIAPHANTA

So methinks; but for your comfort I can tell you we have a doctor in the city that undertakes the cure of such.

JASPERINO

Tush, I know what physic is best for the state of mine own body.

DIAPHANTA

'Tis scarce a well governed state, I believe.

JASPERINO

I could show thee such a thing with an ingredient that we two

123 *What* (*And what* Q) Both metre and sense suggest that Dilke was correct in supposing Q's *And* was repeated from the previous line.
126 *tempt* make trial of, put to the test (*OED* v. I, 1–2)
knew it Scanned as a single syllable (*knew't*).
128 *want* lack means
130 *respect* repute, standing
follows i.e. as a servant; but the simultaneous recognition of Deflores' rank as a gentleman born draws attention to the potential contradiction in his social position (cf. II.i.48–9)
131 *place* social rank; domestic office
132 *mad* wild, extravagant in gaiety; sexually infatuated (*OED* adj. 7a; 4a)
wag mischievous fellow; habitual joker (*OED* n^2 1–2)
134 *doctor* i.e. Alibius. Diaphanta pretends to take 'mad' literally.
135 *physic* medicine – here implying sex (Daalder)
136 *well governed state* healthily regulated condition (*OED govern* v. 4, 6), but playing on the political sense of the words.
137–8 *thing . . . together* i.e. her vagina filled with their combined sexual juices

would compound together, and if it did not tame the maddest blood i'th'town for two hours after, I'll ne'er profess physic again.

DIAPHANTA

A little poppy, sir, were good to cause you sleep.

JASPERINO

Poppy? I'll give thee a pop i'th' lips for that first, and begin there [*Kisses her*]: poppy is one simple indeed, and cuckoo-what-you-call't another. I'll discover no more now; another time I'll show thee all.

BEATRICE

My father, sir.

Enter VERMANDERO *and* SERVANTS

VERMANDERO O Joanna, I came to meet thee.
Your devotion's ended?

BEATRICE For this time, sir.
[*Aside*] I shall change my saint, I fear me: I find
A giddy turning in me. [*Aloud*] Sir, this while
I am beholding to this gentleman
Who left his own way to keep me company;
And in discourse I find him much desirous
To see your castle – he hath deserved it, sir,
If ye please to grant it.

VERMANDERO With all my heart, sir.
Yet there's an article between: I must know

138 *compound* The bawdy pun on 'pound' is enabled by recollection of the (phallic) mortar-and-pestle as the usual instrument for compounding substances in an apothecary's shop.
141 *poppy* opiate
143 *simple* plant or herb employed for medical purposes (*OED* n. 6)
143–4 *cuckoo-what-you-call't* probably Cuckoo-pintle (wild arum), so called after its phallic shape, a diuretic and purgative used to treat digestive problems; or perhaps Cuckoo-spit – a name for Lady's Smock or Cuckoo-flower, another diuretic and expectorant, sometimes used in the treatment of madness
144 *discover . . . show* Bawdy *double entendre.*
147 *devotion* act of worship, religious service (*OED* n. 2)
148 *change . . . saint* (1) change from religious to secular worship; (2) change the object of my adoration (from Piracquo to Alsemero)
149 *giddy* (a) whirling; dizzy (*OED* a. 2c–d); (b) mad (*OED* a. 1a)
turning (a) whirling; vertigo (*OED* n. 1b); (b) conversion, desertion to another side; change (*OED* n. 10, 11)

Your country. We use not to give survey
Of our chief strengths to strangers; our citadels
Are placed conspicuous to outward view,
On promonts' tops, but within are secrets.

ALSEMERO
A Valencian, sir.

VERMANDERO
A Valencian?
That's native, sir – of what name, I beseech you?

ALSEMERO
Alsemero, sir.

VERMANDERO Alsemero! Not the son
Of John de Alsemero?

ALSEMERO The same, sir.

VERMANDERO
My best love bids you welcome.

BEATRICE He was wont
To call me so, and then he speaks a most
Unfeignèd truth.

VERMANDERO O sir, I knew your father;
We two were in acquaintance long ago
Before our chins were worth Iulan down,
And so continued till the stamp of time
Had coined us into silver. Well, he's gone,
A good soldier went with him.

ALSEMERO
You went together in that, sir.

156 *survey* Accent on second syllable here.
157 *strengths* strongholds (*OED* n. 10)
159 *promonts* promontories
within . . . secrets On the trope of secrets in the play, see Neill, 'Hidden Malady', and Introduction, pp. xix–xxvi.
160 *Valencian* Accent on third syllable.
161 *native* i.e. to this region
162–3 *Alsemero* Probably scanned as three syllables in l. 162 (Als[e]méro) and four in l. 163 (Álseméro).
165 *then* i.e. whenever he uses the phrase; in this case he speaks more truly than he knows, since Beatrice does indeed welcome Alsemero.
166 *I . . . father* The prior acquaintance of the two men is not part of Reynolds' story.
168 *Iulan* A coinage from *Iulus* Ascanius, the younger son of Aeneas in Virgil's Aeneid (I, 267), whose name, according to the commentator Servius, derived from a Greek word meaning 'the first growth of beard'.
170 *coined . . . silver* turned our hair silver

VERMANDERO
No, by Saint Jacques, I came behind him.
Yet I have done somewhat too. An unhappy day
Swallowed him at last at Gibraltar
In fight with those rebellious Hollanders –
Was it not so?

ALSEMERO Whose death I had revenged,
Or followed him in fate, had not the late league
Prevented me.

VERMANDERO Ay, ay, 'twas time to breathe.
Oh, Joanna, I should ha' told thee news,
I saw Piracquo lately.

BEATRICE [*Aside*] That's ill news.

VERMANDERO
He's hot preparing for his day of triumph,
Thou must be a bride within this sevennight.

ALSEMERO [*Aside*] Ha!

BEATRICE
Nay, good sir, be not so violent: with speed
I cannot render satisfaction
Unto the dear companion of my soul,
Virginity, whom I thus long have lived with,
And part with it so rude and suddenly.
Can such friends divide never to meet again,
Without a solemn farewell?

173 *Jacques* Disyllabic.

175 *Gibraltar* Accent on first and third syllables. The rebellious Dutch won a decisive victory over their former Spanish masters in a naval engagement here on 15 April 1607. The detail is from Reynolds.

178 *late league* The Treaty of the Hague, 9 April 1609, instituted a twelve year truce between the Dutch and Spanish.

179 *Prevented* Forestalled (*OED* v. II, 5)

182 *hot* ardently, urgently (with a suggestion of sexual excitement (*OED* adv. 2; adj. 6c)
his . . . triumph i.e. his wedding day. In sixteenth and seventeenth-century parlance, the weddings and funerals of the great, along with coronations, royal entries and other forms of street pageantry were included in the category of 'triumphs', along with the celebrations of military conquest modelled on the 'triumphs' of Roman generals. Since the wedding of Alonzo and Beatrice has not so far been mentioned, Dilke's emendation of Q *this* to *his* must be correct.

189 *such friends* Ostensibly Beatrice refers to the allegorized companionship between her soul and virginity, but she is also referring to her reluctance to part with Alsemero (*friend* = lover, *OED* n. 4) – just as 'dear companion' (l. 186) at first seems to refer to Alonzo.

VERMANDERO Tush, tush! There's a toy.

ALSEMERO [*Aside*]

I must now part, and never meet again
With any joy on earth. [*Aloud*] Sir, your pardon,
My affairs call on me.

VERMANDERO How, sir? By no means!
Not changed so soon, I hope? You must see my castle
And her best entertainment ere we part –
I shall think myself unkindly usèd else.
Come, come, let's on. I had good hope your stay
Had been a while with us in Alicant;
I might have bid you to my daughter's wedding.

ALSEMERO [*Aside*]

He means to feast me, and poisons me beforehand.
[*Aloud*] I should be dearly glad to be there, sir,
Did my occasions suit as I could wish.

BEATRICE

I shall be sorry if you be not there
When it is done, sir – but not so suddenly.

VERMANDERO

I tell you, sir, the gentleman's complete,
A courtier and a gallant, enriched
With many fair and noble ornaments:
I would not change him for a son-in-law
For any he in Spain, the proudest he –
And we have great ones, that you know.

ALSEMERO He's much
Bound to you, sir.

VERMANDERO He shall be bound to me,

190 *toy* foolish fancy; trifle (*OED* n. 4, 5); in the context of Beatrice's virginity, a bawdy significance is also possible (see Williams, *Glossary*, pp. 211–12)
194 *changed* Ironic in view of his daughter's aside at l. 148.
195 *entertainment* The bawdy sense, 'sexual diversion', charges Vermandero's invitation with unconscious irony.
196 *unkindly usèd* The metre requires elision of the *y* in *unkindly*, while *used* is disyallabic.
202 *occasions* business affairs (*OED* n.[1] 6a)
suit fit my inclinations (*OED* v. 14a)
204 *but not* but I wish it were not
205 *gentleman's complete* Apparently glancing at Henry Peacham's *The Complete Gentleman* published in the same year that *The Changeling* was first performed (1622), just as the next line probably remembers the original of all such courtesy books, Baldassare Castiglione's *The Courtier* (1528; trans Sir Thomas Hoby, 1561).
211 *bound* obliged; Vermandero plays on an alternative sense, 'tied'.

As fast as this tie can hold him, I'll want
My will else.

BEATRICE [*Aside*] I shall want mine if you do it.

VERMANDERO
But come, by the way, I'll tell you more of him:

ALSEMERO [*Aside*]
How shall I dare to venture in his castle,
When he discharges murderers at the gate?
But I must on, for back I cannot go.

BEATRICE [*Aside*]
Not this serpent gone yet? [*Drops a glove*]

VERMANDERO Look, girl, thy glove's fallen –
Stay, stay – Deflores, help a little.

DEFLORES Here, lady. [*Offers the glove*]

BEATRICE
Mischief on your officious forwardness!
Who bade you stoop? They touch my hand no more:
[*Removes the other glove*]

There! [*Throws it down*] For t'other's sake I part with this –

212–13 *want my will* fail to achieve what I wish for (and mean to bring about)
213 *mine* Beatrice plays on *will* = (sexual) desire.
214 *by* along
216 *murderers* small cannon (typically deployed to protect the entrance to a castle). Alsemero refers to the deadly effect produced on him by Vermandero's announcement of the impending marriage; however, he may also have in mind the 'killing' effect of Beatrice's eyes – a standard trope of love-poetry, in which the lady's eyes were figured as firing darts or bullets at her lover – thus beginning the progressive association of Vermandero's castle with the body of his daughter (see Introduction, pp. xxiii–vi, and Neill, 'Hidden Malady', pp. 179–80, 193–4). Ironically Beatrice herself will soon become a literal murderer.
218 *serpent* One of a number of references in the play that associate Beatrice's fall with the Genesis story. Deflores, like his partial model, Iago in Shakespeare's *Othello*, is identified with the Devil, who in the form of a serpent tempted Eve. Cf. III.iii.165, V.iii.67.
s.d. It is unclear whether the dropping of the glove is accidental, or meant as a conscious invitation to Alsemero; but the fact that it occurs during an aside expressing her pathological aversion to Deflores suggests that it may be unconsciously aimed at him – a suggestion supported by the elaborate play with the phallic suggestiveness of fingers in Deflores' soliloquy, as well as in two later scenes (I.ii.27–31; III.iii.26–38, 88).
219 *Deflores . . . little* The command emphasizes the servile role that Deflores, in spite of his gentle birth, is forced to play in Vermandero's household.
222 s.d. As at 218, 219 and 221, the gesture, while not specified in Q, is clearly implicit in the dialogue. Throwing down a glove was a traditional gesture of challenge, and Beatrice may even emphasize this by striking Deflores in the face with it.

Take 'em, and draw thine own skin off with 'em!
Exeunt VERMANDERO, ALSEMERO, JASPERINO, *and* SERVANTS

DEFLORES

Here's a favour come – with a mischief! Now I know
She had rather wear my pelt tanned in a pair
Of dancing pumps than I should thrust my fingers
Into her sockets here. [*Tries to pull the glove onto his hand*]
I know she hates me,
Yet cannot choose but love her.
No matter: if but to vex her, I'll haunt her still,
Though I get nothing else, I'll have my will. *Exit*

[ACT I. SCENE ii.]

Enter ALIBIUS *and* LOLLIO

ALIBIUS

Lollio, I must trust thee with a secret,
But thou must keep it.

223 *draw . . . skin* as a snake might do; but also, as Daalder points out, drawing attention to the pustular, pock-marked complexion that so obsesses both Beatrice and Deflores himself (II.i.33–45, 53; II.ii.40–1, 72–7, 146)

224 *favour* In the rituals of chivalric or courtly love, gloves were among the most common forms of 'favour' offered by ladies to their knightly 'servants', and often worn in tournaments as tokens of their love. In the 1993 BBC version, Bob Hoskins expressed his physical infatuation by pressing the glove to his nose and inhaling deeply.
with a mischief with a vengeance (*OED* n. 9b).

225 *She had* Metre requires elision here.

227 *sockets* i.e. the fingers of the gloves; but *socket* also = vagina (*OED* n. 4a) the obscene suggestiveness of Deflores' gesture is underlined by Lollio's similarly indecent word-play in the following scene (I.ii.30–1). For a contemporary example of such bawdy symbolism see the story (cited in Chakravorty, p. 147) of Prince Henry's refusal to accept the glove dropped by Frances Howard, Countess of Essex, at a dance, 'saying publicly, he would not have it, it is stretched by another, meaning the Viscount [i.e. her lover, Robert Carr, Viscount Rochester].'

230 *get* (1) possess; (2) beget
will lust; sexual satisfaction

I.ii Author: Rowley. As in much of Rowley's portion of the play, the boundary between verse and prose is often uncertain in this scene. Alibius speaks in verse but is given many irregular or incomplete lines (e.g. 2, 7, 11, 13, 16, 19); Lollio (as befits his lowly rank) generally speaks in prose, but some of his lines seem to fit the verse pattern (e.g. 3, 14, 17).

1 and 3, 8, 17 *secret* Continues the motif of secrets from I.i.159. Cf. also II.ii.68, IV.i.25, 108, IV.ii.111, 139, V.i.6. Lollio characteristically interprets *secret* as = private parts (Williams, *Glossary*, p. 271).

LOLLIO

I was ever close to a secret, sir.

ALIBIUS

The diligence that I have found in thee,
The care and industry already past
Assures me of thy good continuance.
Lollio, I have a wife.

LOLLIO

Fie sir, 'tis too late to keep her secret: she's known to be married all the town and country over.

ALIBIUS

Thou goest too fast, my Lollio. That knowledge
I allow no man can be barred it;
But there is a knowledge which is nearer,
Deeper, and sweeter, Lollio.

LOLLIO

Well, sir, let us handle that between you and I.

ALIBIUS

'Tis that I go about, man – Lollio,
My wife is young.

LOLLIO

So much the worse to be kept secret, sir.

ALIBIUS

Why, now thou meet'st the substance of the point:
I am old, Lollio.

LOLLIO

No, sir, 'tis I am old Lollio.

ALIBIUS

Yet why may not this concord and sympathize?
Old trees and young plants often grow together,
Well enough agreeing.

LOLLIO

Ay, sir, but the old trees raise themselves higher and broader than the young plants.

10 *knowledge* i.e. carnal knowledge
14 *handle* With bawdy implication.
17 *worse* (1) harder (the meaning Alibius is meant to assume); (2) less appropriate
21 *this* i.e. this marriage of January and May
concord agree, be in harmony (*OED* v. 2)
sympathize have an affinity in nature, harmonize (*OED* v. 2)
24–5 *old . . . plants* i.e. his cuckold's horns would make Alibius seem taller (Daalder)

ALIBIUS

Shrewd application – there's the fear man:
I would wear my ring on my own finger;
Whilst it is borrowed it is none of mine,
But his that useth it.

LOLLIO

You must keep it on still, then; if it but lie by, one or other will be thrusting into't.

ALIBIUS

Thou conceiv'st me, Lollio: here thy watchful eye
Must have employment, I cannot always be
At home.

LOLLIO I dare swear you can not.

ALIBIUS I must look out.

LOLLIO

I know't, you must look out, 'tis every man's case.

ALIBIUS

Here, I do say, must thy employment be –
To watch her treadings, and in my absence
Supply my place.

LOLLIO

I'll do my best, sir; yet surely I cannot see who you should have cause to be jealous of.

ALIBIUS

Thy reason for that Lollio? 'Tis a comfortable question.

LOLLIO

We have but two sorts of people in the house, and both under the whip: that's fools and madmen – the one has not wit

27 *I . . . finger* The bawdy implication of Alibius' remark (*ring* = vagina – see Williams, *Glossary*, p. 26) is immediately picked up in Lollio's ensuing lines.
32 *Thou conceiv'st me* You get my point
34 *At . . . out* Lollio normally speaks in prose, but here his speech fits the metre, forming an acceptable hexameter with Alibius' lines. Here (and sometimes elsewhere) the layout of Q makes it impossible to be sure whether verse or prose is intended.
look out leave the house (e.g. on business)
35 *look out* exercise vigilance
case Lollio puns on *case* = sexual organ (Williams, *Glossary*, p. 66).
37 *treadings* (1) where she goes; (2) acts of copulation (*OED* v. *tread* 8a)
38 *Supply . . . place* Fulfil my office (as head of the household); but Lollio will deliberately misunderstand *place* to mean 'vulva' (Williams, *Glossary*, p. 237)
41 *comfortable* reassuring
42 *house* Holdsworth (p. 269) noting that the word could also mean 'playhouse', suggests that 'a knowing glance outwards should accompany the line' (cf. III.iii.108).

enough to be knaves, and the other not knavery enough to be fools.

ALIBIUS

Ay, those are all my patients, Lollio.
I do profess the cure of either sort –
My trade, my living 'tis, I thrive by it –
But here's the care that mixes with my thrift:
The daily visitants, that come to see
My brainsick patients, I would not have
To see my wife. Gallants I do observe
Of quick enticing eyes, rich in habits,
Of stature and proportion very comely –
These are most shrewd temptations, Lollio.

LOLLIO

They may be easily answered, sir: if they come to see the fools and madmen, you and I may serve the turn, and let my mistress alone – she's of neither sort.

ALIBIUS

'Tis a good ward, indeed. Come they to see
Our madmen or our fools, let 'em see no more
Than what they come for; by that consequent
They must not see her: I'm sure she's no fool.

LOLLIO

And I'm sure she's no madman.

47 *cure* A conveniently ambiguous term: (1) care, charge (*OED* n. 3); (2) medical treatment (*OED* n. 5a); (3) restoration to health (*OED* n. 6a).

49 *care* anxiety

50 *daily visitants* Madmen are several times represented on the stage as being a source of entertainment (see e.g. *Northward Ho*, IV.iii.27–36; *Duchess of Malfi*, IV.ii.61–114) It is generally assumed that this was the practice at Bethlehem Hospital, the London madhouse familiarly known as 'Bedlam' on which Alibius' asylum appears to be modelled; Carol Thomas Neely, however, has argued that visiting Bedlam for amusement was a stage convention, and that it was not until the eighteenth century that the madhouse (partly as a result of its representations in the theatre) became a place of entertainment – see *Distracted Subjects: Madness and Gender in Shakespeare and Early Modern Culture* (Ithaca, 2004), Chap. 6, 'Bedlam in History and Drama.'

53 *habits* clothes

54 *comely* handsome

55 *shrewd* wicked, depraved (*OED* a. 1a); dangerous (*OED* n. 2); grievous (*OED* n. 6b); cunning (*OED* a. 13a)

57 *serve the turn* Daalder suggests a play on the bawdy sense ('provide sexual service' – see Williams, *Glossary*, pp. 273–4).

59 *ward* defence (*OED* n.[2] 8); method of keeping watch (*OED* n.[2] 1)

61 *by . . . consequent* consequently

63 *madman* With a play on the gendered sense of 'man'.

ALIBIUS

Hold that buckler fast, Lollio: my trust
Is on thee, and I account it firm and strong.
What hour is't, Lollio?

LOLLIO

Towards belly-hour, sir.

ALIBIUS

Dinner time? Thou mean'st twelve o'clock?

LOLLIO

Yes, sir; for every part has his hour: we wake at six and look about us, that's eye-hour; at seven we should pray, that's knee-hour; at eight walk, that's leg-hour; at nine gather flowers, and pluck a rose, that's nose-hour; at ten we drink, that's mouth-hour; at eleven lay about us for victuals, that's hand-hour; at twelve go to dinner, that's belly-hour.

ALIBIUS

Profoundly, Lollio! It will be long
Ere all thy scholars learn this lesson, and
I did look to have a new one entered – stay,
I think my expectation is come home.

Enter PEDRO, *and* ANTONIO *like an idiot*

PEDRO

Save you, sir. My business speaks it self:
This sight takes off the labour of my tongue.

ALIBIUS

Ay, ay, sir;
'Tis plain enough, you mean him for my patient.

64 *buckler* shield
72 *pluck a rose* urinate
77 *new one* i.e. a new patient
78 *is . . . home* has been fulfilled
s.d. *like an idiot* The frontispiece to Francis Kirkman's collection of drolls, *The Wits* (1672), includes amongst its representations of popular stage characters a figure captioned 'Changeling', wearing a long-skirted gown and a tall pointed cap, with what appears to be a child's primer dangling from his right hand; this is generally taken to be Antonio, and may provide a guide to the original costuming (see Introduction, p. xxiv, and Fig. 4).

PEDRO

And, if your pains prove but commodious, to give but some little strength to his sick and weak part of nature in him. [*Gives him money*] These are but patterns to show you of the whole pieces that will follow to you, beside the charge of diet, washing, and other necessaries fully defrayed.

ALIBIUS

Believe it, sir, there shall no care be wanting.

LOLLIO

Sir, an officer in this place may deserve something: the trouble will pass through my hands.

PEDRO

'Tis fit something should come to your hands then, sir.

[*Gives him money*]

LOLLIO

Yes, sir, 'tis I must keep him sweet, and read to him. What is his name?

PEDRO

His name is Antonio – marry, we use but half to him, only Tony.

LOLLIO

Tony, Tony, 'tis enough, and a very good name for a fool. What's your name, Tony?

ANTONIO

He he he! Well, I thank you cousin, he he he!

83–7 *And ... defrayed* Q prints this passage as verse; and, since most of Pedro's lines, including his other big speech at ll. 100–8, are in verse, it is arguable that Rowley intended to write syllabics here. However the lines are almost impossible to speak as verse.

83 *commodious* beneficial

85 *patterns* samples

86 *pieces* gold coins (*OED* n. 13 b–c)

86–91 *the charge ... hands then* Neely (*Distracted Subjects*, pp. 194–5, 199 n.25) suggests that Alibius was intended as a satirical portrait of Helkiah Crooke, the notoriously corrupt master of Bethlehem from 1619–33, and this episode may allude to his scandalous extortion of fees and donations. Middleton and Rowley may have been familiar with Crooke's anatomical treatise, *Mikrocosmographia* (see V.ii.153).

92 *sweet* clean and sweet-smelling

95 *Tony ... fool OED* suggests that the common use of Tony to mean 'fool' (or, as a verb, 'to make a fool [of someone]'), may actually derive from *The Changeling*, since no other examples are recorded before the 1650s; however Lollio's 'a very good name for a fool' suggests that the term was already in common use (unless some now lost satiric allusion was intended).

LOLLIO

Good boy! Hold up your head. He can laugh: I perceive by that he is no beast.

PEDRO

Well, sir, if you can raise him but to any height,
Any degree of wit – might he attain
(As I might say) to creep but on all four
Towards the chair of wit, or walk on crutches –
'Twould add an honour to your worthy pains,
And a great family might pray for you,
To which he should be heir, had he discretion
To claim and guide his own. Assure you sir,
He is a gentleman.

LOLLIO

Nay, there's nobody doubted that, at first sight I knew him for a gentleman – he looks no other yet.

PEDRO

Let him have good attendance and sweet lodging.

LOLLIO

As good as my mistress lies in, sir; and, as you allow us time and means, we can raise him to the higher degree of discretion.

PEDRO

Nay, there shall no cost want, sir.

LOLLIO

He will hardly be stretched up to the wit of a magnifico.

PEDRO

Oh no, that's not to be expected, far shorter will be enough.

LOLLIO

I'll warrant you I'll make him fit to bear office in five weeks: I'll undertake to wind him up to the wit of constable.

99 *no beast* The idea that laughter is one of the traits that distinguishes men from beasts goes back to Aristotle, *De Partibus Animalium* III, 10.

108 *He . . . gentleman* Compare Deflores' insistence on his own gentle birth at II.i.49.

109–10 *at first . . . other* Given Antonio's appearance '*like an idiot*' this is clearly meant satirically; but it may also suggest that Lollio has seen through his disguise.

111 *have . . . attendance* be well looked after
sweet lodging clean quarters – but Daalder suggests a bawdy *double entendre*

112 *As . . . in* Perhaps implying that Lollio already guesses Antonio's designs.

116 *magnifico* Originally a Venetian magnate – hence any person of distinction and authority.

118 *I'll . . . I'll* ed. (Ile warrant you Q; Bawcutt: I'll warrant you I; Williams: I warrant you I'll)

118–19 Like Dogberry in *Much Ado About Nothing*, constables were presented on the stage as notoriously stupid.

PEDRO

If it be lower than that it might serve turn.

LOLLIO

No, fie, to level him with a headborough, beadle, or watchman were but little better than he is; constable, I'll able him. If he do come to be a justice afterwards, let him thank the keeper. Or I'll go further with you: say I do bring him up to my own pitch, say I make him as wise as my self?

PEDRO

Why there I would have it.

LOLLIO

Well, go to, either I'll be as arrant a fool as he, or he shall be as wise as I, and then I think 'twill serve his turn.

PEDRO

Nay, I do like thy wit passing well.

LOLLIO

Yes, you may; yet if I had not been a fool, I had had more wit than I have too. Remember what state you find me in.

PEDRO

I will, and so leave you. Your best cares I beseech you. *Exit*

ALIBIUS

Take you none with you, leave 'em all with us.

ANTONIO

Oh, my cousin's gone! Cousin, cousin, oh!

LOLLIO

Peace, peace, Tony! You must not cry child – you must be whipped if you do. Your cousin is here still: I am your cousin, Tony.

121 *headborough, beadle, watchman* parish officers ranked successively below the constable.
123 *able him* make him fit for
justice Like constables, justices of the peace were frequently satirized for their stupidity (see e.g. Shallow and Silence in 2 *Henry IV*, and Greedy in Massinger's *A New Way to Pay Old Debts*; and cf. IV.i.125–6).
128 *arrant* absolute, complete; but the Q spelling 'errant' suggests that the meaning 'erring' or 'confused' is also present
129 *serve . . . turn* be adequate for his purposes (perhaps with a bawdy innuendo)
130 *wit* Includes both 'intelligence' and 'good sense'.
passing exceptionally
132 *Remember . . . in* Another appeal for money.
135 *cousin* Need not imply kinship – often simply used as a term of intimacy and affection (*OED* n. 5).

ANTONIO

He, he! Then I'll not cry, if thou be'st my cousin. He, he, he!

LOLLIO

I were best try his wit a little, that I may know what form to place him in.

ALIBIUS

Ay, do, Lollio, do.

LOLLIO

I must ask him easy questions at first. – Tony, how many true fingers has a tailor on his right hand?

ANTONIO

As many as on his left, cousin.

LOLLIO

Good; and how many on both?

ANTONIO

Two less than a deuce, cousin.

LOLLIO

Very well answered! I come to you again, cousin Tony: how many fools goes to a wise man?

ANTONIO

Forty in a day sometimes, cousin.

LOLLIO

Forty in a day? How prove you that?

ANTONIO

All that fall out amongst themselves, and go to a lawyer to be made friends.

LOLLIO

A parlous fool, he must sit in the fourth form at least, I perceive that. I come again, Tony: how many knaves make an honest man?

141 *try* test
form school class
144–5 *true fingers* (1) fingers excluding thumbs; (2) honest fingers – tailors were proverbially dishonest
148 *deuce* pair
150 *goes to* make up; Antonio chooses to understand Lollio as meaning 'visit'. The use of a singular verb with a plural subject is not uncommon in the period (cf. l. 189 and II.ii.10).
153–4 *All . . . friends* Then, as now, jokes at the expense of lawyers were commonplace. Cf. Tilley L130: 'Lawyers's houses are built on the heads of fools'.
155 *parlous* dangerously cunning (originally a contracted form of 'perilous')

ANTONIO

I know not that cousin.

LOLLIO

No, the question is too hard for you. I'll tell you, cousin – there's three knaves may make an honest man: a sergeant, a jailor, and a beadle; the sergeant catches him, the jailor holds him, and the beadle lashes him; and, if he be not honest then, the hangman must cure him.

ANTONIO

Ha ha ha! That's fine sport cousin!

ALIBIUS

This was too deep a question for the fool, Lollio.

LOLLIO

Yes, this might have served yourself, though I say't. Once more, and you shall go play, Tony.

ANTONIO

Ay, play at push-pin cousin. Ha he!

LOLLIO

So thou shalt: say how many fools are here –

ANTONIO

Two, cousin – thou and I.

LOLLIO

Nay, you're too forward there. Tony, mark my question: how many fools and knaves are here? A fool before a knave, a fool behind a knave, between every two fools a knave, how many fools, how many knaves?

ANTONIO

I never learnt so far, cousin.

ALIBIUS

Thou putt'st too hard questions to him, Lollio.

160 *sergeant* court officer charged with arresting offenders and executing legal orders (*OED* n. 4a)
161 *beadle* (here) court officer charged with enforcing discipline
165 *deep* (1) profound; (2) crafty
166 *this . . . yourself* this would have done for someone as intelligent as you (but with the implication that his joke is also well suited to a crafty knave like Alibius)
168 *push-pin* popular children's game (but with obscene innuendo – see Williams, *Dictionary*, p. 1120)
171 *forward* prompt, eager (*OED* n. 6a); presumptuous (*OED* n. 8)
172 *before* (1) in front of; (2) in preference to; (3) before revealing himself as
173 *behind* (1) to the rear of; (2) following (i.e. serving)
between . . . knave (1) a knave stands between each pair of fools; (2) of any two fools, one is likely to be a knave

LOLLIO
I'll make him understand it easily. – Cousin, stand there.

ANTONIO
Ay, cousin.

LOLLIO
Master, stand you next the fool.

ALIBIUS Well, Lollio.

LOLLIO
Here's my place. Mark now, Tony: there a fool before a knave.

ANTONIO
That's I cousin.

LOLLIO
Here's a fool behind a knave, that's I; and between us two fools there is a knave, that's my master: 'tis but we three, that's all.

ANTONIO
We three, we three, cousin.

MADMEN *within*

FIRST MADMAN *(Within)*
Put's head i' th' pillory, the bread's too little.

SECOND MADMAN *(Within)*
Fly, fly, and he catches the swallow.

THIRD MADMAN *(Within)*
Give her more onion, or the devil put the rope about her crag.

181–4 *Here's . . . master* 'The others of course are really the knaves who are trying to make a fool of Alibius' (Bawcutt)

184 *We three* Cf. *Twelfth* Night, II.ii.16–7; alluding to the stock image of two idiots over the caption 'We three, loggerheads be' – the third being the viewer himself (in this case, Alibius).

185 s.d. In the original staging the shrieks and howls of the inmates will have issued from the so-called 'discovery space', until the Madmen finally burst onto the stage in III.ii. In a play much concerned with dark 'secrets' and hidden sickness, their off-stage presence develops a symbolic resonance – one emphasised in Richard Eyre's 1988 National Theatre production, in which the entire performance was framed by a kind of false proscenium made of spiral staircases and scaffolding around which the denizens of the madhouse clung in grotesque postures: this was, in effect, the 'hell' that 'circumscribes' the characters in the final scene (V.iii.164); cf. Introduction, p. xxxv and Fig. 5.

186 *the . . . little* there's not enough bread

187 *Fly . . . swallow* Alluding to a proverbial impossibility: 'Fly and you will catch the swallow' (Tilley S1024); but given that the other Madmen's speeches register hunger, probably punning on *swallow*, as Daalder suggests.

188 *rope* (1) hangman's rope; (2) rope of onions
crag neck

LOLLIO

You may hear what time of day it is, the chimes of Bedlam goes.

ALIBIUS

Peace, peace, or the wire comes!

THIRD MADMAN *(Within)*

Cat-whore, cat-whore! Her Parmesan, her Parmesan!

ALIBIUS Peace, I say! – Their hour's come: they must be fed, Lollio.

LOLLIO

There's no hope of recovery of that Welsh madman was undone by a mouse that spoiled him a parmesan – lost his wits for't.

ALIBIUS

Go to your charge, Lollio; I'll to mine.

LOLLIO

Go you to your madmen's ward, let me alone with your fools.

ALIBIUS

And remember my last charge, Lollio. *Exit*

LOLLIO

Of which your patients do you think I am? Come, Tony, you must amongst your school-fellows now: there's pretty scholars amongst 'em, I can tell you; there's some of 'em at *stultus, stulta, stultum.*

ANTONIO

I would see the madmen, cousin, if they would not bite me.

LOLLIO

No, they shall not bite thee, Tony.

ANTONIO

They bite when they are at dinner, do they not coz?

LOLLIO

They bite at dinner indeed, Tony. Well, I hope to get credit by thee; I like thee the best of all the scholars that ever I brought up, and thou shalt prove a wise man, or I'll prove a fool my self.

Exeunt

189 *chimes of Bedlam* cries of the mad
190 *wire* whip made of wire
191 *Cat-whore . . . Parmesan* Spoken by the 'Welsh madman'. The Welsh were proverbially fond of cheese; and the speaker is abusing his cat for failing to prevent the theft of his Parmesan by a mouse (see l. 206) – *her* being stage-Welsh for 'my'.
194 *spoiled him* despoiled him of
197 *last charge* i.e. to keep a close watch on Alibius' wife
200 *amongst* go amongst, join
201 *at . . . stultum* i.e. they have reached only as far the second declension in their Latin grammars; fittingly, the noun they are declining means 'stupid'.
207 *prove* (1) become; (2) turn out to have been (all along)

ACT II. [SCENE i.]

Enter BEATRICE *and* JASPERINO *severally*

BEATRICE

O Sir, I'm ready now for that fair service,
Which makes the name of friend sit glorious on you.
Good angels and this conduct be your guide – [*Gives a paper*]
Fitness of time and place is there set down, sir.

JASPERINO

The joy I shall return rewards my service. *Exit*

BEATRICE

How wise is Alsemero in his friend!
It is a sign he makes his choice with judgement.
Then I appear in nothing more approved
Than making choice of him;
For 'tis a principle, he that can choose
That bosom well who of his thoughts partakes,
Proves most discreet in every choice he makes.
Methinks I love now with the eyes of judgement,
And see the way to merit, clearly see it.
A true deserver like a diamond sparkles –
In darkness you may see him, that's in absence,
Which is the greatest darkness falls on love;
Yet is he best discernèd then
With intellectual eyesight. What's Piracquo

II.i Author: Middleton

1–2 *service . . . friend* For Jasperino's role as both servant and friend, see *Dramatis Personae* above; but Daalder is probably right to suppose that, since Beatrice is thinking of Vermandero, *service* also carries an erotic suggestion.

3 *conduct* document conferring privilege of entry (not in *OED* – presumably an abbreviation of 'safe-conduct', n. 2)

5 *return* take back (to Alsemero).

10–12 *For . . . makes* Presumably on the grounds that a true friend (as theorists of friendship had insisted from classical times) is a 'second self'.

11 *bosom* intimate friend

13–19 *Methinks . . . eyesight* Beatrice's conviction that her love is the product of insight rather than the notoriously unreliable impressions of the eye is undercut by the repeated emphasis upon her obsession with outward appearances.

15–16 *A . . . him* For the idea that diamonds were luminous, see *Titus Andronicus*, II.iii.226–30; and cf. III.i.30–1.

18 *discernèd* ed. (discern'd Q)

My father spends his breath for? And his blessing
Is only mine as I regard his name,
Else it goes from me, and turns head against me,
Transformed into a curse. Some speedy way
Must be remembered – he's so forward too,
So urgent that way, scarce allows me breath
To speak to my new comforts.

Enter DEFLORES

DEFLORES [*Aside*] Yonder's she.
Whatever ails me, now alate especially
I can as well be hanged as refrain seeing her;
Some twenty times a day – nay not so little –
Do I force errands, frame ways and excuses
To come into her sight; and I have small reason for't,
And less encouragement, for she baits me still
Every time worse than other, does profess herself
The cruellest enemy to my face in town,
At no hand can abide the sight of me,
As if danger, or ill luck hung in my looks.
I must confess my face is bad enough,
But I know far worse has better fortune –

20–1 *his* i.e. Vermandero's
20–3 *blessing . . . curse* Just as, in the formal rite of blessing, a father became the conduit of God's grace, so his curse was the most terrible thing a child could experience.
21 *as . . . name* in so far as I respect his honour (by obeying his wishes)
22 *turns . . . me* rounds on me with all its power (*OED turn* v. 57; *head* n. 29, 57a)
23–4 *Some . . . remembered* i.e. some way of disposing of Alonzo – but at this point Beatrice cannot quite bring herself to say it.
24–5 *he's . . . way* Ambiguous – 'forward' sounds like a complaint against Alonzo's over-zealous suit, but it may (as Daalder supposes) simply refer to Vermandero's eager determination to conclude the match.
26 *my new comforts* i.e. her affair with Alsemero. But note Deflores' entrance (Daalder).
s.d. Though this speech, like ll. 76–88, takes the form of a soliloquy, it is in fact an extended aside. The aside was typically employed for ironic and often comic effect, but a number of the key scenes in Middleton's part of the play (e.g. II.ii, III.iii, IV.i) make extensive use of the device, including such extended passages of reflection, to emphasize the isolation of the characters as they brood over inward secrets.
27 *alate* of late (*OED* adv. *arch.*).
28 *refrain* Stress on first syllable.
32 *baits* bites and tears as dogs attack a chained animal (*OED* v.[1] 3) – cf. ll. 80–1; but perhaps (as Daalder suggests) with a subdued pun on *baits* = tempts (*OED* v.[1] 11)
35 *At no hand* Under no circumstances; On no account
36 *danger* Cf. l. 90.

And not endured alone, but doted on –
And yet such pick-hatched faces, chins like witches,
Here and there five hairs, whispering in a corner
As if they grew in fear one of another,
Wrinkles like troughs, where swine-deformity swills
The tears of perjury that lie there like wash
Fallen from the slimy and dishonest eye –
Yet such a one plucked sweets without restraint,
And has the grace of beauty to his sweet.
Though my hard fate has thrust me out to servitude,
I tumbled into th' world a gentleman –
She turns her blessed eye upon me now,
And I'll endure all storms before I part with't.

BEATRICE [*Aside*]
Again!
This ominous, ill-faced fellow more disturbs me
Than all my other passions.

DEFLORES [*Aside*] Now't begins again:
I'll stand this storm of hail though the stones pelt me.

40 *pick-hatched* Bruster conj. (pickhaird Q); cant term for a brothel – deriving from the 'hatch' or half-door, defended with 'picks' (or spikes) commonly used in the London stews (*OED* picked-hatch) – here presumably indicating a face pock-marked as though from syphilis. Bruster's own text prints *pig-haired* (= bristly), a contemptuous term found in Middleton's *A Trick to Catch the Old One* (IV.iv.298–9). Editors who retain Q take *pick-haired* to mean 'covered in spiky hairs' – i.e. 'bristly', or perhaps 'sparsely bearded'.

44 *wash* (1) watery discharge; (2) pig-swill (*OED* n. 9; 11a)

46 *sweets* pleasures (*OED* n. 3a)

47 *grace of beauty* Deflores may be thinking of the classical Three Graces – thus the 'grace of beauty' would be the goddess of beauty herself; but 'grace' (or 'mercy') was what the courtly lover, imitating the language of religion, sought from his mistress (cf. l. 63).
sweet sweetheart (*OED* n. 4). In the popular character-book, *Sir Thomas Ouerbury: His Wife*, we are told of '*A Serving-man*' that 'His inheritance is the Chamber-mayd, but [he] often purchaseth his Master's daughter, by reason of opportunity' (1618 edition, Sig. E1v).

48–9 *Though . . . gentleman* In fact many gentlemen were employed as upper servants in great households, but Deflores' disdain for service as a form of degrading 'servitude' echoes the complaints of contemporary pamphleteers, such as 'I.M.' in *A Health to the Gentlemanly profession of Servingmen: or, The Servingmans Comfort* (1598), who argued that changing conditions of employment were rendering domestic service no longer suitable for persons of gentle birth.

52–3 *Again . . . me* Q prints this as one line, but its dash after 'Again' – like that after 'So' (l. 77) – may indicate that the word is extra-metrical.

53 *ominous* Cf. I.i.2.

BEATRICE
Thy business? What's thy business?
DEFLORES [*Aside*] Soft and fair!
I cannot part so soon now.
BEATRICE [*Aside*] The villain's fixed. –
[*Aloud*] Thou standing toad-pool.
DEFLORES [*Aside*] The shower falls amain now.
BEATRICE
Who sent thee? What's thy errand? Leave my sight.
DEFLORES
My lord your father charged me to deliver
A message to you.
BEATRICE What, another since?
Do't and be hanged, then! Let me be rid of thee.
DEFLORES
True service merits mercy.
BEATRICE What's thy message?
DEFLORES
Let beauty settle but in patience,
You shall hear all.
BEATRICE A dallying, trifling torment!
DEFLORES
Signor Alonzo de Piracquo, lady,
Sole brother to Tomazo de Piracquo –

56 *Soft and fair* Directed at himself – cf. Tilley S601: 'Soft and fair goes far'; and Proverbs 15:1 'A soft answer turneth away wrath'.

57 *fixed* (1) immoveable; (2) transfixed (i.e. by the sight of her)

58 *standing toad-pool* stagnant water in which poisonous toads were generated (cf. *Othello* IV.ii.62–3: 'a cistern for foul toads / To knot and gender in') *amain* with full force

59–61 *thee . . . you* The social distance between Beatrice and Deflores is registered by the way that Beatrice uses the singular pronouns (*thee, thou, thy*) customarily used in addressing servants, children and social inferiors, while Deflores employs the more respectful plural forms (*you, your*). Cf. also II.ii.72, III.iii.168–70.

63 *True . . . mercy* Begins a series of equivocations, elaborated in II.ii and III.iii, on the meanings of service. Delivering messages belongs to Deflores' function as a household servant, but by using the term *mercy* he seeks to cast himself in the role of a courtly lover offering a more exalted kind of *service* to the lady of the castle. The lady's grant of 'mercy' often involved a 'favour' such as Deflores claims at I.i.224. Cf. also l. 48 and Introduction, p. xxx.

65 *dallying* (1) idly chattering, time wasting (*OED* v. 1, 4); (2) playing mockingly (*OED* v. 3); (3) amorously playful
trifling (1) mocking, deceitful (*OED* v.); (2) frivolously time-wasting. Gordon Williams (*Dictionary*, p. 1422) notes that the verb *trifle* was 'used with the sense of coit from c. 1560.'

BEATRICE
Slave, when wilt make an end?
DEFLORES [*Aside*] Too soon I shall.
BEATRICE
What all this while of him?
DEFLORES The said Alonzo,
With the foresaid Tomazo –
BEATRICE Yet again!
DEFLORES
Is new alighted.
BEATRICE Vengeance strike the news!
Thou thing most loathed, what cause was there in this
To bring thee to my sight?
DEFLORES My lord your father
Charged me to seek you out.
BEATRICE Is there no other
To send his errand by?
DEFLORES It seems 'tis my luck
To be i'th' way still.
BEATRICE Get thee from me.
DEFLORES [*Aside*] So!
Why, am not I an ass to devise ways
Thus to be railed at? I must see her still;
I shall have a mad qualm within this hour again –
I know't, and, like a common Garden-bull,
I do but take breath to be lugged again.
What this may bode I know not; I'll despair the less
Because there's daily precedents of bad faces
Beloved beyond all reason: these foul chops
May come into favour one day 'mongst his fellows.
Wrangling has proved the mistress of good pastime;

68 *Slave* While the regime of service in early modern England did not include literal slavery, 'slave' persisted as term expressing extreme social contempt.
77 *devise* Accent on first syllable.
78 *still* all the time
79 *qualm* bout of sickness – like Alsemero's at I.i.24 Deflores' desire is figured as an illness; and cf. Beatrice's fits of trembling below (l. 91)
80 *common Garden-bull* i.e one of the bulls kept for baiting at Paris Garden, near the theatres in Southwark
81 *lugged* worried, baited (as by dogs)
84 *chops* Literally 'jaws' – here a metonym for the face.
85 *his fellows* other faces as deformed as mine

As children cry themselves asleep, I ha' seen
Women have chid themselves a-bed to men. *Exit*

BEATRICE

I never see this fellow, but I think
Of some harm towards me, danger's in my mind still,
I scarce leave trembling of an hour after.
The next good mood I find my father in,
I'll get him quite discarded – Oh, I was
Lost in this small disturbance and forgot
Affliction's fiercer torrent that now comes
To bear down all my comforts.

Enter VERMANDERO, ALONZO, TOMAZO

VERMANDERO
You're both welcome;
But an especial one belongs to you, sir,
To whose most noble name our love presents
The addition of a son, our son Alonzo.

ALONZO

The treasury of honour cannot bring forth
A title I should more rejoice in, sir.

VERMANDERO

You have improved it well. Daughter, prepare:
The day will steal upon thee suddenly.

BEATRICE [*Aside*]

Howe'er, I will be sure to keep the night,
If it should come so near me.

[BEATRICE *and* VERMANDERO *talk apart*]

91 *of* for
hour Scanned as two syllables.

98 *our* Vermandero makes use of the royal plural on this formal occasion, no doubt because in confirming the betrothal he speaks for his entire lineage.

99 *addition . . . son* title of my son, together with the marks of honour belonging to that dignity (cf. *King Lear* I.i.136: 'the name and all th'addition to a king')

100 *treasury of honour* the entire store of noble titles

102 *improved it well* amply augmented the honour belonging to that title (*OED improve* v.[2] 4a)

104 *keep the night* preserve the night for myself. Beatrice plays on Vermandero's 'steal' to suggest that the wedding will involve a kind of theft (of her virginity), and implies that she will not allow the marriage to be consummated – an ironic anticipation (as Daalder points out) of what will actually happen on the night of her wedding to Alsemero.

105 *If . . . near* (1) If that day should actually come; (2) If it should affect me so intimately (*OED near* adv.[2] 16b)

TOMAZO Alonzo.

ALONZO Brother?

TOMAZO
In troth I see small welcome in her eye.

ALONZO
Fie, you are too severe a censurer
Of love in all points – there's no bringing on you:
If lovers should mark every thing a fault,
Affection would be like an ill-set book,
Whose faults might prove as big as half the volume.

BEATRICE
That's all I do entreat.

VERMANDERO It is but reasonable,
I'll see what my son says to't. – Son Alonzo,
Here's a motion made but to reprieve
A maidenhead three days longer; the request
Is not far out of reason, for indeed
The former time is pinching.

ALONZO Though my joys
Be set back so much time as I could wish
They had been forward, yet, since she desires it,
The time is set as pleasing as before;
I find no gladness wanting.

VERMANDERO May I ever
Meet it in that point still. You're nobly welcome, sirs.

Exeunt VERMANDERO *and* BEATRICE

TOMAZO
So. Did you mark the dullness of her parting now?

ALONZO
What dullness? Thou art so exceptious still.

108 *all points* every respect
bringing on you (1) advancing your attitude, educating you; (2) exciting you sexually. Q has no punctuation after *you*, and Frost suggests that the meaning might therefore be 'I cannot make you realise that . . .'; but the syntax seems strained, and Dilke was surely right to suppose an error by the compositor.
110 *ill-set* badly type-set
114 *motion* application (as to a court) (*OED* n. 8b)
117 *pinching* pressing; troublesome (*OED* v. 7)
121 *wanting* lacking
121–2 *May . . . still* May I always satisfy your wish for happiness in such matters (*OED satisfy* v. 7)
123 *dullness* gloomy lack of interest (*OED* n. 3)
124 *exceptious* disposed to find fault

TOMAZO

Why let it go, then: I am but a fool
To mark your harms so heedfully.

ALONZO Where's the oversight?

TOMAZO

Come, your faith's cozened in her, strongly cozened:
Unsettle your affection with all speed
Wisdom can bring it to – your peace is ruined else.
Think what a torment 'tis to marry one
Whose heart is leapt into another's bosom:
If ever pleasure she receive from thee,
It comes not in thy name, or of thy gift –
She lies but with another in thine arms,
He the half-father unto all thy children
In the conception; if he get 'em not,
She helps to get 'em for him in this passion;
And how dangerous
And shameful her restraint may go in time to,
It is not to be thought on without sufferings.

ALONZO

You speak as if she loved some other, then.

TOMAZO

Do you apprehend so slowly?

ALONZO Nay, and that
Be your fear only, I am safe enough:
Preserve your friendship and your counsel brother
For times of more distress; I should depart
An enemy, a dangerous, deadly one
To any but thyself that should but think
She knew the meaning of inconstancy,
Much less the use and practice. Yet we're friends:

126 *To . . . heedfully* To be so much on the lookout for things that may harm you
Where's the oversight? What have I overlooked?

127 *cozened* deceived, cheated

137 *in this passion* ed. (in his passions Q; Bruster, *conj.* Sampson: in his absence) i.e. the state of sexual arousal produced by the fantasy that she lies in her lover's embrace

138–9 *And . . . to* 'and what dangerous and shameful consequences will eventually result from restraining her' (Frost)

142 *and* if

149 *Yet* (1) Nevertheless; (2) Still (with the implication that if Tomazo persists it will destroy their friendship)
we're Q *corr.* (w'are; we are Q *uncorr.*)

Pray let no more be urged, I can endure
Much, till I meet an injury to her;
Then I am not myself. Farewell, sweet brother –
How much we're bound to heaven to depart lovingly! *Exit*

TOMAZO
Why here is love's tame madness, thus a man
Quickly steals into his vexation. *Exit*

[ACT II. SCENE ii.]

Enter DIAPHANTA *and* ALSEMERO

DIAPHANTA
The place is my charge; you have kept your hour,
And the reward of a just meeting bless you!
I hear my lady coming. Complete gentleman!
I dare not be too busy with my praises,
They're dangerous things to deal with. *Exit*

ALSEMERO This goes well:
These women are their ladies' cabinets,

153 *bound* obligated

154 *love's tame madness* picking up the theme of love-sickness and linking it to the sub-plot (cf. e.g. IV.iii.1–4). The idea that love constituted a form of madness is elaborated at great length in the section on love melancholy in Robert Burton's *Anatomy of Melancholy* (1621) – see also Introduction, pp. xvi–xvii.

155 *vexation* Scanned as four syllables.

II.ii Author: Middleton

1 *charge* responsibility

3 *Complete gentleman* Perfect gentleman – as at I.i.205, the phrase probably alludes to Henry Peacham's conduct book, *The Complete Gentleman*, published in the year of *The Changeling*'s first performance.

4–5 *I . . . with* i.e. if Diaphanta is too effusive in her praise of Alsemero, Beatrice may become jealous

6–7 *These . . . 'em* In *Gerardo*, Isdaura's waiting maid, Julia, is described as 'Secretary to my most hidden thoughts' (sig. H5); compare also the character of '*A Chamber-maide*' in Overbury's *Wife*: 'She is her mistresses she Secretary, and keepes the box of her teeth, her haire, & her painting very priuate' (1618 edition, sig. G7v).

6 *women* waiting-women

their ed. (the Q)

cabinets either (a) a small, private room (in which costly paintings and other treasures were often kept), or (b) a chest for jewels and other precious possessions; figuratively (c) a secret receptacle (*OED* n. 4–6). In *Othello*, the waiting-woman Emilia is similarly described by Othello as 'A closet, lock and key of villainous secrets' (4.1.22).

Things of most precious trust are locked into 'em.

Enter BEATRICE

BEATRICE

I have within mine eye all my desires:
Requests that holy prayers ascend heaven for,
And brings 'em down to furnish our defects,
Come not more sweet to our necessities
Than thou unto my wishes.

ALSEMERO We're so like
In our expressions, lady, that unless I borrow
The same words, I shall never find their equals.

BEATRICE

How happy were this meeting, this embrace,
If it were free from envy! This poor kiss
It has an enemy, a hateful one,
That wishes poison to't. How well were I now
If there were none such name known as Piracquo,
Nor no such tie as the command of parents!
I should be but too much blessed.

ALSEMERO One good service
Would strike off both your fears, and I'll go near it too,
Since you are so distressed: remove the cause,
The command ceases; so there's two fears blown out
With one and the same blast.

BEATRICE Pray let me find you, sir.
What might that service be so strangely happy?

7 *locked* ed. (lock Q)
10 *brings 'em down* i.e. the prayers succeed in bringing the things requested back to earth. For the irregular grammar here, see I.ii.150.
furnish our defects supply us with what we lack, make up for our deficiencies
11 *our necessities* what we need
17–18 *an enemy . . . to't* i.e. Alonso, who would wish their kiss poisoned, if he knew of it; ironically, as we learn at l. 57, their entire rendezvous is being watched by an even more dangerous enemy, Deflores – the 'poison' that Beatrice is destined to 'kiss' (see V.iii.67).
21 *service* As ll. 27–8 show, it is chivalric 'service' that Alsemero has in mind.
23–4 *remove . . . ceases* A paraphrase of the scholastic tag, *ablata causa, tollitur effectus* ('the cause removed, the effect ceases').
25 *blast* puff of breath
find understand
26 *happy* fortunate

ALSEMERO
The honourablest piece about man – valour.
I'll send a challenge to Piracquo instantly.

BEATRICE
How? Call you that extinguishing of fear
When 'tis the only way to keep it flaming?
Are not you ventured in the action,
That's all my joys and comforts? Pray no more, sir.
Say you prevailed, you're danger's and not mine then:
The law would claim you from me, or obscurity
Be made the grave to bury you alive.
I'm glad these thoughts come forth – O keep not one
Of this condition, sir! Here was a course
Found to bring sorrow on her way to death:
The tears would ne'er ha' dried till dust had choked 'em.
Blood-guiltiness becomes a fouler visage,
And now I think on one – [*Aside*] I was to blame,
I ha' marred so good a market with my scorn:
'T had been done questionless. The ugliest creature
Creation framed for some use, yet to see
I could not mark so much where it should be.

ALSEMERO
Lady!

BEATRICE [*Aside*]Why men of art make much of poison,
Keep one to expel another. Where was my art?

ALSEMERO
Lady, you hear not me.

BEATRICE I do especially, sir.

27 *about* ed. ('bout Q – another instance of unnecessary colloquial contraction)
31 *ventured* put at risk
32 *That's* Who are
33 *you're* ed. (your Q)
34–5 *The law . . . alive* either you'd fall victim to the law or you'd have to go into hiding
36–7 *one . . . condition* one thought of this kind
38 *to bring . . . death* to make me die of grief
41 s.d. Most eds. begin the aside at the beginning of the line, but Q's dash after *one* suggests that the first part of the line is spoken aloud and that *I think on one* probably means 'I am thinking about [how to find] one' rather than 'I have one in mind'.
42 *marred . . . market* Semi-proverbial (cf. Tilley M672: 'He has made a good market').
43 *done questionless* (1) 'there is no doubt it would have been done by now;' (2) 'done with no questions asked'
46 *make . . . poison* turn to poison to good account (*OED* v.[1] 18d)
47 *Keep . . . another* A standard nostrum of early modern medicine, enshrined in the proverb 'one poison expels [drives out] another' (Tilley P477).

The present times are not so sure of our side
As those hereafter may be: we must use 'em then
As thrifty folks their wealth, sparingly now,
Till the time opens.

ALSEMERO You teach wisdom, lady.

BEATRICE [*Calling*]
Within there, Diaphanta!

Enter DIAPHANTA

DIAPHANTA Do you call, madam?

BEATRICE
Perfect your service, and conduct this gentleman
The private way you brought him.

DIAPHANTA I shall, madam.

ALSEMERO
My love's as firm as love e'er built upon.

Exeunt DIAPHANTA *and* ALSEMERO

Enter DEFLORES

DEFLORES [*Aside*]
I have watched this meeting, and do wonder much
What shall become of t'other; I'm sure both
Cannot be served unless she transgress. Happily
Then I'll put in for one; for if a woman

49 *not . . . side* favourable to our cause
52 *time opens* future unfolds
54 *service* Ricks (p. 299) suggests an ironic *double entendre* – Diaphanta will 'serve' Alsmero in a way she does not yet imagine.
55 *private way* Perhaps another ironic *double entendre* (Ricks).
56 *My . . . upon* My love for you is as unshakeable as any on which a mistress ever rested her hopes
57 *I have watched* Possibly an indication that an earlier stage direction has been lost: Deflores was perhaps meant to appear 'above', like Lollio in the parallel episode at III.ii.170 ff., to spy on the lovers – as he did in the 1978 Royal Shakespeare Company production.
58 *t'other* Alonzo
59 *served* sexually satisfied
Happily Perhaps
60 *put . . . one* apply for a share (with sexual innuendo – cf. IV.iii.34)

Fly from one point, from him she makes a husband,
She spreads and mounts then like arithmetic –
One, ten, a hundred, a thousand, ten thousand –
Proves in time sutler to an army royal.
Now do I look to be most richly railed at,
Yet I must see her.

BEATRICE [*Aside*] Why, put case I loathed him
As much as youth and beauty hates a sepulchre,
Must I needs show it? Cannot I keep that secret,
And serve my turn upon him? See he's here –
[*Aloud*] Deflores.

DEFLORES [*Aside*] Ha! I shall run mad with joy:
She called me fairly by my name, Deflores,
And neither 'rogue' nor 'rascal'.

BEATRICE What ha' you done
To your face alate? You've met with some good physician;
You've pruned yourself, methinks: you were not wont
To look so amorously.

DEFLORES Not I.
[*Aside*] 'Tis the same physnomy to a hair and pimple
Which she called scurvy scarce an hour ago:
How is this?

BEATRICE Come hither – nearer, man.

DEFLORES [*Aside*]
I'm up to the chin in heaven.

BEATRICE Turn, let me see –

61–2 *Fly . . . mounts* 'De Flores uses the language of falconry . . . with [a] sexual suggestion' (Bawcutt 1998).

61 *point* position; with a quibble on *point* = penis (Williams, *Glossary*, p. 241)

64 *sutler* supplier of provisions; 'if a woman, sometimes a prostitute' (Bawcutt (1998))
army royal grand army (*OED* royal a. 10b)

66 *put case* suppose

68 *secret* Cf. I.ii.1–8.

69 *serve . . . him* make use of him for my own purposes; but with an unconscious sexual innuendo (cf. I.ii.57)

72 *you* Beatrice's flattering approach is marked by her switch to the respectful plural pronoun.

74 *pruned* preened, decked out (*OED* v.[1] 1–2)

75 *look so amorously* (1) look so lovable, desirable (*OED amorous* a. II); (2) gaze so fondly, lustfully [at me] (*OED amorous* a. I, 2)

76 *physnomy* physiognomy

77 *scurvy* (1) covered with diseased scabs (*OED* a. 1); (2) worthless, contemptible (*OED* a. 2)

Faugh! 'Tis but the heat of the liver, I perceiv't;
I thought it had been worse.

DEFLORES [*Aside*] Her fingers touched me –
She smells all amber!

BEATRICE
I'll make a water for you shall cleanse this
Within a fortnight.

DEFLORES With your own hands, lady?

BEATRICE
Yes, mine own, sir: in a work of cure
I'll trust no other.

DEFLORES [*Aside*] 'Tis half an act of pleasure
To hear her talk thus to me.

BEATRICE When we're used
To a hard face, 'tis not so unpleasing,
It mends still in opinion, hourly mends –
I see it by experience.

DEFLORES [*Aside*] I was blest
To light upon this minute, I'll make use on't.

BEATRICE
Hardness becomes the visage of a man well,
It argues service, resolution, manhood,
If cause were of employment.

DEFLORES 'Twould be soon seen,
If e'er your ladyship had cause to use it.
I would but wish the honour of a service
So happy as that mounts to.

80 *Faugh!* The exclamation is extra-metrical.
heat of the liver In Galenic medicine the liver was the seat of love and the passions; an overheated liver could produce excess of desire, but might also result in physical symptoms.

81 *fingers* Already eroticised by Deflores' play with Beatrice's glove at I.i.224–7.

82 *amber* ambergris – an ingredient of costly perfumes. The detail shows how Deflores' erotic excitement is directly linked to Beatrice's rank and wealth.

83 *water* medicinal tincture (*OED* n. 16a); however, Deflores' response at ll. 86–7 suggests that he chooses to understand it as meaning 'semen' (Williams, *Glossary*, p. 332).

94 *employment* Like *service* capable of a sexual interpretation.

95 *use* With the additional sense 'employ sexually'.

96 *honour of a service* Deflores emphasises the chivalric sense of *service*; but *honour* also = virginity (and hence vagina – Williams, *Glossary*, pp. 161–2).

97 *mounts* bawdy *double entendre*

BEATRICE We shall try you –
Oh, my Deflores!

DEFLORES How's that?
[*Aside*] She calls me hers already, 'my Deflores'! –
[*Aloud*] You were about to sigh out somewhat, madam.

BEATRICE
No, was I? I forgot – Oh!

DEFLORES There 'tis again,
The very fellow on't.

BEATRICE You are too quick, sir.

DEFLORES
There's no excuse for't now I heard it twice, madam:
That sigh would fain have utterance, take pity on't,
And lend it a free word – 'las how it labours
For liberty, I hear the murmur yet
Beat at your bosom.

BEATRICE Would creation –

DEFLORES
Ay, well said, that's it!

BEATRICE Had formed me man!

DEFLORES
Nay, that's not it.

BEATRICE Oh, 'tis the soul of freedom!
I should not then be forced to marry one
I hate beyond all depths; I should have power
Then to oppose my loathings – nay, remove 'em
For ever from my sight.

DEFLORES O blest occasion!
Without change to your sex, you have your wishes:
Claim so much man in me.

97 *try* put to the test (*OED* v. 7a; with unconscious sexual innuendo – see Williams, *Dictionary*, p. 1430: *try* = 'have sexual experience of')

102 *on't* of it
quick Perhaps with an unconscious play on *quick* n. = sexual centre (see Williams, *Dictionary*, p. 1129).

103 *for't now I* This edition (for't, now I Q; for't now; I Dilke and most eds).
now I heard given that I have now heard

107 *creation* Four syllables, stress on final syllable.

112–13 *remove . . . sight* Beatrice's euphemism for murder takes her obsession with eyesight and appearance to its logical extreme.

113 *occasion* opportunity (*OED* n. 1a)

BEATRICE In thee, Deflores?
There's small cause for that.
DEFLORES Put it not from me:
It's a service that I kneel for to you. [*Kneels*]
BEATRICE
You are too violent to mean faithfully,
There's horror in my service, blood and danger:
Can those be things to sue for?
DEFLORES If you knew
How sweet it were to me to be employed
In any act of yours, you would say then
I failed, and used not reverence enough
When I receive the charge on't.
BEATRICE [*Aside*] This is much methinks;
Belike his wants are greedy, and to such
Gold tastes like angels' food. – [*Aloud*] Rise.
DEFLORES
I'll have the work first.
BEATRICE [*Aside*] Possible his need
Is strong upon him – [*Gives him money*] there's to
encourage thee:
As thou art forward and thy service dangerous,
Thy reward shall be precious.
DEFLORES That I have thought on;
I have assured myself of that beforehand,
And know it will be precious – the thought ravishes.
BEATRICE
Then take him to thy fury.

117 *It's . . . you* Deflores adopts the supplicant posture of a knight seeking acceptance as his lady's 'servant' (cf. also Antonio's offer of himself as Isabella's 'servant' at III.ii.117, and Alsemero's offer of 'service' to Beatrice at II.ii.21).
118 *too . . . faithfully* too passionate to mean what you say
122 *act* (1) action; (2) sexual congress (Williams, *Glossary*, p. 24)
124 *the charge on't* your instructions for it
126 *angels' food* manna (see Psalm 78:24–5)
129 *forward* eager (to carry out my will), bold (*OED* a. 6a, c)
131 *myself of that* Q *corr* (myselfe that Q *uncorr.*)
132 *ravishes* enraptures; but the sexual sense ('rapes'), which Beatrice does not hear, emphasizes the gap between the two kinds of 'reward' they envisage.
133 *Then . . . fury* In the 1993 BBC version Beatrice joined the kneeling Deflores on this line, as though mimicking the ritual of marriage vows – which she appeared to seal with the kiss she gave Deflores at l. 147, after her contemptuous aside about 'his dog-face'.

DEFLORES I thirst for him.
BEATRICE
Alonzo de Piracquo.
DEFLORES His end's upon him:
He shall be seen no more.
BEATRICE How lovely now
Dost thou appear to me! Never was man
Dearlier rewarded.
DEFLORES I do think of that.
BEATRICE
Be wondrous careful in the execution.
DEFLORES
Why, are not both our lives upon the cast?
BEATRICE
Then I throw all my fears upon thy service.
DEFLORES
They ne'er shall rise to hurt you. [*Rises*]
BEATRICE When the deed's done,
I'll furnish thee with all things for thy flight:
Thou may'st live bravely in another country.
DEFLORES
Ay, ay, we'll talk of that hereafter.
BEATRICE [*Aside*] I shall rid
Myself of two inveterate loathings at one time:
Piracquo and his dog-face. *Exit*
DEFLORES O my blood!
Methinks I feel her in mine arms already,
Her wanton fingers combing out this beard,

133 *thirst* Cf. Deflores' metaphors of sexual desire as thirst for 'blood' of a different kind (III.iii.107–8; V.iii.170–1; and below l. 146).
135 *He . . . more* Deflores cleverly exploits Beatrice's self-deceiving euphemism at ll. 112–13.
lovely Not only 'beautiful', but also 'lovable' and 'amorous' (*OED* a. 1–3).
137 *Dearlier* (1) More richly; (2) Lovingly; (3) At greater cost (*OED* a. 2a, 3, 4a, 5a, 6a)
139 *upon the cast* dependent on the throw of this dice
141 s.d. Most eds. insert this s.d. at l. 135, but the visual pun created by the sight of Deflores rising even as he speaks of Beatrice's 'rising fears' is entirely in accord with Middleton's ironic technique.
143 *bravely* splendidly, ostentatiously (*OED* adv. 2)
146 *his dog-face* Beatrice imagines Deflores as one of those monstrous dog-headed humans (*cynopheli*) described by Pliny and his medieval successors, including the fabled Sir John Mandeville; Bawcutt (1958) suggests that Beatrice may be coining a mock-title for Deflores, 'His Dog-Face' (on the model of His Lordship).
blood sexual desire

And, being pleased, praising this bad face.
Hunger and pleasure, they'll commend sometimes
Slovenly dishes, and feed heartily on 'em –
Nay, which is stranger, refuse daintier for 'em.
Some women are odd feeders – I'm too loud:
Here comes the man goes supperless to bed,
Yet shall not rise tomorrow to his dinner.

Enter ALONZO

ALONZO
Deflores.

DEFLORES My kind, honourable lord?

ALONZO
I am glad I've met with thee.

DEFLORES Sir.

ALONZO Thou canst show me
The full strength of the castle?

DEFLORES That I can, sir.

ALONZO
I much desire it.

DEFLORES And if the ways and straits
Of some of the passages be not too tedious for you,
I will assure you, worth your time and sight, my lord.

ALONZO
Pooh! That shall be no hindrance.

DEFLORES I'm your servant, then.
'Tis now near dinner time; 'gainst your lordship's rising
I'll have the keys about me.

ALONZO Thanks, kind Deflores.

151 *Slovenly* Nasty, disgusting (*OED* a. 3)
154–5 *supperless . . . rise . . . dinner* Extends the sexual metaphor from ll. 150–3.
159 *ways* doorways, gateways (*OED* n. 1f)
straits narrow places (*OED* n. 1a; and cf. a. 3a)
160 *tedious* irksome (*OED* a. 2)
163 *'gainst . . . rising* i.e. until such time as you rise from the table
164 *keys* For the symbolic significance of these instruments in Deflores' 'work of secrecy' (III.i.27), cf. the key with which Beatrice opens Alsemero's closet to discover '*The Book of Experiment / Called Secrets in Nature*' (IV.i.18–25), and the 'key of [the] wardrobe' which Isabella obtains from Lollio in order to penetrate the secret of Antonio's and Franciscus' disguise (IV.iii.44). See also Introduction, p. xx.

DEFLORES
He's safely thrust upon me beyond hopes *Exeunt*

In the act-time DEFLORES *hides a naked rapier*

ACT III. [SCENE i.]

Enter ALONZO *and* DEFLORES

DEFLORES
Yes, here are all the keys: I was afraid, my lord,
I'd wanted for the postern – this is it.
I've all, I've all, my lord – this for the sconce.

ALONZO
'Tis a most spacious and impregnable fort.

DEFLORES
You'll tell me more, my lord. This descent
Is somewhat narrow, we shall never pass
Well with our weapons, they'll but trouble us.
[*Takes off his sword*]

ALONZO
Thou sayest true.

DEFLORES
Pray let me help your lordship.
[*Takes off* ALONZO*'s sword*]

165 *safely* securely, without any risk (to me) – ironic
s.d. *act-time* Unlike outdoor playhouses, such as the Globe, where the action was continuous, the so-called 'private' theatres, including the Cockpit and Salisbury Court, allowed for intervals between the acts, during which music was customarily played.
s.d. *DEFLORES . . . rapier* An altogether unusual stage-direction, since the interval between acts is a kind of non-time from which the characters are conventionally excluded: Deflores' exploitation of it becomes a way of representing his unfettered access to the castle's innermost 'secrets'.

III.i Author: Middleton.
2 *postern* rear door or gate
3 *sconce* small fort designed to defend a castle gate (*OED* n.[3] 1). Holdsworth, 'Notes on *The Changeling*,' *N&Q* ns. 234 (1989) 344–6, suggests a pun on *sconce* n.[2] = jocular term for the head, and argues that 'this must mean that he intends to club Alonzo with one of the large, heavy keys he is carrying, the very one he is now showing his victim'; Bruster inserts stage directions to this effect at III.i.24 ff.
5 *tell me more* 'have more to say, be even more impressed [when you have seen more]' – with an ironic innuendo

ALONZO
'Tis done. Thanks, kind Deflores.

DEFLORES
Here are hooks, my lord,
To hang such things on purpose.

ALONZO
Lead, I'll follow thee.

Exeunt at one door and enter at the other

DEFLORES
All this is nothing; you shall see anon
A place you little dream on.

ALONZO
I am glad
I have this leisure; all your master's house
Imagine I ha' taken a gondola.

DEFLORES
All but myself, sir, [*Aside*] which makes up my safety.
[*Aloud*] My lord, I'll place you at a casement here
Will show you the full strength of all the castle.
Look, spend your eye a while upon that object.

ALONZO
Here's rich variety, Deflores.

DEFLORES
Yes, sir.

ALONZO
Goodly munition.

DEFLORES
Ay, there's ordnance, sir –
No bastard metal – will ring you a peal like bells
At great men's funerals. Keep your eye straight, my lord,
Take special notice of that sconce before you:
There you may dwell awhile. [*Takes up the rapier*]

9 *lord* Scanned as two syllables here.
10 s.d. This helps the actors to mime the narrow, winding descent. Most editions begin a separate scene at this point, but since the s.d. indicates that the action is effectively continuous, there seems no point in doing so.
12 *A place . . . on* i.e. the grave
16 *casement* Corruption of *casemate* (*OED casement* n. 4) which is the word in Reynolds: 'A vaulted chamber built in the thickness of the ramparts of a fortress, with embrasures for the defence of the place' (*OED casemate* n. 1).
20 *munition* fortification
21 *bastard metal* corrupt alloy
peal (1) changes rung on a set of bells; (2) discharge of cannons, esp. in salute (*OED* n. 2, 3)
22 *great men's funerals* a by-word for hypocritical behaviour (see Webster, *White Devil*, V.ii.296–7)
24 *dwell* (1) fix your attention; (2) remain when dead

ALONZO I am upon't.

DEFLORES
And so am I. [*Stabs him*]

ALONZO Deflores! O Deflores,
Whose malice hast thou put on?

DEFLORES Do you question
A work of secrecy? I must silence you. [*Stabs him*]

ALONZO
Oh, oh, oh!

DEFLORES I must silence you. [*Kills him*]
So, here's an undertaking well accomplished.
This vault serves to good use now – Ha! what's that
Threw sparkles in my eye? – Oh, 'tis a diamond
He wears upon his finger. It was well found:
This will approve the work. What, so fast on?
Not part in death? I'll take a speedy course then:
Finger and all shall off. So, now I'll clear
The passages from all suspect or fear. *Exit with the body*

[ACT III. SCENE ii.]

Enter ISABELLA *and* LOLLIO

ISABELLA
Why, sirrah? Whence have you commission
To fetter the doors against me? If you
Keep me in a cage, pray whistle to me,
Let me be doing something.

24 *I . . . upon't* I can see it. Deflores' reply twists the phrase to mean 'I have found my target'.
30 *vault* Presumably represented by the curtained 'discovery space' at the rear of the stage.
31 *sparkles . . . diamond* Uncanny echo of II.i.15.
33 *approve* serve as proof of
34 *Not . . . death* An ironic recollection of the marriage vow 'till death us do part' – cf. III.iv.37–8.
III.ii Author: Rowley
1 *sirrah* term of address expressing authority, reprimand or contempt

LOLLIO

You shall be doing, if it please you: I'll whistle to you, if you'll pipe after.

ISABELLA

Is it your master's pleasure or your own
To keep me in this pinfold?

LOLLIO

'Tis for my master's pleasure, lest, being taken in another man's corn, you might be pounded in another place.

ISABELLA

'Tis very well, and he'll prove very wise.

LOLLIO

He says you have company enough in the house, if you please to be sociable, of all sorts of people.

ISABELLA

Of all sorts? Why here's none but fools and madmen.

LOLLIO

Very well – and where will you find any other, if you should go abroad? There's my master and I to boot too.

ISABELLA

Of either sort one – a madman and a fool.

LOLLIO

I would even participate of both then, if I were as you: I know you're half mad already; be half foolish too.

ISABELLA

You're a brave, saucy rascal! Come on, sir,
Afford me then the pleasure of your bedlam:
You were commending once today to me

5 *doing* fornicating
5–6 *I'll . . . after* Daalder suggests that Lollio plays on the proverbial expression 'to dance after someone's pipe' (*Oxford Dictionary of English Proverbs*, p. 166); the proverb is not in Tilley, but is recorded in *OED* (v. 1 e) from 1562.
6 *pipe* obscene *double entendre* (*pipe* = penis; Williams, *Glossary*, p. 236)
8 *pinfold* pound for stray livestock; place of confinement. Daalder suggests a play on *pin* = penis (Williams, *Glossary*, pp. 235–6).
10 *pounded* (1) held in a pound; (2) pounded with a (phallic) pestle
another place obscene innuendo
16 *abroad* into the world at large
to boot as well
19 *participate* partake (i.e. sexually)
20 *brave* bold (in a pejorative sense)
saucy insolent; lascivious (*OED* a. 2a–b)
21 *bedlam* See above, I.ii.50.
22 *once* earlier

Your last come lunatic – what a proper
Body there was without brains to guide it,
And what a pitiful delight appeared
In that defect, as if your wisdom had found
A mirth in madness; pray sir, let me partake,
If there be such a pleasure.

LOLLIO

If I do not show you the handsomest, discreetest madman – one that I may call the understanding madman – then say I am a fool.

ISABELLA

Well, a match: I will say so.

LOLLIO

When you have a taste of the madman, you shall (if you please) see Fools' College o' th'other side. I seldom lock there: 'tis but shooting a bolt or two, and you are amongst 'em. *Exit*

Enters presently [drawing FRANCISCUS *after him]*

Come on, sir; let me see how handsomely you'll behave yourself now.

FRANCISCUS

How sweetly she looks! Oh, but there's a wrinkle n her brow as deep as philosophy. Anacreon, drink to my mistress' health, I'll pledge it. Stay, stay, there's a spider in the cup – no, 'tis but a grape-stone; swallow it, fear nothing, poet; so, so, lift higher.

23 *last come* most recently arrived
proper handsome (*OED* a. 9)
26 *In . . . defect* i.e in your description of it
32 *a match* it's a deal
34 *o' th'other side* ed. (o'th' side Q)
35 *shooting a bolt* undoing a bolt – with a play both on the proverb 'A fool's bolt is soon shot' (Tilley, F515) and on the obscene meanings of 'bolt' and 'shoot'
36 *handsomely* decently (*OED* adv. 5)
39 *Anacreon* Greek poet who celebrated the pleasures of wine (probably addressed to Lollio)
40 *spider . . . cup* According to folk-belief, since spiders were venomous, they could poison a drink, and to swallow one could be fatal (cf. *Winter's Tale*, II.i.39–45).
41 *grape-stone* Pliny (*Natural History* VII, vii) records the legend that Anacreon choked to death on a grapeseed.

ISABELLA

Alack, alack, 'tis too full of pity
To be laughed at. How fell he mad? Canst thou tell?

LOLLIO

For love, mistress. He was a pretty poet too, and that set him forwards first; the Muses then forsook him, he ran mad for a chambermaid – yet she was but a dwarf neither.

FRANCISCUS

Hail, bright Titania!
Why standst thou idle on these flowery banks?
Oberon is dancing with his Dryades;
I'll gather daisies, primrose, violets,
And bind them in a verse of poesy. [*Approaches* ISABELLA]

LOLLIO

Not too near – you see your danger.
[*Threatens* FRANCISCUS *with a whip*]

FRANCISCUS

O hold thy hand, great Diomed!
Thou feedst thy horses well, they shall obey thee;
[*Drops onto all fours*] Get up, Bucephalus kneels. [*Kneels*]

LOLLIO

You see how I awe my flock: a shepherd has not his dog at more obedience.

42–3 *Alack . . . tell* l. 42 is one syllable short, l. 43 one syllable too long. Dilke may have been right to read 'it is' for *'tis*, and *canst thou tell* may similarly be a mistake for 'canst tell'; but the scansion in these sub-plot scenes of mingled verse and prose is often unusually rough.

44–5 *set . . . forwards* started him off. Poetic inspiration (like love) was sometimes thought of as a kind of divine madness, the *furor poeticus* – cf. *A Midsummer Night's Dream*, V.i.12–20.

47, 49 *Titania, Oberon* 'Oberon' was the traditional name for the fairy king, but the conjunction with 'Titania', the name given to Oberon's consort in *A Midsummer Night's Dream*, suggests that Franciscus is probably remembering Shakespeare's comedy (see Introduction, pp. xviii–xix).

49 *Dryades* wood-nymphs. Lollio implies that Isabella's husband is entertaining himself with other women.

50 *daisies . . . violets* Daalder notes the symbolism of these flowers (freshness, excellence, and chastity).

51 *poesy* (1) poetry; (2) posy of flowers (*OED* n. 1, 4)

53 *Diomed* Diomedes, King of the Bistonians in Thrace, who fed his horses on human flesh; Hercules tamed these savage steeds by feeding them Diomedes' own corpse.

55 *Get up* Mount
Bucephalus the mighty charger of Alexander the Great, which only the king himself could ride
s.d. '*Kneels*' Repeats Deflores' gesture at II.ii.117.

ISABELLA

His conscience is unquiet; sure that was
The cause of this. A proper gentleman!

FRANCISCUS

Come hither, Aesculapius, hide the poison.

LOLLIO

Well, 'tis hid. [*Puts away the whip.* FRANCISCUS *rises*]

FRANCISCUS

Didst thou never hear of one Tiresias,
A famous poet?

LOLLIO

Yes, that kept tame wild geese.

FRANCISCUS

That's he, I am the man.

LOLLIO

No!

FRANCISCUS

Yes, but make no words on't: I was a man
Seven years ago.

LOLLIO

A stripling, I think you might.

FRANCISCUS

Now I'm a woman, all feminine.

LOLLIO

I would I might see that.

FRANCISCUS

Juno struck me blind.

LOLLIO

I'll ne'er believe that; for a woman they say, has an eye more than a man.

59 *proper* (1) handsome; (2) complete, thorough (*OED* a. 9, 7)
60 *Aesculapius* Greek god of medicine
poison i.e. the whip, but picking up the image from l. 40.
61 *hid* A visual parallel with Deflores' concealment of the rapier at the beginning of Act III may be intended here.
62–3 *Tiresias . . . poet* Not a poet, but a blind prophet from Thebes.
64 *wild geese* prostitutes (see Williams, *Dictionary*, pp. 143–4)
67–70 *I was . . . woman* Tiresias spent seven years as a woman, before changing back into a man.
69 *might* might have been
72 *Juno . . . blind* When Tiresias revealed that women derived more pleasure from sex than men, the marriage goddess, Juno, punished him with blindness.
73–4 *eye . . . man* i.e. between her legs – an ironic gloss on Beatrice's 'eyes of judgement' (II.i.13)

FRANCISCUS

I say she struck me blind.

LOLLIO

And Luna made you mad: you have two trades to beg with.

FRANCISCUS

Luna is now big-bellied, and there's room
For both of us to ride with Hecate;
I'll drag thee up into her silver sphere,
And there we'll kick the dog and beat the bush
That barks against the witches of the night;
The swift lycanthropi that walks the round,
We'll tear their wolvish skins, and save the sheep.

LOLLIO

Is't come to this? Nay, then my poison comes forth again.
[*Shows the whip*] Mad slave indeed – abuse your keeper!

ISABELLA

I prithee, hence with him, now he grows dangerous.

FRANCISCUS [*Sings*]

Sweet love, pity me:
Give me leave to lie with thee.

LOLLIO

No, I'll see you wiser first: to your own kennel.

FRANCISCUS

No noise, she sleeps; draw all the curtains round,

76 *Luna* The moon goddess. Not only was the moon credited with the power to drive people 'lunatic', but, as the planet of change, it was supposed to exercise particular influence upon women, because of their monthly cycles – rendering them especially liable to fickleness, change, and emotional instability (cf. V.iii.196 ff.). Lollio implies Tiresias'/ Franciscus' time as a woman made him unusually vulnerable to the malign influence of the moon
two trades i.e. blindness and madness
beg beg with

77 *big-bellied* Franciscus' conceit is that the full moon is pregnant.

78 *Hecate* Greek goddess of witchcraft, frequently identified with the moon goddess Diana/ Artemis, and hence often used as a synonym for the moon itself

80 *dog . . . bush* conventional properties of the man-in-the-moon (see *A Midsummer Night's Dream*, V.i.251–3). The bawdy implication is that Franciscus himself means to be the man in *her* moon.

80–1 *bush / That barks* Franciscus' confused syntax is perhaps encouraged by a pun on *barks*.

82 *lycanthropi* sufferers from lycanthropia who (like Duke Ferdinand in *The Duchess of Malfi*) imagine themselves transformed into wolves. Q prints a comma rather than a semi-colon after *night*, and it may be that *lycanthropi* are being imagined as witches of a sort.

90–2 *No . . . mouse-hole* Noting the rhymes on 'sleeps/creeps', 'round/sound', 'soul/hole', Bruster suggests that these lines may have been intended as a continuation of Antonio's song, forming a lyric with alternating long and short lines.

Let no soft sound molest the pretty soul
But love, and love creeps in at a mouse-hole.

LOLLIO

I would you would get into your hole.

Exit FRANCISCUS

Now, mistress, I will bring you another sort: you shall be fooled another while – [*Calls*] Tony, come hither, Tony!

Enter ANTONIO

Look who's yonder, Tony.

ANTONIO

Cousin, is it not my aunt?

LOLLIO

Yes, 'tis one of 'em, Tony.

ANTONIO

He, he! how do you, uncle?

LOLLIO

Fear him not mistress, 'tis a gentle nidget: you may play with him as safely with him as with his bauble.

ISABELLA

How long hast thou been a fool?

ANTONIO

Ever since I came hither, cousin.

ISABELLA

Cousin? I'm none of thy cousins, fool.

LOLLIO

O mistress, fools have always so much wit as to claim their kindred.

92 *mouse-hole* obscene ('mouse' being a term of affection for women)
95 s.d. ed. (*after* 'yonder, Tony' Q)
97 *aunt* (also) prostitute (Williams, *Glossary*, p. 31)
99 *uncle* Daalder suggests this may have the cant meaning of 'procurer' – a conjecture made more plausible by the fact that, in *Troilus and Cressida*, Cressida is pimped by Pandarus, whom she repeatedly addresses as 'uncle'.
100 *nidget* colloquial contraction of 'an idiot'
play copulate (Williams, *Glossary*, p. 238)
101 *bauble* (1) fool's baton (usually with a carved fool's head at its tip); (2) penis (Williams, *Glossary*, pp. 36–7)
103 *cousin* Isabella probably interprets *cousin* as a euphemism for 'lover'.

MADMAN (*Within*)
Bounce, bounce! He falls, he falls!

ISABELLA
Hark you – your scholars in the upper room
Are out of order.

LOLLIO
Must I come amongst you there? Keep you the fool, mistress. I'll go up and play left-handed Orlando amongst the madmen.

Exit

ISABELLA
Well, sir.

ANTONIO
'Tis opportuneful now, sweet lady! Nay,
Cast no amazing eye upon this change.

ISABELLA
Ha!

ANTONIO
This shape of folly shrouds your dearest love,
The truest servant to your powerful beauties,
Whose magic had this force thus to transform me.

ISABELLA
You are a fine fool indeed.

ANTONIO
Oh, 'tis not strange:
Love has an intellect that runs through all
The scrutinous sciences; and, like
A cunning poet, catches a quantity
Of every knowledge, yet brings all home

107 *bounce* the noise made by an explosion, the explosion itself (*OED* n.[1] 2), often (as probably here) representing gunfire (cf. *King John*, II.i.462; *2 Henry IV*, III.ii.280)
falls i.e from a shot or explosion; but here with a sexual innuendo

108 *upper room* Perhaps includes a satiric glance at the audience, since 'room' was the contemporary term for a theatre 'box' (see Holdsworth, *Casebook*, p. 269).

111 *left-handed Orlando* clumsy imitation (*OED left-handed* a. 2) of the hero of Ariosto's epic *Orlando Furioso*

113–14 *'Tis . . . change* Antonio's abandonment of his fool persona is signified by his shift to a slightly pompous style of blank verse. His reference to this 'change' acts as reminder of his own role as the nominal 'changeling' of the title (see also l. 118).

114 *amazing* full of amazement; but Antonio may also be referring to the power of her eye to throw a lover into confusion and bewilderment. Literally speaking, to be 'amazed' is to be trapped in a maze or labyrinth – a recurrent motif in *The Changeling* (cf. III.iii.71; IV.iii.98–100; V.iii.148).

121 *scrutinous* searching
sciences branches of learning

122 *cunning* skilful

Into one mystery, into one secret
That he proceeds in.

ISABELLA You're a parlous fool.

ANTONIO
No danger in me: I bring nought but Love
And his soft wounding shafts to strike you with –
Try but one arrow; if it hurt you,
I'll stand you twenty back in recompence. [*Kisses her*]

ISABELLA
A forward fool, too!

ANTONIO This was Love's teaching:
A thousand ways he fashioned out my way,
And this I found the safest and the nearest
To tread the galaxia to my star.

ISABELLA
Profound withal! Certain you dreamed of this –
Love never taught it waking.

ANTONIO Take no acquaintance
Of these outward follies; there is within
A gentleman that loves you.

ISABELLA When I see him,
I'll speak with him; so in the meantime
Keep your habit, it becomes you well enough.
As you are a gentleman, I'll not discover you –
That's all the favour that you must expect.
When you are weary, you may leave the school,
For all this while you have but played the fool.

Enter LOLLIO

124 *mystery* religious truth known by revelation (hence part of the religious language of courtly love); hidden or secret thing (*OED* n. 2, 5a). Cf. also IV.i.25, 38. For the bawdy sense of *mystery* and *secret*, see Williams, *Glossary*, pp. 212, 271, and above I.ii.1.
125 *proceeds* advances in a course of study (as to a university degree)
parlous (1) dangerously cunning; (a) awful, extraordinary (*OED* a. 2)
126 *Love* i.e. Cupid /Amor
127–8 *soft . . . arrow* Antonio exploits the phallic suggestiveness of Cupid's arrows.
129 *stand* give
130 *forward* (1) presumptuous; (2) lustful – see Ricks (pp. 298–300)
131 *he* ed. (she Q)
132 *the nearest* ed. (nearest Q)
133 *tread* The bawdy sense ('copulate') is probably hinted at.
galaxia i.e the Milky Way
136 *outward . . . within* Continues the motif of secrets within (cf. I.i.159).
discover expose

ANTONIO [*Seeing him*]
And must again. – He he! I thank you, cousin,
I'll be your valentine tomorrow morning.

LOLLIO
How do you like the fool, mistress?

ISABELLA
Passing well, sir.

LOLLIO
Is he not witty, pretty well for a fool?

ISABELLA
If he hold on as he begins, he is like
To come to something!

LOLLIO
Ay, thank a good tutor: you may put him to't; he begins to answer pretty hard questions. – Tony, how many is five times six?

ANTONIO
Five times six, is six times five.

LOLLIO
What arithmetician could have answered better? How many is one hundred and seven?

ANTONIO
One hundred and seven, is seven hundred and one, cousin.

LOLLIO
This is no wit to speak on: will you be rid of the fool now?

ISABELLA
By no means, let him stay a little.

MADMAN (*Within*)
Catch there, catch the last couple in hell!

LOLLIO
Again! Must I come amongst you? Would my master were come home! I am not able to govern both these wards together. *Exit*

145 *valentine ... morning* Perhaps influenced by a song that the mad Ophelia sings in *Hamlet* (IV.v.48–66).

147 *Passing* Exceedingly

150 *come to something* With a bawdy *double entendre* (Williams, *Glossary*, pp. 75, 306–7).

151 *put him to't . . . hard* Bawdy *double entendre* (*put to* = insert penis; see Williams, *Glossary*, p. 251).

160 *Catch ... hell* Cry from the popular game known as 'Barley-brake', referred to by Deflores at V.ii.162–4. The game was played by couples holding hands: one couple were confined to a circle, known as 'hell', and would try to catch the other couples as they ran through it; those caught would have to replace the couple in hell, and the game continued until every pair had served its term there.

ANTONIO

Why should a minute of love's hour be lost?

ISABELLA

Fie, out again! I had rather you kept
Your other posture; you become not your tongue,
When you speak from your clothes.

ANTONIO How can he freeze
Lives near so sweet a warmth? Shall I alone
Walk through the orchard of the Hesperides
And cowardly not dare to pull an apple?
This with the red cheeks I must venture for. [*Kisses her*]

Enter LOLLIO *above*

ISABELLA

Take heed, there's giants keep 'em.

LOLLIO [*Aside*]

How now fool, are you good at that? Have you read Lipsius? He's past *Ars Amandi*; I believe I must put harder questions to him, I perceive that –

ISABELLA

You are bold – without fear, too.

ANTONIO What should I fear,
Having all joys about me? Do you but smile,

164 *out* out of your role

166 *you . . . clothes* you talk unbecomingly when you speak in a way that does not match your fool's costume

167 *Lives* That lives

168 *orchard of the Hesperides* At the rim of the Western world, this orchard, tended by the nymphs of the evening (Hesperides), bore golden apples that were guarded by a ferocious dragon. Hercules' penultimate task was to pluck three of its apples.

170 s.d.2 Lollio enters to spy on Isabella, as Deflores has previously done on Beatrice-Joanna in II.ii. In both scenes the treacherous servant plans to use his discoveries to blackmail erotic favours from his mistress. For the possibility that the original staging may have given visual emphasis to the parallel, see II.ii.57.

171 *giants keep 'em* A mocking reference to Alibius and Lollio as keepers of the madhouse; Isabella's substitution of giants for the dragon of the original myth may be an indication that she has caught sight of Lollio above.

172 *Lipsius* renaissance scholar and populariser of neo-Stoic moral philosophy; but included here for the pun on 'lips'

173 *Ars Amandi* Ovid's much imitated poem *The Art of Love* was the most popular erotic manual of the day.

176 *but smile* ed. (smile Q) – Lollio's otherwise completely accurate repetition of this speech at ll. 217–24 suggests that the compositor accidentally omitted 'but' from a line he had already had difficulty accommodating.

And Love shall play the wanton on your lip,
Meet and retire, retire and meet again;
Look you but cheerfully, and in your eyes
I shall behold mine own deformity,
And dress my self up fairer; I know this shape
Becomes me not, but in those bright mirrors
I shall array me handsomely.

LOLLIO Cuckoo, cuckoo – *Exit*

[*Enter*] MADMEN *above, some as birds, others as beasts,* [*uttering fearful cries*]

ANTONIO
What are these?

ISABELLA Of fear enough to part us,
Yet are they but our schools of lunatics,
That act their fantasies in any shapes
Suiting their present thoughts: if sad, they cry;
If mirth be their conceit, they laugh again;
Sometimes they imitate the beasts and birds,
Singing, or howling, braying, barking – all
As their wild fancies prompt 'em.

Enter LOLLIO.

ANTONIO These are no fears.

ISABELLA
But here's a large one, my man.

ANTONIO
Ha he! That's fine sport indeed, cousin.

LOLLIO [*Aside*]
I would my master were come home! 'Tis too much for one

178 *Meet and retire* Kissing is imagined as a kind of playful combat, orchestrated by Cupid.
179–80 *in . . . deformity* Compare the way in which Deflores is forced to contemplate his own 'deformity' in Beatrice's eyes (see e.g. II.i.26–51).
183 *cuckoo* Suggesting that Alibius is about to be cuckolded ('cuckold' derives from 'cuckoo').
s.d. Appearing as though in response to Lollio's cry of 'cuckoo', the madmen's grotesquerie appears like a quasi-allegorical representation of the bestial passions hidden beneath the surface of the play-world, just as their madness mirrors the love-madness that possesses so many of the play's superficially sane characters.

shepherd to govern two of these flocks; nor can I believe that one churchman can instruct two benefices at once: there will be some incurable mad of the one side, and very fools on the other. – [*Aloud*] Come, Tony.

ANTONIO

Prithee, cousin, let me stay here still.

LOLLIO

No, you must to your book, now you have played sufficiently.

ISABELLA

Your fool is grown wondrous witty.

LOLLIO

Well, I'll say nothing; but I do not think but he will put you down one of these days.

Exeunt LOLLIO *and* ANTONIO

ISABELLA

Here the restrainèd current might make breach,
Spite of the watchful bankers. Would a woman stray,
She need not gad abroad to seek her sin –
It would be brought home one ways or other:
The needle's point will to the fixèd north,
Such drawing Arctics women's beauties are.

Enter LOLLIO

LOLLIO

How dost thou, sweet rogue?

ISABELLA

How now?

LOLLIO

Come, there are degrees – one fool may be better than another.

ISABELLA

What's the matter?

196 *one churchman . . . at once* The corrupt practice of drawing income from more than one living at a time was widely denounced in the period.

202–3 *put you down* (1) beat or surpass you (*OED* v. 42 e–f); (2) subdue you sexually (Williams, *Glossary*, pp. 250–1)

205 *bankers* builders of protective banks and dikes (*OED* n.[3] 2)

208 *needle's point* Phallic *double-entendre.*

LOLLIO

Nay, if thou giv'st thy mind to fools'-flesh, have at thee!
[*Tries to kiss her*]

ISABELLA

You bold slave, you!

LOLLIO

I could follow now as t'other fool did:
'What should I fear,
Having all joys about me? Do you but smile,
And Love shall play the wanton on your lip,
Meet and retire, retire and meet again;
Look you but cheerfully, and in your eyes
I shall behold my own deformity,
And dress my self up fairer; I know this shape
Becomes me not –'
And so as it follows; but is not this the more foolish way? Come, sweet rogue: kiss me, my little Lacedemonian. Let me feel how thy pulses beat. Thou hast a thing about thee would do a man pleasure, I'll lay my hand on't. [*Grabs indecently at her*]

ISABELLA

Sirrah, no more! I see you have discovered
This love's knight-errant, who hath made adventure
For purchase of my love. Be silent, mute –
Mute as a statue – or his injunction
For me enjoying shall be to cut thy throat:
I'll do it, though for no other purpose;
And be sure he'll not refuse it.

LOLLIO

My share, that's all! I'll have my fool's part with you.

ISABELLA

No more – your master!

Enter ALIBIUS

226 *Lacedemonian* Spartan – i.e. 'whore' (by analogy with Helen of Troy, the adulterous former Queen of Sparta; and perhaps involving, as Sampson suggests, a play on 'laced mutton' – a cant term for a prostitute).

227 *thing* i.e. her sex

228 s.d. This edition (*not in* Q)

230 *knight-errant . . . purchase* The bathetic descent from the 'adventure' of knight-errantry (associated with courtly love) to the merchant venturing of 'purchase' is significant.

236 *part* (1) share; (2) role; (3) sexual organ (Williams, *Glossary*, p. 247) – cf. the fool's 'bauble' (above, l. 101)

ALIBIUS Sweet, how dost thou?

ISABELLA
Your bounden servant, sir.

ALIBIUS Fie, fie, sweetheart,
No more of that!

ISABELLA You were best lock me up.

ALIBIUS
In my arms and bosom, my sweet Isabella,
I'll lock thee up most nearly. Lollio,
We have employment, we have task in hand.
At noble Vermandero's, our castle-captain,
There is a nuptial to be solemnized –
Beatrice Joanna, his fair daughter, bride –
For which the gentleman hath bespoke our pains:
A mixture of our madmen and our fools,
To finish, as it were, and make the fag
Of all the revels, the third night from the first;
Only an unexpected passage-over
To make a frightful pleasure, that is all –
But not the all I aim at: could we so act it,
To teach it in a wild, distracted measure,
Though out of form and figure, breaking Time's head,
It were no matter, 'twould be healed again
In one age or other, if not in this.
This, this, Lollio! [*Shows him money*]
There's a good reward begun,
And will beget a bounty, be it known.

LOLLIO
This is easy, sir, I'll warrant you – you have about you fools and

238 *bounden* (1) under obligation for favours received; (2) tied with the bonds of matrimony; (3) made fast in bonds or prison (*OED* ppl. a. 4, 2c, 2a)
241 *nearly* (1) intimately; (2) narrowly, under close surveillance (*OED* adv. 2, 1a)
248 *fag* fag-end (*OED* n.[2] 2)
250–1 *unexpected . . . pleasure* the madmen will give the guests a delightful frisson of alarm by suddenly rushing through the festivities
253 *measure* dance
254 *out . . . figure* ignoring all the customary patterns of the dance
breaking . . . head Alibius's conceit imagines a dance so extravagantly out of time as to break the head of Father Time himself.
257–8 This passage (like much of Alibius' excited speech) has caused commentators some difficulty; but it makes best sense to assume that *This, this* refers to the first part of their reward, an advance payment from Vermandero, which Alibius flourishes as an earnest of the even greater *bounty* (l. 258) that will follow, if they succeed.

madmen that can dance very well; and 'tis no wonder: your best dancers are not the wisest men – the reason is, with often jumping they jolt their brains down into their feet, that their wits lie more in their heels than in their heads.

ALIBIUS
Honest Lollio, thou giv'st me a good reason,
And a comfort in it.

ISABELLA You've a fine trade on't:
Madmen and fools are a staple commodity!

ALIBIUS
O wife, we must eat, wear clothes, and live:
Just at the lawyers' haven we arrive,
By madmen and by fools we both do thrive.

Exeunt

[ACT III. SCENE iii.]

Enter VERMANDERO, ALSEMERO, JASPERINO, *and* BEATRICE

VERMANDERO
Valencia speaks so nobly of you, sir,
I wish I had a daughter now for you.

ALSEMERO
The fellow of this creature were a partner
For a king's love.

VERMANDERO I had her fellow once, sir;
But heaven has married her to joys eternal,
'Twere sin to wish her in this vale again.
Come, sir, your friend and you shall see the pleasures
Which my health chiefly joys in.

ALSEMERO
I hear the beauty of this seat largely.

268–9 *Just . . . thrive* Asylum keepers and lawyers both grow rich by exploiting the same victims, because only a fool or a madman would put his faith in lawyers (or the law).

III.iii Author: Middleton

6 *vale* i.e. the world (as in the proverbial 'vale of tears')

9 *largely* [proclaimed] generally, in the world at large (*OED* adv. 4)

VERMANDERO
It falls much short of that.
Exeunt, except for BEATRICE

BEATRICE So, here's one step
Into my father's favour – time will fix him.
I have got him now the liberty of the house.
So wisdom by degrees works out her freedom:
And if that eye be darkened that offends me –
I wait but that eclipse – this gentleman
Shall soon shine glorious in my father's liking
Through the refulgent virtue of my love.

Enter DEFLORES

DEFLORES
My thoughts are at a banquet for the deed;
I feel no weight in't, 'tis but light and cheap
For the sweet recompense, that I set down for't.
BEATRICE
Deflores?
DEFLORES Lady?
BEATRICE Thy looks promise cheerfully.
DEFLORES
All things are answerable: time, circumstance,
Your wishes and my service.
BEATRICE Is it done, then?
DEFLORES
Piracquo is no more.
BEATRICE
My joys start at mine eyes; our sweet'st delights
Are evermore born weeping.

11 *fix him* install him permanently (*OED* v. 8c)
14 *eye . . . offends* Cf. Matthew 18:9, Mark 9:47: 'And if thine eye offend thee, pluck it out'; the ironic implication is that the true offence lies in her own eye.
14–15 *darkened . . . eclipse* Beatrice refers to the moment when the light of life is extinguished in Alonzo; but her conceit also depends on the old idea of the sun as the 'eye of heaven'.
17 *refulgent* radiantly reflecting
virtue (1) power, (superhuman) influence; (2) moral goodness (*OED* n. 1–2)
19 *weight* i.e. of sin
20 *For* Compared with

DEFLORES I've a token for you.

BEATRICE
For me?

DEFLORES But it was sent somewhat unwillingly –
[*Shows the finger*]
I could not get the ring without the finger.

BEATRICE
Bless me! What hast thou done?

DEFLORES Why, is that more
Than killing the whole man? I cut his heart-strings!
A greedy hand thrust in a dish at court
In a mistake hath had as much as this.

BEATRICE
'Tis the first token my father made me send him.

DEFLORES
And I made him send it back again
For his last token; I was loath to leave it
And I'm sure dead men have no use of jewels –
He was as loath to part with't, for it stuck
As if the flesh and it were both one substance.

BEATRICE
At the stag's fall the keeper has his fees –
'Tis soon applied: all dead men's fees are yours, sir,
I pray bury the finger, but the stone
You may make use on shortly – the true value
(Take't of my truth) is near three hundred ducats.

31–2 *A greedy . . . this* A recognised peril of contemporary banqueting tables, when diners helped themselves from communal dishes with the aid of sharp knives: a similar episode, involving the poet Thomas Randolph, is recounted in William Heminges' satiric 'Elegy on Randolph's Finger' (1632).

31 *thrust . . . dish* Suspecting a bawdy *double entendre* in *dish* (= 'woman as sexual object' – see *Anthony and Cleopatra,* II.vii.125), Daalder sees *thrust* as underlining the phallic suggestiveness of the finger.

36 *jewels* also = 'maidenheads'

38 *As . . . substance* Echoing the biblical notion (repeated in the Anglican marriage service) that man and wife 'shall be one flesh' (Genesis 2:21–4; Matthew 19:6), the ring serves as a reminder that the bond between Alonzo and Beatrice is theoretically unbreakable, since for most purposes a formal betrothal was granted the full moral force of matrimony.

39 *At . . . fees* A warden or 'keeper' could claim the skin, head, and other parts of any deer killed in his killed in his game-park.

40 *applied* i.e. the proverb-like remark can be readily applied to Deflores' situation.

43 *three hundred ducats* i.e. about 135 pounds (a gold ducat was worth about nine shillings) – a gentleman could live modestly on 100 pounds per annum

DEFLORES

'Twill hardly buy a capcase for one's conscience, though,
To keep it from the worm, as fine as 'tis.
Well, being my fees, I'll take it –
Great men have taught me that, or else my merit
Would scorn the way on't.

BEATRICE It might justly, sir.
Why thou mistak'st, Deflores: 'tis not given
In state of recompence.

DEFLORES No? I hope so, lady:
You should soon witness my contempt to't then.

BEATRICE

Prithee, thou look'st as if thou wert offended.

DEFLORES

That were strange, lady: 'tis not possible
My service should draw such a cause from you.
Offended? Could you think so? That were much
For one of my performance, and so warm
Yet in my service.

BEATRICE

'Twere misery in me to give you cause, sir.

DEFLORES

I know so much, it were so – misery
In her most sharp condition.

BEATRICE 'Tis resolved then.
Look you, sir, here's three thousand golden florins:
I have not meanly thought upon thy merit.

44 *capcase* travelling case, casket, or chest

45 *worm* the gnawings of remorse. Frost suggests a further allusion to the sufferings of hell – 'where their worm dieth not, and the fire is never quenched' (Mark 9:46, 48) – described in the same passage echoed at l. 15 above.

50 *state* way

53–7 *'tis . . . service* In *Gerardo*, the lecherous Biscayner similarly prefaces his sexual conquest of Isdaura by demanding gratitude for 'my good deeds and service' (sig. H4). Deflores' language, though ostensibly referring to his murder of Alonzo, is full of sexual innuendo (*performance . . . warm . . . service*).

54 *cause* accusation (*OED* n. 9)

56 *warm* energetic, ardent (*OED* a. 10a)

58 *'Twere . . . me* It would make me miserable
misery miserliness

61 *three . . . florins* about three hundred pounds (a florin was worth about two shillings)

DEFLORES
What, salary? Now you move me!
BEATRICE How, Deflores?
DEFLORES
Do you place me in the rank of verminous fellows
To destroy things for wages? Offer gold?
The life blood of man! Is any thing
Valued too precious for my recompence?
BEATRICE
I understand thee not.
DEFLORES I could ha' hired
A journeyman in murder at this rate,
And mine own conscience might have slept at ease,
And have had the work brought home.
BEATRICE [*Aside*] I'm in a labyrinth:
What will content him? I would fain be rid of him.
[*Aloud*] I'll double the sum, sir.
DEFLORES You take a course
To double my vexation, that's the good you do.
BEATRICE [*Aside*]
Bless me! I am now in worse plight than I was;
I know not what will please him. [*Aloud*] For my fear's sake,

63 *salary* financial reward (*OED* n. 2)
move enrage (*OED* n. 9b)

64–5 *Do ... wages* The degradation of feudal service (seen as dependent on reciprocal bonds of obligation) into a mere wage-relationship is a recurrent theme amongst early modern writers on service, such as 'I.M.', who deplore how the old 'kind usage and friendly familiarity', which made domestic service in a great household a suitable calling for a gentleman, has been replaced by the humiliation of 'reward only with bare wages' (pp. 147–58). See Introduction, p. xxviii.

64 *rank* In the context of *verminous* (= infested with parasites) a play on *rank* = evil-smelling is likely.

69 *journeyman* 'one who, having served his apprenticeship to a handicraft or trade, is qualified to work at it for days' wages . . . as the servant or employee of another' *OED* n. 1) – in the mouth of the gentleman-born, Deflores, the term is charged with intense social contempt.

70 *slept at ease* ed. (*not in* Q). Most editors accept this conjecture, since the Q line is obviously incomplete.

71 *brought home* either (i) 'delivered to me by someone who had already carried it out' (Daalder); or (ii) 'brought to its intended conclusion' (*OED home* adv. 4a); or perhaps (iii) 'have got someone else to carry out the job in a forcible manner' – cf. l. 87 (Bawcutt 1998)
labyrinth Sounded as two syllables here ('lab'rinth'). The audience are probably expected to remember the original *labyrinth* of ancient Crete, at whose centre lurked the hideous Minotaur, monstrous offspring of Queen Pasiphae's adultery with a bull, which brought death to anyone penetrating the maze (cf. III.ii.114; IV.iii.97–100; V.iii.148).

I prithee make away with all speed possible;
And if thou be'st so modest not to name
The sum that will content thee, paper blushes not –
Send thy demand in writing, it shall follow thee;
But prithee take thy flight.

DEFLORES You must fly too then.

BEATRICE
I?

DEFLORES I'll not stir a foot else.

BEATRICE What's your meaning?

DEFLORES
Why are not you as guilty, in (I'm sure)
As deep as I? And we should stick together.
Come, your fears counsel you but ill: my absence
Would draw suspect upon you instantly;
There were no rescue for you.

BEATRICE He speaks home.

DEFLORES
Nor is it fit we two, engaged so jointly,
Should part and live asunder. [*Tries to kiss her*]

BEATRICE How now, sir?
This shows not well.

DEFLORES What makes your lip so strange?
This must not be betwixt us.

BEATRICE [*Aside*] The man talks wildly.

DEFLORES
Come kiss me with a zeal now.

BEATRICE [*Aside*] Heaven, I doubt him!

DEFLORES
I will not stand so long to beg 'em shortly.

BEATRICE
Take heed, Deflores, of forgetfulness:
'Twill soon betray us.

84 *stick* Significantly, the same verb used to describe the bond between ring and finger (l. 37).
86 *suspect* Accent on second syllable.
87 *speaks home* addresses the very heart of the matter (*OED* adv. 5a)
88 *engaged so jointly* so mutually committed to this business (*OED engage* v. 13); but quibbling on *engaged* and *joint*, as a reminder of the bond symbolised by ring and finger
90 *strange* like that of a stranger
92 *doubt* dread
94 *forgetfulness* i.e. of your rank and station

DEFLORES Take you heed first!
Faith, you're grown much forgetful, you're to blame in't.

BEATRICE
He's bold, and I am blamed for't.

DEFLORES I have eased you
Of your trouble – think on't: I'm in pain,
And must be eased of you; 'tis a charity.
Justice invites your blood to understand me.

BEATRICE
I dare not.

DEFLORES Quickly.

BEATRICE Oh, I never shall!
Speak it yet further off, that I may lose
What has been spoken, and no sound remain on't.
I would not hear so much offence again
For such another deed.

DEFLORES Soft, lady, soft –
The last is not yet paid for! Oh, this act
Has put me into spirit; I was as greedy on't
As the parched earth of moisture when the clouds weep.
Did you not mark, I wrought my self into't –
Nay, sued and kneeled for't? Why was all that pains took?
You see I have thrown contempt upon your gold:
Not that I want it not, for I do piteously –
In order I will come unto't, and make use on't –
But 'twas not held so precious to begin with,
For I place wealth after the heels of pleasure;
And were I not resolved in my belief

96 *forgetful* i.e. of your obligations to me (and of the situation in which the crime has placed you)

97 *eased* (1) relieved from pain; (2) purged (*OED* v. 1a; 1c) – compare the dying Beatrice's metaphor at V.iii.150–3. In *Gerardo* the Biscayner similarly presses his affections on Isdaura by presenting his desire as a 'torment . . . mischief and sickness' for which only she can serve as 'the antidote and wholesome physician' (sig. H4–H4v).

100 *your blood* (1) your aristocratic nature; (2) your desire; (3) your bloody disposition; (4) the blood with which your crime has stained you

105 *Soft* Exclamation to enjoin silence or deprecate haste (*OED* adv. 8a).

107 *spirit* (1) courage (*OED* n. 13a); (2) sexual desire – sometimes used as a euphemism for the penis, or for semen (Williams, *Glossary*, pp. 284–5)

107–8 *I . . . moisture* Cf. II.ii.133.

112 *it not* ed. (it Q). The emendation is required by both sense and metre.

That thy virginity were perfect in thee,
I should but take my recompense with grudging,
As if I had but half my hopes I agreed for.

BEATRICE
Why 'tis impossible thou canst be so wicked,
Or shelter such a cunning cruelty,
To make his death the murderer of my honour.
Thy language is so bold and vicious,
I cannot see which way I can forgive it
With any modesty.

DEFLORES Push! You forget yourself:
A woman dipped in blood, and talk of modesty?

BEATRICE
O misery of sin! Would I had been bound
Perpetually unto my living hate
In that Piracquo, than to hear these words.
Think but upon the distance that creation
Set 'twixt thy blood and mine, and keep thee there.

DEFLORES
Look but into your conscience, read me there –
'Tis a true book, you'll find me there your equal.
Push! Fly not to your birth, but settle you
In what the act has made you, you're no more now;
You must forget your parentage to me –
You're the deed's creature: by that name
You lost your first condition; and I challenge you,
As peace and innocency has turned you out
And made you one with me.

BEATRICE With thee, foul villain?

DEFLORES
Yes, my fair murd'ress; do you urge me?
Though thou writ'st 'maid', thou whore in thy affection,

136 *to me* when talking to me; as far as I am concerned
137 *creature* (1) creation (like the fallen Eve, Beatrice has lost her innocent 'first condition' and been, in effect, created anew); (2) puppet, slave (*OED* n. 1a; 5)
138 *challenge you* assert my title to you
140 *one with me* i.e. Beatrice has become 'one flesh' with Deflores (elucidating the new symbolism of the finger and ring)
foul (1) wicked, guilty; (2) physically loathsome, ugly (*OED* a. 7a–b; 1a)
141 *urge* provoke to anger (*OED* v. 7b)
142 *whore . . . heart* Cf. Matthew 5:28.

'Twas changed from thy first love – and that's a kind
Of whoredom in thy heart – and he's changed now
To bring thy second on, thy Alsemero,
Whom (by all sweets that ever darkness tasted!)
If I enjoy thee not, thou ne'er enjoy'st:
I'll blast the hopes and joys of marriage,
I'll confess all – my life I rate at nothing.

BEATRICE
Deflores –

DEFLORES I shall rest from all love's plagues then,
I live in pain now: that flame-shooting eye
Will burn my heart to cinders.

BEATRICE O sir, hear me!

DEFLORES
She that in life and love refuses me,
In death and shame my partner she shall be.

BEATRICE
Stay, hear me once for all! [*Kneels*] I make thee master
Of all the wealth I have in gold and jewels:
Let me go poor unto my bed with honour,
And I am rich in all things.

DEFLORES Let this silence thee,
The wealth of all Valencia shall not buy
My pleasure from me.
Can you weep Fate from its determined purpose?
So soon may you weep me.

143–5 *'Twas . . . Alsemero* Cf. V.ii.197–8.
143 *first love* In contrast to Reynolds, Middleton and Rowley never suggest that Piracquo was simply foisted on Beatrice by her father.
144 *changed* i.e. by death
146 *sweets* sexual pleasures
149 *confess* Stress on first syllable.
150 *love's* ed. (lovers Q)
151 *flame-shooting* This edition (shooting Q; Dyce: love-shooting; Craik: fire-shooting). The line is metrically deficient and some addition is also needed to clarify the sense. The idea of darts or flames being discharged from the mistress' eyes is a common trope in Renaissance love-poetry (cf. I.i.216).
155 s.d. *Kneels* Deflores' 'Come, rise' at l. 166 makes it clear that Beatrice kneels at some point in this closing dialogue – by echoing Deflores' kneeling at II.ii.117, the gesture expresses the reversed power-relationship between them. In the 1993 BBC production, Deflores knelt with her on 'Let this silence thee'.
155 *master* A loaded word, in the context of Deflores' servile position in the household.
161 *determined* (1) resolute; (2) pre-ordained, predestined (*OED* ppl. a. 7a; 4)
162 *you* ed. (*not in* Q)

BEATRICE Vengeance begins:
Murder, I see, is followed by more sins.
Was my creation in the womb so cursed,
It must engender with a viper first?

DEFLORES
Come, rise, and shroud your blushes in my bosom.
[*Raises her*]
Silence is one of pleasure's best receipts:
Thy peace is wrought for ever in this yielding.
'Las, how the turtle pants! Thou'lt love anon
What thou so fear'st and faint'st to venture on.
Exeunt

ACT IV. [SCENE i.]

[*Dumb show*]

Enter GENTLEMEN, VERMANDERO *meeting them with action of wonderment at the flight of* PIRACQUO. *Enter* ALSEMERO, *with* JASPERINO *and* GALLANTS; VERMANDERO *points to him, the* GENTLEMEN *seeming to applaud the choice.*

[*Exeunt in procession* VERMANDERO,] ALSEMERO, JASPERINO, *and* GENTLEMEN. [*Enter*] BEATRICE *the Bride following* [*them*

165 *viper* Cf. I.i.218.
167 *receipts* (1) recipes – or drugs compounded from a recipe; (2) things received, payments (*OED* n. 1–2; 3)
168–70 *Thy . . . thou* Deflores' sudden switch from the respectful 'you' marks a turning-point in the play: here the singular pronoun expresses intimacy, but also registers the reversal of power-relations between mistress and servant as a consequence of his 'master-sin' (V.ii.199); in the 1993 BBC version Beatrice kissed Deflores on 'Thoul't love anon . . .'.
168 *peace* Perhaps emphasising Beatrice's newly subordinate position by playing on the *quietus est* that marked a master's formal discharge of a servant from duty.
169 *'Las . . . on* Middleton may intend an ironic echo of the Epithalamium in Ben Jonson's, marriage masque, *Hymenaei*, written to celebrate Frances Howard's first wedding: 'Shrink not, soft virgin, you will love / Anon what you so fear to prove' – see Lisa Hopkins, 'Beguiling the Master of the Mystery,' *MRDE* 9 (1997), 149–61 (154–5).
turtle turtle-dove (a symbol of love)
pants For panting as an expression of orgasmic excitement, see Williams, *Glossary*, p. 121 (citing *Othello*, II.i.81, and *Anthony and Cleopatra*, IV.ix.16).
IV.i Author: Middleton

across the stage] in great state, accompanied with DIAPHANTA, ISABELLA, *and other* GENTLEWOMEN. [*Enter*] DEFLORES *after all, smiling at the accident;* ALONZO'S *Ghost appears to* DEFLORES *in the midst of his smile, startles him, showing him the hand whose finger he had cut off. They pass over in great solemnity* [*and exeunt*].

Enter BEATRICE

BEATRICE

This fellow has undone me endlessly:
Never was bride so fearfully distressed.
The more I think upon th'ensuing night,
And whom I am to cope with in embraces –
One that's ennobled both in blood and mind,
So clear in understanding (that's my plague now),
Before whose judgement will my fault appear
Like malefactors' crimes before tribunals,
(There is no hiding on't) – the more I dive
Into my own distress. How a wise man
Stands for a great calamity! There's no venturing
Into his bed, what course soe'er I light upon,
Without my shame, which may grow up to danger:
He cannot but in justice strangle me
As I lie by him, as a cheater use me.
'Tis a precious craft to play with a false die
Before a cunning gamester: here's his closet,

1 *fellow* (1) person of humble station, servant; (2) accomplice (*OED* n. 10a; 1b)
undone (1) destroyed; (2) ruined by seducing (*OED* v. 8a; 8d)
endlessly eternally
2 *fearfully distressed* terribly tormented; tormented by fear
4 *cope with* have to do with (*OED* v. 5); encounter sexually (Williams, *Glossary*, p. 81)
5 *that's* ed. (both Q)
11 *Stands for* Can be reckoned as (*OED* v. 71 f)
16 *precious* Ironic (= 'worthless', *OED* a. 4b).
die dice (original singular form)
17 *Before* Under the attention of
closet small private room or study; or, a private repository of valuables (*OED* n. 1a, c; 3a). For the closet as a place of secrets, see Angel Day, *The English Secretary* (1586), ii. 103 (cited in *OED*) 'We do call the most secret place in the house appropriate unto our own private studies . . . a Closet.' Because in early modern households the closet was one of the few rooms likely to be locked, in allegorized descriptions of the human body it was frequently used to figure the privacies of the heart.

The key left in't, and he abroad i'th' park –
Sure, 'twas forgot; I'll be so bold as look in't.
Bless me! A right physician's closet 'tis,
Set round with vials, every one her mark too.
Sure he does practise physic for his own use,
Which may be safely called your great man's wisdom.
What manuscript lies here? '*The Book of Experiment,*
Called Secrets in Nature' – so 'tis, 'tis so:
'How to know whether a woman be with child or no' –
I hope I am not yet – if he should try though!
Let me see: folio forty-five – here 'tis,
The leaf tucked down upon't, the place suspicious:
'If you would know whether a woman be with child or not, give her two spoonfuls of the white water in Glass C' –
Where's that Glass C? Oh, yonder I see't now –
'and if she be with child, she sleeps full twelve hours after, if not, not.'
None of that water comes into my belly:
I'll know you from a hundred; I could break you now
Or turn you into milk, and so beguile
The master of the mystery, but I'll look to you.
Ha! That which is next, is ten times worse:
'How to know whether a woman be a maid, or not.'
If that should be applied, what would become of me?
Belike he has a strong faith of my purity,
That never yet made proof; but this he calls
'A merry sleight, but true experiment' –
The author 'Antonius Mizaldus':

21 *every one her mark* each duly labelled (*OED mark* n. 11a)
22 *physic* medicine
23 *Which ... wisdom* Because great men are vulnerable to attempts on their lives, especially through poisoning
24–5 *The ... Nature* The title translates that of a work by the French scholar Antonius Mizaldus (1520–78), *De Arcanis Naturae.* However, the tests discovered by Beatrice do not appear in that book – though similar ones are described in his *Centuriae IX. Memorabilium.* The fact that Mizaldus is mentioned by name in the passage quoted at ll. 44 ff. suggests that this is a manuscript compilation put together by Alsemero himself.
35 *water* Cf. II.ii.83.
38 *master of the mystery* Apparently echoing Jonson's *Alchemist*, 4.1.122, where Sir Epicure Mammon, relishing the prospect of success in his alchemical project, declares himself 'master of the mastery'.
mystery (1) highly technical practice in a trade or art; (2) secret (*OED* n. 8; 5a)
look to watch out for
43 *That... proof* Who has never put it to the test

'Give the party you suspect the quantity of a spoonful of the water in the glass M, which upon her that is a maid makes three several effects: 'twill make her incontinently gape, then fall into a sudden sneezing, last into a violent laughing – else dull, heavy and lumpish.'
Where had I been?
I fear it, yet 'tis seven hours to bedtime.

Enter DIAPHANTA

DIAPHANTA
Cuds, madam, are you here?
BEATRICE [*Aside*] Seeing that wench now,
A trick comes in my mind: 'tis a nice piece
Gold cannot purchase; [*Aloud*] I come hither, wench,
To look my lord.
DIAPHANTA [*Aside*] Would I had such a cause
To look him too. [*Aloud*] Why, he's i' th' park, madam.
BEATRICE
There let him be.
DIAPHANTA Ay, madam, let him compass
Whole parks and forests, as great rangers do,
At roosting-time a little lodge can hold 'em.
Earth-conquering Alexander, that thought the world
Too narrow for him, in the end had but his pit-hole.

46–50 *Give . . . lumpish* Although the Alsemero's virginity test may appear absurd to modern eyes, it is not so different from some of those seriously propounded in contemporary medical treatises (see Dale J. Randall, 'Some Observations on the Theme of Chastity in *The Changeling*', *ELR* 14 (1984), 347–66).
48 *several* different
incontinently immediately
50 *lumpish* stupidly lethargic
51 *Where . . . been* What would have become of me (if I had not found out)
53 *Cuds* Contraction of 'God save me'.
54 *nice* scrupulous (*OED* a. 7d)
piece woman (Williams, *Glossary*, p. 234)
56 *look* seek (*OED* v. 6d)
59 *parks and forests* With sexual innuendo (for *park* = 'woman as sexual landscape', see Williams, *Glossary*, p. 228)
ranger (1) forest officer, gamekeeper; (2) rover, rake (*OED* n. 2a; 1a)
60 *roosting-time* bedtime
61–2 *Earth . . . pit-hole* For another example of this trope, which can be traced back to Juvenal, *Satire* X, 168–72, see *Hamlet*, V.i.192 ff.
62 *pit-hole* (1) grave; (2) vagina (see Williams, *Glossary*, pp. 159, 237).

BEATRICE
I fear thou art not modest, Diaphanta.
DIAPHANTA
Your thoughts are so unwilling to be known, madam;
'Tis ever the bride's fashion towards bedtime
To set light by her joys, as if she owed 'em not.
BEATRICE
Her joys? Her fears thou wouldst say.
DIAPHANTA
Fear of what?
BEATRICE
Art thou a maid, and talkst so to a maid?
You leave a blushing business behind,
Beshrew your heart for't!
DIAPHANTA
Do you mean good sooth, madam?
BEATRICE
Well, if I'd thought upon the fear at first,
Man should have been unknown.
DIAPHANTA
Is't possible?
BEATRICE
I will give a thousand ducats to that woman
Would try what my fear were, and tell me true
Tomorrow, when she gets from't: as she likes,
I might perhaps be drawn to't.
DIAPHANTA
Are you in earnest?
BEATRICE
Do you get the woman, then challenge me,
And see if I'll fly from't; but I must tell you
This by the way: she must be a true maid,
Else there's no trial, my fears are not hers else.
DIAPHANTA
Nay, she that I would put into your hands, madam
Shall be a maid.

66 *owed* owned
68 *maid* virgin
70 *Beshrew* A plague on
mean . . . sooth really mean what you say
72 *Man . . . unknown* (1) I never would have had anything to do with men; (2) I would have avoided carnal knowledge
75 *when . . . from't* when it's all over
as she likes depending on how much she enjoyed it
77 *Do you get* Imperative.
78 *fly from't* renege on my promise

BEATRICE You know I should be shamed else,
Because she lies for me.
DIAPHANTA 'Tis a strange humour!
But are you serious still? Would you resign
Your first night's pleasure, and give money too?
BEATRICE
As willingly as live; alas, the gold
Is but a by-bet to wedge in the honour.
DIAPHANTA [*Aside*]
I do not know how the world goes abroad
For faith or honesty; there's both required in this.
[*Aloud*] Madam, what say you to me? And stray no further:
I've a good mind in troth to earn your money.
BEATRICE
You're too quick, I fear, to be a maid.
DIAPHANTA
How? Not a maid? Nay, then you urge me, madam!
Your honourable self is not a truer
With all your fears upon you –
BEATRICE [*Aside*] Bad enough, then.
DIAPHANTA
Than I with all my lightsome joys about me.
BEATRICE
I'm glad to hear't: then you dare put your honesty
Upon an easy trial.
DIAPHANTA Easy? – Anything.
BEATRICE
I'll come to you straight. [*Goes to the closet*]

83 *lies* (1) deceives; (2) lies with a man
humour mood, caprice (*OED* n. 5, 6a)

86–7 *alas . . . honour* Most eds. treat this as an aside, but there is no reason why Beatrice should not further encourage Diaphanta by adding honour to gold and pleasure as motives for sleeping with her master.

87 *by-bet* side-bet (*OED*, citing only this example)
wedge in secure

88–89 *how . . . honesty* how much good faith and truthfulness is to be found in the world nowadays. But *honesty* also carries the senses 'honour, reputation', and (ironically) 'female chastity' (*OED* 1c, 3b).

92 *quick* (1) quick to respond; (2) alive [sexually]; (3) pregnant (*OED* a. 21a; 2a; 4b)

93 *urge* Cf. III.iii.141.

96 *lightsome* light-hearted

DIAPHANTA [*Aside*] She will not search me? Will she?
Like the forewoman of a female jury?
BEATRICE [*Aside*]
Glass M. Ay, this is it. [*Aloud*] Look, Diaphanta,
You take no worse than I do. [*Drinks*]
DIAPHANTA And in so doing,
I will not question what 'tis, but take it. [*Drinks*]
BEATRICE [*Aside*]
Now if the experiment be true, 'twill praise itself,
And give me noble ease. [*Diaphanta gapes*] – Begins already:
There's the first symptom; and what haste it makes
To fall into the second, [*Diaphanta sneezes*] there by this time!
Most admirable secret! On the contrary,
It stirs not me a whit, which most concerns it.
DIAPHANTA
Ha ha ha!
BEATRICE [*Aside*] Just in all things and in order
As if 'twere circumscribed; one accident
Gives way unto another.
DIAPHANTA Ha ha ha!
BEATRICE
How now wench?
DIAPHANTA Ha ha ha! I am so – so light
At heart! Ha ha ha! So pleasurable!
But one swig more, sweet madam?
BEATRICE Ay, tomorrow;
We shall have time to sit by't.
DIAPHANTA Now I'm sad again.

99–100 *She . . . jury* Alluding to the notorious divorce action of 1613 in which Frances Howard, Countess of Essex, having been examined by a panel of noblewomen and matrons, secured a divorce on the grounds of non-consummation, and was freed to marry her lover, Robert Carr, Earl of Somerset, King James' favourite. The pair were subsequently imprisoned for complicity in the murder of Carr's client, Sir Thomas Overbury, who had opposed the match. Interest in the case seems to have been reignited by the pair's release from prison in January 1622, shortly before this play was licensed.
104 *praise* demonstrate its value
109 *which . . . it* (although that is) the very thing it is specifically designed to do
110 *Just* By the book
111 *circumscribed* confined to the prescribed sequence
accident symptom (*OED* n. 3)
116 *sit by't* 'sit and enjoy its effects at leisure' (Bawcutt 1998)

BEATRICE
It lays itself so gently too. Come, wench –
Most honest Diaphanta I dare call thee now.

DIAPHANTA
Pray tell me, madam, what trick call you this?

BEATRICE
I'll tell thee all hereafter; we must study
The carriage of this business:

DIAPHANTA I shall carry't well,
Because I love the burden.

BEATRICE About midnight
You must not fail to steal forth gently,
That I may use the place.

DIAPHANTA Oh, fear not, madam,
I shall be cool by that time. [*Aside*] The bride's place,
And with a thousand ducats! I'm for a justice now –
I bring a portion with me, I scorn small fools.

Exeunt

[ACT IV. SCENE ii.]

Enter VERMANDERO *and* SERVANT

VERMANDERO
I tell thee, knave, mine honour is in question,
A thing till now free from suspicion,
Nor ever was there cause. Who of my gentlemen
Are absent? Tell me and truly, how many, and who?

SERVANT
Antonio, sir, and Franciscus.

VERMANDERO
When did they leave the castle?

117 *lays itself* subsides (*OED* v. 3a)
121 *The carriage of* how to carry out
121–2 *carry't . . . burden* Bawdy *double entendre.*
124 *use* resort to (*OED* v. 17a)
126–7 *I'm . . . fools* now that I have a dowry, I need not bother with petty fools, I can look to marry a great one – like a justice of the peace (cf. I.ii.123).
IV.ii Author: Rowley 1–16; Middleton 17–150

SERVANT

Some ten days since, sir – the one intending to Briamata, th'other for Valencia.

VERMANDERO

The time accuses 'em: a charge of murder
Is brought within my castle gate – Piracquo's murder;
I dare not answer faithfully their absence.
A strict command of apprehension
Shall pursue 'em suddenly, and either wipe
The stain off clear, or openly discover it.
Provide me wingèd warrants for the purpose.
See, I am set on again.

Exit SERVANT

Enter TOMAZO

TOMAZO

I claim a brother of you.

VERMANDERO You're too hot,
Seek him not here.

TOMAZO Yes, 'mongst your dearest bloods!
If my peace find no fairer satisfaction,
This is the place must yield account for him,
For here I left him, and the hasty tie
Of this snatched marriage, gives strong testimony
Of his most certain ruin.

VERMANDERO Certain falsehood!
This is the place indeed: his breach of faith
Has too much marred both my abusèd love –
The honourable love I reserved for him –
And mocked my daughter's joy. The prepared morning
Blushed at his infidelity; he left
Contempt and scorn to throw upon those friends
Whose belief hurt 'em. Oh, 'twas most ignoble

7 *Briamata* the name of Vermandero's country house in Reynolds
11 *answer* be accountable for (*OED* v. 1b)
14 *discover* Cf. III.ii.140.
16 *set on* harried (by Tomazo)
17 *hot* passionate, angry
18 *bloods* kindred (*OED* n. 10a)
26, 27 *reserved, prepared* Stress on first syllable.
30 *belief* i.e. in Alonzo's good faith

To take his flight so unexpectedly,
And throw such public wrongs on those that loved him!

TOMAZO
Then this is all your answer.

VERMANDERO 'Tis too fair
For one of his alliance; and I warn you
That this place no more see you. *Exit*

Enter DEFLORES

TOMAZO The best is,
There is more ground to meet a man's revenge on. –
Honest Deflores!

DEFLORES That's my name indeed.
Saw you the bride? Good sweet sir, which way took she?

TOMAZO
I have blest mine eyes from seeing such a false one.

DEFLORES [*Aside*]
I'd fain get off: this man's not for my company;
I smell his brother's blood when I come near him.

TOMAZO
Come hither, kind and true one; I remember
My brother loved thee well.

DEFLORES O purely, dear sir!
[*Aside*] Methinks I am now again a-killing on him,
He brings it so fresh to me.

TOMAZO Thou canst guess, sirrah –
An honest friend has an instinct of jealousy –
At some foul guilty person?

DEFLORES
'Las, sir, I am so charitable, I think none
Worse then my self – you did not see the bride then?

TOMAZO
I prithee name her not! Is she not wicked?

34 *alliance* kinsmen
36 *There . . . on* There are other ways for a man to achieve revenge
37 *Honest Deflores* A reminder that the character of Deflores is partly modelled on that of another disloyal servant, whose sobriquet of 'Honest Iago' belies his real nature as a hypocrite and diabolical tempter (see Introduction, pp. vii, xiii, xxviii).
43 *purely* absolutely, entirely (*OED* adv. 2b)
46 *An honest* ed. (One honest Q)

DEFLORES
No, no, a pretty, easy, round-packed sinner,
As your most ladies are – else you might think
I flattered her – but sir, at no hand wicked,
Till they're so old their chins and noses meet,
And they salute witches. – I am called, I think, sir.
[*Aside*] His company even o'erlays my conscience. *Exit*

TOMAZO
That Deflores has a wondrous honest heart –
He'll bring it out in time, I'm assured on't.
Oh, here's the glorious master of the day's joy;
'Twill not be long till he and I do reckon.

Enter ALSEMERO

Sir!

ALSEMERO You are most welcome.

TOMAZO You may call that word back:
I do not think I am, nor wish to be.

ALSEMERO
'Tis strange you found the way to this house, then.

TOMAZO
Would I'd ne'er known the cause! I'm none of those, sir,
That come to give you joy, and swill your wine;
'Tis a more precious liquor that must lay
The fiery thirst I bring.

ALSEMERO Your words and you
Appear to me great strangers.

TOMAZO Time and our swords
May make us more acquainted. This the business:

51 *round-packed sinner* i.e. one 'firm in her curves and solid with sin' (Frost)
54 *chins and noses* ed. (sins and vices Q)
55 *salute* greet, kiss; begin an acquaintance with (*OED* v. 2a, e; 4) – as themselves looking like witches
56 *o'erlays* distresses, weighs down (*OED* v. 2a–b)
58 *bring it out* either (i) 'show his honest heart', or (ii) 'discover the truth about Alonzo's disappearance'
59 *glorious* vainglorious (*OED* a. 1a)
60 *'Twill* ed. (I will Q)
reckon settle our accounts – i.e. come to blows (*OED* v. 11a)
60–1 *reckon. / Sir!* ed. (reckon sir. Q)
s.d. After 'sir' Q.
66 *lay* appease (*OED* v[1] 3a)

I should have had a brother in your place –
How treachery and malice have disposed of him,
I'm bound to enquire of him which holds his right,
Which never could come fairly.

ALSEMERO
You must look
To answer for that word, sir.

TOMAZO
Fear you not:
I'll have it ready drawn at our next meeting.
Keep your day solemn. Farewell, I disturb it not;
I'll bear the smart with patience for a time. *Exit*

ALSEMERO
'Tis somewhat ominous this: a quarrel entered
Upon this day. My innocence relieves me,

Enter JASPERINO

I should be wondrous sad else. – Jasperino,
I have news to tell thee, strange news.

JASPERINO
I ha' some too,
I think as strange as yours. Would I might keep
Mine, so my faith and friendship might be kept in't!
Faith sir, dispense a little with my zeal,
And let it cool in this.

ALSEMERO
This puts me on,
And blames thee for thy slowness.

JASPERINO
All may prove nothing,
Only a friendly fear that leapt from me, sir.

70 *have had* ed. (have Q)
72 *holds his right* possesses what is rightfully his (i.e. Beatrice)
73 *come fairly* come about by lawful means (*OED fairly* adv. 4b)
75 *have . . . drawn* (1) have my answer already drawn up; (2) have my sword drawn and at the ready
76 *Keep . . . solemn* Observe your wedding day with proper ceremony and reverence (*OED keep* v. 12, *solemn* a. 1)
77 *smart* pain, suffering (*OED* n. 1–2)
83 *so . . . in't* provided that I could preserve my faith and friendship to you by keeping it back
85 *let . . . this* allow some cooling in the warmth of my zeal to serve you, so far as passing on this news is concerned
puts me on urges me onward (*OED* v. 47h)

ALSEMERO
No question it may prove nothing; let's partake it, though.
JASPERINO
'Twas Diaphanta's chance – for to that wench
I pretend honest love, and she deserves it –
To leave me in a back part of the house,
A place we chose for private conference;
She was no sooner gone, but instantly
I heard your bride's voice in the next room to me;
And, lending more attention, found Deflores
Louder then she.
ALSEMERO Deflores? Thou art out now.
JASPERINO
You'll tell me more anon.
ALSEMERO Still I'll prevent thee:
The very sight of him is poison to her.
JASPERINO
That made me stagger too, but Diaphanta
At her return confirmed it.
ALSEMERO Diaphanta!
JASPERINO
Then fell we both to listen, and words passed
Like those that challenge interest in a woman.
ALSEMERO
Peace, quench thy zeal – 'tis dangerous to thy bosom.
JASPERINO
Then truth is full of peril.
ALSEMERO Such truths are.
Oh, were she the sole glory of the earth,
Had eyes that could shoot fire into kings' breasts,

88 *No . . . though* Provided the first *it* is elided ('question't') this line forms a rough but acceptable hexameter.
90 *pretend* profess (*OED* v. 3)
honest honourable
96 *out* wide of the mark, mistaken
97 *prevent* forestall (*OED* v. 5)
102 *challenge* lay claim to (*OED* v. 5)
interest right, title (*OED* n. 1). Daalder reads this passage to mean that the exchange between Deflores and Beatrice excited *Diaphanta*'s interest (especially after her promise to act as Beatrice's substitute on the wedding night); but Jasperino's 'like those that . . .' makes it plain that an act of interpretation is involved: the eavesdroppers have heard words that sound as if the servant were asserting a physical claim over his mistress.

And touched, she sleeps not here! Yet I have time,
Though night be near, to be resolved hereof;
And prithee do not weigh me by my passions.

JASPERINO
I never weighed friend so.

ALSEMERO
Done charitably.
That key will lead thee to a pretty secret
By a Chaldean taught me – and I've spent
My study upon some. Bring from my closet
A glass inscribed there with the letter M;
And question not my purpose.

JASPERINO
It shall be done, sir.

ALSEMERO
How can this hang together? Not an hour since,
Her woman came pleading her lady's fears,
Delivered her for the most timorous virgin
That ever shrunk at man's name, and so modest,
She charged her weep out her request to me,
That she might come obscurely to my bosom.

Enter BEATRICE

BEATRICE [*Aside*]
All things go well: my woman's preparing yonder
For her sweet voyage, which grieves me to lose;
Necessity compels it; I lose all else.

ALSEMERO [*Aside*]
Push! Modesty's shrine is set in yonder forehead.
I cannot be too sure, though. [*Aloud*] My Joanna!

BEATRICE
Sir, I was bold to weep a message to you –
Pardon my modest fears.

107 *And touched* And if she has had sexual contact with someone (*OED* v. 2a)
111 *pretty* ingenious; admirable (*OED* a. 2b; 3)
112 *Chaldean* seer, soothsayer (after the people described in Daniel 2:2–12, famous for such practices)
spent Bruster (*not in* Q; Bawcutt: made)
118 *Delivered her for* Described her as (*OED* v. 11a)
121 *obscurely* in the dark (cf. *OED obscure* a. 2)

ALSEMERO [*Aside*] The dove's not meeker.
She's abused questionless.

Enter JASPERINO

[*Aloud*] Oh, are you come, sir?

BEATRICE [*Aside*]
The glass, upon my life! I see the letter.

JASPERINO
Sir, this is M.

ALSEMERO 'Tis it.

BEATRICE [*Aside*] I am suspected.

ALSEMERO
How fitly our bride comes to partake with us!

BEATRICE
What is't, my lord?

ALSEMERO No hurt.

BEATRICE Sir, pardon me –
I seldom taste of any composition.

ALSEMERO
But this, upon my warrant, you shall venture on.
[*Gives her the glass*]

BEATRICE
I fear 'twill make me ill.

ALSEMERO Heaven forbid that.

BEATRICE [*Aside*]
I'm put now to my cunning: th'effects I know,
If I can now but feign 'em handsomely. [*Drinks*]

ALSEMERO [*To* JASPERINO]
It has that secret virtue it ne'er missed, sir,
Upon a virgin. [BEATRICE *gapes, then sneezes*]

JASPERINO [*To* ALSEMERO] Treble qualitied!

129 *abused* maligned, libelled (*OED* v. 7)
s.d. *Enter* JASPERINO (*after . . . come, sir?* Q)
134 *composition* substance composed of a mixture of ingredients (*OED* n. 20a)
135 *upon my warrant* I swear
138 *handsomely* skilfully (*OED* adv. 3)
139 *secret* kept from the knowledge of the uninitiated (*OED* a. 1e)
virtue power, efficacy (*OED* n. 11a)
140 *Treble qualitied* Referring to the three symptoms Beatrice exhibits.

ALSEMERO [*To* JASPERINO]
By all that's virtuous, it takes there, proceeds!
JASPERINO [*To* ALSEMERO]
This is the strangest trick to know a maid by.
BEATRICE
Ha ha ha!
You have given me joy of heart to drink, my lord.
ALSEMERO
No, thou hast given me such joy of heart,
That never can be blasted.
BEATRICE
What's the matter sir?
ALSEMERO [*To* JASPERINO]
See now, 'tis settled in a melancholy
Keeps both the time and method. [*To* BEATRICE] My Joanna,
Chaste as the breath of heaven, or morning's womb
That brings the day forth, thus my love encloses thee!
[*Embraces her*]
Exeunt

[ACT IV. SCENE iii.]

Enter ISABELLA *and* LOLLIO

ISABELLA
O heaven! Is this the waxing moon?
Does love turn fool, run mad, and all at once?
Sirrah, here's a madman, akin to the fool too,
A lunatic lover.

141 *virtuous* Playing on the efficacious *virtue* of the drug and its proof of Beatrice's moral *virtue*.
takes is having the intended result (*OED* v. 11c)
proceeds takes effect (*OED* v. 5)
146 *blasted* blighted (*OED* v. 8)
148 *Keeps* ed. (keep Q)
Keeps . . . method Follows both the [prescribed] timing and sequence
IV.iii Author: Rowley
1 *waxing* ed. (waiting Q). It is difficult to make sense of Q *waiting*, and in some hands *x* could easily be misread as *it*. Since lunatics were thought to be governed by the moon (*luna*), madness could be expected to increase as it moved towards the full.
2 *at* ed. (*not in* Q)

LOLLIO

No, no! Not he I brought the letter from?

ISABELLA

Compare his inside with his out, and tell me.

[*Gives him the letter*]

LOLLIO

The out's mad, I'm sure of that, I had a taste on't.

[*Reads*] 'To the bright Andromeda, chief chambermaid to the Knight of the Sun, at the sign of Scorpio, in the middle region, sent by the bellows-mender of Æolus. Pay the post.' This is stark madness.

ISABELLA [*Takes the letter*]

Now mark the inside.

[*Reads*] 'Sweet lady, having now cast off this counterfeit cover of a madman, I appear to your best judgement a true and faithful lover of your beauty.'

LOLLIO

He is mad still.

ISABELLA

'If any fault you find, chide those perfections in you which have made me imperfect: 'tis the same sun that causeth to grow, and enforceth to wither –'

LOLLIO

O rogue!

6 *Compare . . . out* (1) Compare the contents of the letter with what is written on its outside; (2) Compare his inner self with his outward guise

8–10 *To . . . Aeolus* A deliberate jumble of astrological and mythical material, laced with bawdy *double entendre.*

8 *bright Andromeda* Both the brilliant constellation and the beautiful heroine of classical myth (= Isabella) whom Perseus rescued from the dragon (= Alibius).

8–9 *chambermaid . . . Sun* A mock-astrological description of the relationship between the constellation Andromeda and the Sun, but also recalling the character of 'A Chamber-Mayde' in Overbury's *Wife,* whose lascivious behaviour is encouraged by her passion for chivalric romance; in particular 'She . . . is so carried away with *The Mirror of Knighthood,* she is many times resolved to run out of herself, and become a lady errant' (sig. G8) – the reference is to a popular Spanish romance translated and published in nine parts between 1578 and 1601 – one of whose heroes is the Knight of the Sun. Cf. also *chamber* = vagina (Williams, *Glossary*, p. 67).

9 *sign of Scorpio* (1) the name of the inn where Andromeda is imagined to be lodging; (2) the astrological sign supposed to govern the private parts

middle region (1) fifth to eighth months of the astrological year; (2) private parts

10 *Aeolus* god of the winds – hence linked by bawdy association with *the middle region.* Daalder suggests *bellows* = phallus.

post messenger (*OED* n.[2] 2a)

18 *imperfect* Referring to his degrading disguise as a madman.

18–19 *'tis . . . wither* Cf. Tilley, S980: 'The same sun softens wax and hardens clay.'

ISABELLA

'– shapes and trans-shapes, destroys and builds again. I come in winter to you dismantled of my proper ornaments: by the sweet splendour of your cheerful smiles, I spring and live a lover.'

LOLLIO

Mad rascal still!

ISABELLA

'Tread him not under foot, that shall appear an honour to your bounties. I remain, mad till I speak with you from whom I expect my cure, yours all, or one beside himself, Franciscus.'

LOLLIO

You are like to have a fine time on't: my master and I may give over our professions – I do not think but you can cure fools and madmen faster then we, with little pains too.

ISABELLA

Very likely.

LOLLIO

One thing I must tell you, mistress: you perceive that I am privy to your skill; if I find you minister once and set up the trade, I put in for my thirds – I shall be mad or fool else.

ISABELLA

The first place is thine – believe it, Lollio –
If I do fall –

LOLLIO I fall upon you.

ISABELLA So.

LOLLIO

Well, I stand to my venture.

ISABELLA

But thy counsel now: how shall I deal with 'em?

22 *dismantled . . . ornaments* stripped of the garments and trappings appropriate to one of my rank
25–6 *that . . . bounties* whose love will bring honour to you if you treat him generously
33 *skill* (1) in curing fools and madmen; (2) in erotic matters
minister . . . trade (1) treat one patient and set yourself up as a practitioner; (2) commit adultery and become a whore
33–4 *I . . . thirds* Note the echo of Deflores' 'I'll put in for one' (II.ii.60).
thirds share (financial and sexual). 'Thirds' were the third share of captures or of certain fines due to the crown; also the third part of a husband's estate due to his widow (*OED* n. 3; 2).
37 *stand to* stand by (with bawdy *double entendre*)
venture commercial enterprise, speculation (*OED* n. 4a)

LOLLIO

Why, do you mean to deal with 'em?

ISABELLA

Nay, the fair understanding – how to use 'em.

LOLLIO

Abuse 'em! That's the way to mad the fool, and make a fool of the madman, and then you use 'em kindly.

ISABELLA

'Tis easy – I'll practise. Do thou observe it.
The key of thy wardrobe?

LOLLIO

There – fit yourself for 'em, and I'll fit 'em both for you.
[*Gives her the key*]

ISABELLA

Take thou no further notice than the outside. *Exit*

LOLLIO

Not an inch, I'll put you to the inside.

Enter ALIBIUS

ALIBIUS

Lollio, art there? Will all be perfect, think'st thou?
Tomorrow night, as if to close up the solemnity,
Vermandero expects us.

LOLLIO

I mistrust the madmen most; the fools will do well enough: I have taken pains with them.

ALIBIUS

Tush, they cannot miss! The more absurdity,

39 *Why* ed. (We Q)
deal Lollio deliberately misunderstands her to mean 'copulate' (Williams, *Glossary*, p. 92).
40 *the fair understanding* understand my words in the decent sense I intended. Ironically *use* could also mean 'employ sexually' (Williams, *Glossary*, pp. 320–21).
41 *Abuse* (1) Maltreat; (2) Deceive; (3) Ravish, Defile sexually (*OED* v. 5; 4; 6)
42 *kindly* (1) considerately; (2) as creatures of their kind deserve
43 *practise* plot, employ an artifice or stratagem (*OED* v. 9)
44–7 *The key . . . inside* Compare Beatrice's opening of the closet with Alsemero's key in IV.i – the 'wardrobe' like the 'closet' will presumably have been represented either by the discovery space at the rear of the Phoenix stage or by the same stage-door.
45 *fit* (1) make ready; (2) prepare for copulation (Williams, *Glossary*, p. 127)
47 *put . . . inside* 'I'll allow you intimate access to your lovers' (Bawcutt 1998); but see also Williams, *Glossary*, p. 251: *put to* 'of phallic insertion'
49 *solemnity* i.e. the wedding celebration

The more commends it, so no rough behaviours
Affright the ladies – they are nice things, thou know'st.

LOLLIO

You need not fear, sir: so long as we are there with our commanding pizzles, they'll be as tame as the ladies themselves.

ALIBIUS

I will see them once more rehearse before they go.

LOLLIO

I was about it, sir. Look you to the madmen's morris, and let me alone with the other. There is one or two that I mistrust their fooling: I'll instruct them, and then they shall rehearse the whole measure.

ALIBIUS

Do so – I'll see the music prepared. But, Lollio,
By the way, how does my wife brook her restraint?
Does she not grudge at it?

LOLLIO

So, so – she takes some pleasure in the house, she would abroad else. You must allow her a little more length, she's kept too short.

ALIBIUS

She shall along to Vermandero's with us:
That will serve her for a month's liberty.

LOLLIO

What's that on your face, sir?

ALIBIUS Where, Lollio, I see nothing.

LOLLIO

Cry you mercy, sir, 'tis your nose; it showed like the trunk of a young elephant.

55 *nice* delicate; coy, shy; fastidious, refined (*OED* a. 4c; 5a; 7a)
57 *pizzles* whips made from dried bull-penises
59 *morris* morris-dance – grotesque dance usually representing characters from the Robin Hood story
60 *the other* i.e. the fools' performance
62 *measure* dance – usually of a grave and stately kind (*OED* n. 20a)
64 *bròok* tolerate, endure
65 *grudge* grumble
66 *pleasure* With sexual *double entendre.*
67 *allow . . . length* give her more rope – but (cf. *short*, l. 68) with an obscene reference to the length of a penis (see Williams, *Dictionary*, p. 800).
70 *month's* Disyllabic, as the Q spelling *moneths* indicates.
72–3 *nose . . . elephant* Lollio implies that Alibius is easily led by the nose; but a phallic joke may also be involved.

ALIBIUS

Away, rascal! I'll prepare the music, Lollio. *Exit*

LOLLIO

Do, sir; and I'll dance the whilst. [*Calls*] Tony! Where art thou, Tony?

Enter ANTONIO

ANTONIO

Here, cousin, where art thou?

LOLLIO

Come, Tony, the footmanship I taught you.

ANTONIO

I had rather ride, cousin.

LOLLIO

Ay, a whip take you! But I'll keep you out. Vault in, look you, Tony: fa, la, la, la, la. [*Dances*]

ANTONIO Fa, la, la, la, la. [*Dances*]

LOLLIO

There, an honour. [*Bows*]

ANTONIO

Is this an honour, coz? [*Bows*]

LOLLIO

Yes, and it please your worship.

ANTONIO

Does honour bend in the hams, coz?

LOLLIO

Marry does it: as low as worship, squireship – nay, yeomanry itself sometimes; from whence it first stiffened, there rises a caper.

78 *footmanship* skill in dancing (cf. *OED* n. 1)
79 *ride* Bawdy *double entendre.*
82 *honour* bow (*OED* n. 5b)
83 *coz* cousin (cf. I.ii.135)
84 *and* if
85 *bend in the hams* (1) bow, make obeisance; (2) show the bent posture of someone suffering from venereal disease (Williams, *Glossary*: 'ham', p. 150)
86 *Marry* Abbreviation of 'By Mary'.
87 *from . . . stiffened* If honour can bend, Lollio suggests, it must first have stiffened (with pride) as it rose from the mere yeomanry into the honourable ranks of the lesser gentry (*worship, squireship*); a quibble on phallic erection is also involved.
rises ed. (rise Q)
88 *caper* (1) leap; (2) fantastical proceeding, freak (*OED* n. 1a)

ANTONIO

Caper after an honour, coz?

LOLLIO

Very proper: for honour is but a caper, rises as fast and high, has a knee or two, and falls to th'ground again. You can remember your figure, Tony? *Exit*

ANTONIO

Yes, cousin, when I see thy figure, I can remember mine.

Enter ISABELLA [*like a madwoman*]

ISABELLA

Hey, how he treads the air! Shough, shough, t'other way – he burns his wings else. Here's wax enough below, Icarus – more than will be cancelled these eighteen moons.

[ANTONIO *falls*]

He's down, he's down! What a terrible fall he had!
Stand up, thou son of Cretan Daedalus,
And let us tread the lower labyrinth;
I'll bring thee to the clew. [*Pulls him*]

ANTONIO

Prithee, coz, let me alone.

90–1 *has a knee* Cf. 'makes a knee' = bows.

92 *figure* (1) set of dance movements; (2) appearance (*OED* n. 16; 1c)

94–100 Q prints this entire passage as verse, but its lineation corresponds to no discernible metrical pattern. Editors have made several attempts to re-line the whole speech, but none is entirely satisfactory. Lines 94 and 98–100 make reasonably good iambic verse, but the rest of the speech is clearly prose. The oscillation between metre and prose rhythms, which is also apparent in some of Antonio's and Franciscus' speeches, is a way of representing the disordered quality of mad utterance.

94 *he* ed. (she Q)

Shough Exclamation still used by beaters when driving game birds towards the guns – an obsolete, slightly gutteral form of 'shoo' (*OED*).

94–9 *he burns . . . labyrinth* Referring to the myth of the labyrinth built by King Minos of Crete. Daedalus, the architect of this maze, was imprisoned there with his son, Icarus, but engineered their escape with the aid of artificial wings; Icarus, however, flew too close to the sun, melting the wax with which his wings were attached, and plunged to his death in the Icarian Sea (cf. III.ii.114; III.iii.71; V.iii.148).

95–6 *more . . . moons* more than will be used up in sealing eighteen months' worth of legal documents

99 *tread . . . labyrinth* Obscene *double entendre* (see Williams, *Glossary*: 'tread' = copulate, p. 313).

100 *clew* the ball of thread, given to Theseus by Minos's daughter, Ariadne, which enabled the hero to escape from the labyrinth after he had slain the monstrous Minotaur

ISABELLA Art thou not drowned?
About thy head I saw a heap of clouds
Wrapped like a Turkish turban, on thy back
A crook'd chameleon-coloured rainbow hung
Like a tiara down unto thy hams.
Let me suck out those billows in thy belly, [*Bends over him*]
Hark how they roar and rumble in the straits!
Bless thee from the pirates!

ANTONIO
Pox upon you, let me alone! [*Rises*]

ISABELLA
Why shouldst thou mount so high as Mercury,
Unless thou hadst reversion of his place?
Stay in the moon with me, Endymion,
And we will rule these wild rebellious waves,
That would have drowned my love.

ANTONIO
I'll kick thee if again thou touch me,
Thou wild, unshapen antic; I am no fool,
You bedlam.

ISABELLA But you are, as sure as I am, mad.
Have I put on this habit of a frantic,
With love as full of fury, to beguile
The nimble eye of watchful jealousy,
And am I thus rewarded? [*Reveals herself*]

ANTONIO
Ha! Dearest beauty!

ISABELLA
No, I have no beauty now,

105 *tiara* raised head-dress or turban worn by Persians and other Eastern peoples (*OED* n. 1), here with a long tail-piece at the back
106 *suck . . . belly* 'Probably . . . an indecent advance under the guise of an insane allusion to the myth' (Frost).
107 *straits* (streets Q)
110 *Mercury* winged messenger of the Gods
111 *reversion of his place* entitlement to succeed him in his office
112 *Endymion* beautiful youth with whom the moon-goddess fell in love
113 *rule . . . waves* The moon-goddess controlled the tides.
116 *antic* grotesque performer, clown (*OED* n. 4)
117 *bedlam* lunatic (after Bethlehem Hospital, see above I.ii.50)
118 *frantic* frenzied person, lunatic
122 *Ha . . . beauty* Metrically amphibious, forming a loose pentameter line with either or both of ll. 120 and 122.

Nor never had, but what was in my garments.
You a quick-sighted lover? Come not near me!
Keep your caparisons, you're aptly clad;
I came a feigner to return stark mad. *Exit*

Enter LOLLIO

ANTONIO
Stay, or I shall change condition,
And become as you are.

LOLLIO
Why Tony, whither now? Why, fool?

ANTONIO
Whose fool, usher of idiots? You coxcomb,
I have fooled too much.

LOLLIO
You were best be mad another while then.

ANTONIO
So I am, stark mad; I have cause enough,
And I could throw the full effects on thee,
And beat thee like a Fury.

LOLLIO
Do not, do not! I shall not forbear the gentleman under the fool, if you do. Alas, I saw through your fox-skin before now! Come, I can give you comfort: my mistress loves you, and there is as arrant a mad-man i' th' house as you are a fool – your rival, whom she loves not. If, after the masque, we can rid her of him, you earn her love, she says, and the fool shall ride her.

ANTONIO
May I believe thee?

LOLLIO
Yes, or you may choose whether you will or no.

ANTONIO
She's eased of him, I have a good quarrel on't.

126 *caparisons* trappings
131 *usher* door-keeper; assistant schoolmaster (*OED* n. 1; 4)
coxcomb fool – after the cap, decorated with a cock's comb worn by jesters (*OED* n. 3)
136 *Fury* In classical mythology, one of the three avenging spirits sent from the underworld to punish crimes; generally, a tormenting spirit.
137 *forbear* spare
142 *ride her* Obscene word-play on 'rid her' (l. 141).
145 *eased* relieved (cf. III.iii.99)

LOLLIO
Well, keep your old station yet, and be quiet.

ANTONIO
Tell her I will deserve her love. [*Exit*]

LOLLIO
And you are like to have your desire.

Enter FRANCISCUS

FRANCISCUS [*Sings*]
'Down, down, down a-down a-down'; and then with a horse-trick
To kick Latona's forehead, and break her bowstring.

LOLLIO
This is t'other counterfeit – I'll put him out of his humour [*Takes out letter and reads*]: 'Sweet Lady, having now cast this counterfeit cover of a mad-man, I appear to your best judgement a true and faithful lover of your beauty.' This is pretty well for a madman.

FRANCISCUS
Ha! What's that?

LOLLIO
'Chide those perfections in you which made me imperfect.'

FRANCISCUS
I am discovered to the fool.

LOLLIO
I hope to discover the fool in you, e're I have done with you. 'Yours all, or one beside himself, Franciscus.' This madman will mend sure.

FRANCISCUS
What do you read, sirrah?

146 *old station* existing position (as a fool)

149 *Down . . . a-down* Daalder suggests a deliberate echo of Ophelia's mad song in *Hamlet* (IV.v.167).
horse-trick Cf. 'horse-play' and 'trick' = feat of dexterity (*OED* n. 5a) – so probably an extravagant dance-leap; but the bawdy sense of 'trick' = sexual act (Williams, *Glossary*, p. 313) suggests that the familiar horse/whores pun is also involved (cf. *Anthony and Cleopatra*, I.v.21).

150 *Latona* mother of the goddess Diana, but here apparently confused with Diana herself, typically depicted as a hunter with a bow

152 *off* ed. (*not in* Q; but cf. l. 13)

158 *discovered* exposed, revealed

LOLLIO

Your destiny, sir: you'll be hanged for this trick, and another that I know.

FRANCISCUS

Art thou of counsel with thy mistress?

LOLLIO

Next her apron-strings.

FRANCISCUS

Give me thy hand.

LOLLIO

Stay, let me put yours in my pocket first [*Puts away the letter*]: your hand is true, is it not? It will not pick? I partly fear it, because I think it does lie.

FRANCISCUS

Not in a syllable.

LOLLIO

So, if you love my mistress so well as you have handled the matter here, you are like to be cured of your madness.

FRANCISCUS

And none but she can cure it.

LOLLIO

Well, I'll give you over then, and she shall cast your water next.

FRANCISCUS

Take for thy pains past. [*Gives him money*]

LOLLIO

I shall deserve more, sir, I hope. My mistress loves you, but must have some proof of your love to her.

FRANCISCUS

There I meet my wishes.

LOLLIO

That will not serve, you must meet her enemy and yours.

FRANCISCUS

He's dead already.

163 *another* i.e. his 'whore's-trick' with Isabella (l. 149)
168 *yours* your hand(writing) – i.e. the letter
169 *hand is true* (1) your handwriting is correct; (2) what you have written is truthful; (3) your hand is honest (*OED* a. 4a–b; 3d; 2)
pick steal (*OED* v. 9a)
175 *give you over* abandon you
cast your water diagnose your condition with a urine sample
180 *meet* fight a duel with (*OED* v. 3a)

LOLLIO

Will you tell me that, and I parted but now with him?

FRANCISCUS

Show me the man!

LOLLIO

Ay, that's a right course now: see him before you kill him in any case; and yet it needs not go so far neither – 'tis but a fool that haunts the house and my mistress in the shape of an idiot: bang but his fool's coat well-favouredly, and 'tis well.

FRANCISCUS

Soundly, soundly!

LOLLIO

Only reserve him till the masque be past; and if you find him not now in the dance yourself, I'll show you. In, in! My master! [*Dances*]

FRANCISCUS

He handles him like a feather. Hey! [*Exit dancing*]

Enter ALIBIUS

ALIBIUS

Well said! In a readiness, Lollio?

LOLLIO

Yes, sir.

ALIBIUS

Away then, and guide them in, Lollio;
Entreat your mistress to see this sight.
Hark, is there not one incurable fool
That might be begged? I have friends.

LOLLIO

I have him for you – one that shall deserve it too. [*Exit*]

182 *and* given that
187 *well-favouredly* thoroughly
189 *Only . . . you* The fact the promised face-off between Antonio and Franciscus, like the masque of madmen itself, never takes place suggests either that there was a change of plan on the part of the dramatists, or (as some scholars have suggested) that a scene has been cut from the surviving text.
192 *him* himself
193 *Well said* Well done
197–8 *fool . . . begged* In cases where an heir was legally declared a congenital idiot, his estate passed to the management of the crown; anyone who wished to enjoy its revenue could 'beg a fool' – i.e. apply through the Court of Wards to be made his guardian.

ALIBIUS

Good boy, Lollio.

[*Enter* ISABELLA, *and* LOLLIO *ushering in the* MADMEN *and* FOOLS.]
The MADMEN *and* FOOLS *dance*

'Tis perfect! Well, fit but once these strains,
We shall have coin and credit for our pains.

Exeunt

ACT V. [SCENE i.]

Enter BEATRICE. *A clock strikes one*

BEATRICE

One struck, and yet she lies by't! O my fears!
This strumpet serves her own ends, 'tis apparent now,
Devours the pleasure with a greedy appetite,
And never minds my honour or my peace,
Makes havoc of my right; but she pays dearly for't –
No trusting of her life with such a secret,
That cannot rule her blood to keep her promise.
Beside, I have some suspicion of her faith to me,
Because I was suspected of my lord,

201 *fit . . . strains* only fit the music (to the wild dance)
V.i Author: Middleton
1–6 *One . . . secret* In *Gerardo*, the maid Julia, similarly substituting for her mistress on her wedding night, is guilty of the same careless indulgence: 'she belike either wearied, or taken with the sweet of so much pleasure, contrary to the order I had given her, fell asleep, and now I knew not which in me was most, my jealousy or fear, and my rage increased the more, when (hearing the clock strike three) I saw so little memory in her of my danger.' Isdaura, 'taking her to be too shallow a vessel for my secrets,' then resolves to kill her (H5–H5v).
1 *lies by't* continues in sin (*OED* v. 3a); Daalder suggests an indecent play on *lie* and *it* (= sexual act; Williams, *Glossary*, p. 172).
2 *serves . . . ends* A play on sexual 'service' and on 'end' = genital area (Williams, *Glossary*, pp. 273–4, 113–14) is unavoidable here.
7 *blood* lustful desires
9 *of* by

And it must come from her. – Hark, by my horrors,
Another clock strikes two! [*Clock*] *strike*[*s*] *two*

Enter DEFLORES.

DEFLORES Psst! Where are you?

BEATRICE
Deflores!

DEFLORES Ay – is she not come from him yet?

BEATRICE
As I am a living soul not.

DEFLORES Sure the devil
Hath sowed his itch within her! Who'd trust
A waiting-woman?

BEATRICE
I must trust somebody.

DEFLORES
Push! They are termagants;
Especially when they fall upon their masters
And have their ladies' first-fruits, they're mad whelps,
You cannot stave 'em off from game royal. Then
You are so harsh and hardy, ask no counsel –
And I could have helped you to a 'pothecary's daughter
Would have fallen off before eleven, and thanked you too.

BEATRICE
O me! Not yet? This whore forgets herself.

14 *itch* sexual urge (Williams, *Glossary*, p. 172)
16 *I . . . somebody* Metrically amphibious.
17 *termagants* viragos
18 *fall upon* attack (with sexual innuendo – see Williams, *Dictionary*, p. 460)
19 *first-fruits* Ironically, given its bawdy meaning here, the phrase is biblical and referred originally to the harvest offerings required by God (see e.g. Exodus 23:16, Leviticus 23:10; Numbers 28:26); but St Paul employs it as a figure for Christ's sacrifice as 'the first fruits of them that sleep' (1 Corinthians 15:20); significantly, in view of the extended play on 'falling' and 'rising' in this passage of dialogue, St Paul is discussing the resurrection of Christ and the rising of the dead.
20 *stave . . . royal* keep them from worrying game which belongs exclusively to the monarch; but 'game' also = wantonness (Williams, *Glossary*, p. 137), so that *game royal* could mean something like 'extravagant sexual indulgence'
21 *harsh* rough, rude – perhaps here 'headstrong'
hardy foolhardy (*OED* a. 2)
22 *a 'pothecary's* Dyce (a Apothecaries Q; an apothecary's Dilke)
23 *thanked* ed. (thank Q)

DEFLORES
The rascal fares so well – look, you're undone,
The day-star by this hand! See Phosphorus plain yonder.

BEATRICE
Advise me how to fall upon some ruin;
There is no counsel safe else.

DEFLORES
Peace! I ha't now,
For we must force a rising, there's no remedy.

BEATRICE
How? Take heed of that.

DEFLORES
Tush! Be you quiet,
Or else give over all.

BEATRICE
Prithee, I ha' done then.

DEFLORES
This is my reach: I'll set some part a-fire
Of Diaphanta's chamber.

BEATRICE
How? Fire, sir?
That may endanger the whole house.

DEFLORES
You talk of danger when your fame's on fire?

BEATRICE
That's true, do what thou wilt now.

DEFLORES
Push! I aim
At a most rich success, strikes all dead sure:
The chimney being a-fire, and some light parcels
Of the least danger in her chamber only,
If Diaphanta should be met by chance then,
Far from her lodging – which is now suspicious –
It would be thought her fears and affrights then,

26 *Phosphorus* ed. (Bosphorus Q); the morning star – ironically, as Frost points out, *Lucifer* in Latin; see also Isaiah 14:12 ff. 'How art thou fallen from heaven, O day star, son of the morning . . .' – here, however, Lucifer rises.
27 *how* ed. (now Q)
fall upon have recourse to (*OED* v. 70d)
ruin (1) downfall (*OED* n. 6a) – but with *fall* picking up the reference to Lucifer at l. 26; (2) dishonour, loss of virginity (*OED* n. 6b)
29 *force a rising* drive everyone out of bed – but with a sardonic play on the fall/resurrection motif (cf. ll. 18, 23, 26, 27)
32 *reach* scheme (*OED* n. 2a)
37 *strikes . . . sure* will make everything safe and secure (but with an ironic quibble on 'strikes . . . dead')
38–9 *light . . . danger* inconsiderable bits and pieces unlikely to cause a major fire
41 *is now* would otherwise be

Drove her to seek for succour; if not seen
Or met at all – as that's the likeliest –
For her own shame she'll hasten towards her lodging.
I will be ready with a piece high-charged,
As 'twere to cleanse the chimney – there 'tis proper,
But she shall be the mark.

BEATRICE I'm forced to love thee now,
'Cause thou provid'st so carefully for my honour.

DEFLORES
'Slid! It concerns the safety of us both,
Our pleasure and continuance.

BEATRICE One word now:
Prithee, how for the servants?

DEFLORES I'll dispatch them,
Some one way, some another in the hurry,
For buckets, hooks, ladders. Fear not you:
The deed shall find its time, and I've thought since
Upon a safe conveyance for the body too.
How this fire purifies wit! Watch you your minute.

BEATRICE
Fear keeps my soul upon't, I cannot stray from't.

Enter ALONZO*'s ghost*

DEFLORES
Ha! What art thou that tak'st away the light
'Twixt that star and me? I dread thee not:
'Twas but a mist of conscience – all's clear again. *Exit*

BEATRICE
Who's that, Deflores? Bless me! It slides by. [*Exit ghost*]

46 *piece* gun
high-charged with a double loading of powder and shot
47 *there . . . proper* it would be appropriate for that purpose
proper ed. (proper now Q); *now* probably picked up by eye-skip from l. 48
50 *'Slid* Contraction of 'By God's (eye)lid'.
56 *conveyance* riddance (*OED* n. 3)
57 *How . . . wit* Fire was an instrument of purification, used both in alchemical experiment, and (more mundanely) to cleanse foul air: Deflores' remark is itself witty, his conceit being that the very idea of the fire he will light has served to purify his wit (intelligence, ingenuity) – familiarly imagined in metaphors of fire and sparks. In terms of humoral psycho-physiology, heat would nourish wit, whilst the cold and damp of melancholy would dull it.
60 *that star* i.e. Phosphorus/Lucifer

Some ill thing haunts the house, 't has left behind it
A shivering sweat upon me – I'm afraid now.
This night hath been so tedious. Oh, this strumpet!
Had she a thousand lives, he should not leave her
Till he had destroyed the last – [*Clock strikes three*]
List! O my terrors,
Three struck by St Sebastian's!

[VOICES] *Within* Fire, fire, fire!

BEATRICE

Already! How rare is that man's speed!
How heartily he serves me! His face loathes one,
But look upon his care, who would not love him?
The east is not more beauteous than his service.

[VOICES] *Within*

Fire, fire, fire!

Enter DEFLORES [*with*] *servants.* [*They*] *pass over* [*the stage. A bell rings*].

DEFLORES

Away! Dispatch! Hooks, buckets, ladders! That's well said!
The fire bell rings, the chimney works, my charge
The piece is ready. *Exit*

Enter DIAPHANTA

BEATRICE Here's a man worth loving! –
[*Sees* DIAPHANTA]

65 *tedious* long and wearisome; painful; slow (*OED* a. 1; 2; 4)
67 s.d. ed. (*'Struck 3 a clock' after* St Sebastian's Q)
69 *rare* exceptional; remarkably good (*OED* a. 5a; 6a)
70 *loathes* excites loathing in (*OED* v. 3)
72 *east . . . beauteous* The beauty of sunrise is traditionally charged with a Christian symbolism that contrasts ironically with the rising of Deflores' Phosphorus/Lucifer (l. 26).
service The bawdy sense is unmistakeable here, although Beatrice is hardly conscious of it.
73 s.d.2 This edition (*Enter Deflores servants: passe over, ring a Bell* Q)
74, 90 *well said* Cf. IV.iii.193.
75 *my charge* the task entrusted to me – with a play on 'charge' = powder and shot for his 'piece'

Oh, you're a jewel!

DIAPHANTA Pardon frailty, madam:
In troth I was so well, I ev'n forgot myself.

BEATRICE
Y'have made trim work!

DIAPHANTA What?

BEATRICE Hie quickly to your chamber;
Your reward follows you.

DIAPHANTA I never made
So sweet a bargain. *Exit*

Enter ALSEMERO

ALSEMERO O my dear Joanna,
Alas, art thou risen too? I was coming,
My absolute treasure.

BEATRICE When I missed you,
I could not choose but follow.

ALSEMERO Th'art all sweetness!
The fire is not so dangerous.

BEATRICE Think you so, sir?

ALSEMERO
I prithee, tremble not. Believe me, 'tis not.

Enter VERMANDERO, JASPERINO.

VERMANDERO
O bless my house and me!

ALSEMERO My lord your father.

Enter DEFLORES *with a piece*

VERMANDERO
Knave, whither goes that piece?

DEFLORES
To scour the chimney. *Exit*

VERMANDERO
Oh, well said, well said!
That fellow's good on all occasions.

80 *reward* i.e. death
89 *To . . . chimney* Metrically amphibious.

BEATRICE
A wondrous necessary man, my lord.

VERMANDERO
He hath a ready wit, he's worth 'em all, sir.
Dog at a house on fire – I ha' seen him singed ere now.
The piece goes off
Ha! There he goes!

BEATRICE [*Aside*] 'Tis done.

ALSEMERO Come, sweet, to bed now;
Alas, thou wilt get cold.

BEATRICE Alas, the fear keeps that out.
My heart will find no quiet till I hear
How Diaphanta, my poor woman, fares –
It is her chamber, sir, her lodging chamber.

VERMANDERO
How should the fire come there?

BEATRICE
As good a soul as ever lady countenanced,
But in her chamber negligent and heavy.
She 'scaped a mine twice.

VERMANDERO Twice?

BEATRICE Strangely twice, sir.

VERMANDERO
Those sleepy sluts are dangerous in a house,
And they be ne'er so good.

Enter DEFLORES [*with the body of* DIAPHANTA]

DEFLORES O poor virginity,
Thou hast paid dearly for't!

94 *Dog at* i.e. he's a dog at – expert in dealing with (*OED* n. 17i)
on ed. (of Q)
s.d. ed. (*after* goes Q)
101 *countenanced* favoured, gave patronage to (*OED* v. 5)
102 *heavy* stupid; clumsy, sluggish (*OED* a. 18; 19)
103 *mine* undermining stratagem, blowing up (*OED* n. 3). Beatrice claims that Diaphanta's carelessness has twice come close to involving her in a fatal accident.
105 *And* Even, if
s.d. *with* ... DIAPHANTA ed. (*not in* Q). Although some editors have disputed this emendation, it is difficult to know what else 'that' and 'thing' (ll. 106–7) can refer to.
105–6 *poor* ... *for't* you have paid a high price for preserving your wretched and unremunerative virginity

VERMANDERO Bless us! What's that?

DEFLORES
A thing you all knew once – Diaphanta's burnt.

BEATRICE
My woman, oh my woman!

DEFLORES Now the flames
Are greedy of her – burnt, burnt, burnt to death, sir!

BEATRICE
O my presaging soul!

ALSEMERO Not a tear more,
I charge you by the last embrace I gave you
In bed before this raised us.

BEATRICE Now you tie me:
Were it my sister now she gets no more.

Enter SERVANT

VERMANDERO
How now?

SERVANT
All danger's past; you may now take your rests, my lords, the fire is thoroughly quenched. Ah, poor gentlewoman, how soon was she stifled!

BEATRICE
Deflores, what is left of her inter,
And we as mourners all will follow her;
I will entreat that honour to my servant,
Ev'n of my lord himself.

ALSEMERO Command it, sweetness.

BEATRICE
Which of you spied the fire first?

DEFLORES 'Twas I, madam.

BEATRICE
And took such pains in't too? A double goodness!
'Twere well he were rewarded.

VERMANDERO He shall be –
Deflores, call upon me.

113 *no more* i.e. tears
s.d. ed. (*after* How now? Q)

ALSEMERO And upon me, sir.
Exeunt

DEFLORES
Rewarded? Precious! Here's a trick beyond me!
I see in all bouts both of sport and wit,
Always a woman strives for the last hit. *Exit*

[ACT V. SCENE ii.]

Enter TOMAZO

TOMAZO
I cannot taste the benefits of life
With the same relish I was wont to do.
Man I grow weary of, and hold his fellowship
A treacherous bloody friendship; and because
I am ignorant in whom my wrath should settle,
I must think all men villains, and the next
I meet, whoe'er he be, the murderer
Of my most worthy brother – ha! What's he?

Enter DEFLORES, *passes over the stage*

Oh, the fellow that some call honest Deflores!
But methinks honesty was hard bestead
To come there for a lodging, as if a queen
Should make her palace of a pest-house.
I find a contrariety in nature
Betwixt that face and me: the least occasion

126 *Precious* Abbreviation of 'By God's precious body', but a relatively mild oath in the abbreviated form. In the context of 'rewarded' a quibble on the pecuniary sense is unavoidable.
127 *sport* (1) fencing; (2) fornication (Williams, *Glossary*, p. 285)
128 *hit* (1) strike in fencing; (2) act of coition (Williams, *Glossary*, p. 158)
V.ii Author: Middleton
10 *hard bestead* hard put to it (*OED* p. ppl. 5)
12 *pest-house* plague hospital

Would give me game upon him; yet he's so foul
One would scarce touch him with a sword he loved
And made account of; so most deadly venomous,
He would go near to poison any weapon
That should draw blood on him – one must resolve
Never to use that sword again in fight,
In way of honest manhood, that strikes him;
Some river must devour it, 'twere not fit
That any man should find it. – What again?

Enter DEFLORES

He walks a-purpose by, sure to choke me up,
To infect my blood.

DEFLORES My worthy noble lord!

TOMAZO
Dost offer to come near and breathe upon me?
[*Strikes him*]

DEFLORES
A blow! [*Draws his sword*]

TOMAZO Yea, are you so prepared? [*Draws*]
I'll rather like a soldier die by th'sword
Than like a politician by thy poison. [*Advances on him*]

DEFLORES
Hold, my lord, as you are honourable.

TOMAZO
All slaves that kill by poison are still cowards!

DEFLORES [*Aside*]
I cannot strike: I see his brother's wounds
Fresh bleeding in his eye, as in a crystal.
[*Aloud*] I will not question this, I know you're noble:

15 *give me game* Meaning unclear; Schelling's suggestion, 'cause me to fight with him', has been favoured by most editors, but the passage may be corrupt.
16 *him* ed. (*not in* Q)
he 'i.e. one' (Daalder)
22 *devour it* ed. (devour't Q)
29 *politician* crafty schemer, practiser of machiavellian 'policy' (*OED* n. 1)
31 *still* always
33 *Fresh bleeding* Probably alluding, as Bawcutt suggests, to the belief that a corpse would bleed again in its murderer's presence.
crystal piece of rock-crystal used by seers in magical art (*OED* n. 4)

I take my injury with thanks given, sir,
Like a wise lawyer, and as a favour
Will wear it for the worthy hand that gave it.
[*Aside*] Why this from him, that yesterday appeared
So strangely loving to me?
Oh, but instinct is of a subtler strain;
Guilt must not walk so near his lodge again –
He came near me now! *Exit*

TOMAZO
All league with mankind I renounce forever,
Till I find this murderer. Not so much
As common courtesy, but I'll lock up:
For in the state of ignorance I live in,
A brother may salute his brother's murderer,
And wish good speed to th'villain in a greeting.

Enter VERMANDERO, ALIBIUS and ISABELLA

VERMANDERO
Noble Piracquo!

TOMAZO
Pray keep on your way, sir;
I've nothing to say to you.

VERMANDERO
Comforts bless you, sir.

TOMAZO
I have forsworn compliment; in troth I have, sir.
As you are merely man, I have not left
A good wish for you, nor any here.

VERMANDERO
Unless you be so far in love with grief
You will not part from't upon any terms,
We bring that news will make a welcome for us.

35–7 *I . . . gave it* Deflores presumably means that a prudent lawyer will pretend to take a humiliating blow as a token of honour rather than expose himself to the physical and legal dangers of a duel.

42 *came near* touched me to the quick, affected me deeply (*OED near* adv. 12b, 16b); 'almost found me out' (Bawcutt 1998)

45 *lock up* suppress

48 *speed* luck, success

51 *compliment* courtesies of speech

55 *You will* That you will

56 *news will* news that will

TOMAZO
What news can that be?
VERMANDERO Throw no scornful smile
Upon the zeal I bring you; 'tis worth more, sir.
Two of the chiefest men I kept about me,
I hide not from the law, or your just vengeance.
TOMAZO Ha!
VERMANDERO
To give your peace more ample satisfaction,
Thank these discoverers.
TOMAZO If you bring that calm,
Name but the manner I shall ask forgiveness in
For that contemptuous smile upon you;
I'll perfect it with reverence that belongs
Unto a sacred altar. [*Kneels*]
VERMANDERO Good sir, rise!
Why now you overdo as much o' this hand,
As you fell short o' t'other. Speak, Alibius.
ALIBIUS
'Twas my wife's fortune – as she is most lucky
At a discovery – to find out lately
Within our hospital of fools and madmen,
Two counterfeits slipped into these disguises:
Their names, Franciscus and Antonio.
VERMANDERO
Both mine, sir, and I ask no favour for 'em.
ALIBIUS
Now that which draws suspicion to their habits:
The time of their disguisings agrees justly
With the day of the murder.
TOMAZO O blest revelation!
VERMANDERO
Nay more, nay more, sir – I'll not spare mine own
In way of justice – they both feigned a journey

65 *perfect* Accent on first syllable.
72 *these disguises* i.e. of fool and madman – though Daalder suggests that Alibius may be carrying the actual disguises as evidence.

To Briamata, and so wrought out their leaves,
My love was so abused in't.

TOMAZO Time's too precious
To run in waste now; you have brought a peace
The riches of five kingdoms could not purchase.
Be my most happy conduct, I thirst for 'em:
Like subtle lightning will I wind about 'em,
And melt their marrow in 'em.

Exeunt

[ACT V. SCENE iii.]

Enter ALSEMERO *and* JASPERINO

JASPERINO
Your confidence, I'm sure, is now of proof:
The prospect from the garden has showed
Enough for deep suspicion.

ALSEMERO The black mask
That so continually was worn upon't
Condemns the face for ugly ere't be seen –
Her despite to him, and so seeming bottomless.

JASPERINO
Touch it home then: 'tis not a shallow probe

80 *Briamata* Treated as three syllables (as the Q spelling *Bramata* may indicate). At IV.ii.7–8 the Servant informed Vermandero that one had pretended to travel to Valencia. *leaves* permission to depart

84 *conduct* guide (*OED* n. 3)

85 *Like . . . 'em* A figure for secret murder, based on the belief that lightning could melt the marrow without damaging the skin; Bawcutt (1958) compares Chapman's *Bussy D'Ambois*: 'A politician must like lightning melt / The very marrow, and not taint the skin' (IV.ii.188–9).

V.iii Author: Rowley (and Middleton?)

1 *of proof* (1) armoured, impenetrable; (2) shown to be founded on truth (*OED* n. 10a–b, a. 1a; n. 1a)

2–3 *prospect . . . suspicion* The detail derives from *Gerardo* (sig. H1v); but here 'garden' inevitably picks up the resonances of the play's recurrent Fall motif.

2 *garden* If spoken with a rolled *r* this word becomes (as Daalder suggests) effectively trisyllabic, making the line a regular pentameter.

3 *black mask* i.e. her treacherous show of scorn (*despite*, l. 6) for Deflores. However, Bawcutt (1998) suggests that Beatrice, like other ladies of fashion may actually have worn a black mask to protect her complexion from the sun.

7 *Touch . . . home* Probe deeply (*OED* v. 2d)

Can search this ulcer soundly; I fear you'll find it
Full of corruption. – 'Tis fit I leave you:
She meets you opportunely from that walk;
She took the back door at his parting with her. *Exit*

ALSEMERO
Did my fate wait for this unhappy stroke
At my first sight of woman? – She is here.

Enter BEATRICE

BEATRICE
Alsemero!

ALSEMERO How do you?

BEATRICE How do I?
Alas, sir! How do you? You look not well.

ALSEMERO
You read me well enough, I am not well.

BEATRICE
Not well, sir? Is't in my power to better you?

ALSEMERO
Yes.

BEATRICE Nay, then you're cured again.

ALSEMERO
Pray resolve me one question, lady.

BEATRICE
If I can.

ALSEMERO
None can so sure. Are you honest?

BEATRICE
Ha ha ha! That's a broad question, my lord.

10 *that walk* Jasperino gestures at one of the stage doors, imagined as being the entrace to a garden 'walk'.
12–13 *Did . . . woman* Cf. I.i.1–12.
13 *She is* ed. (She's Q)
15 *sir* ed. (*not in* Q). Not only is the Q line one syllable short, but Craik's emendation ensures that the proper stress will fall on the first *you.*
15–18 *You . . . cured* Returns to the motif of love as a sickness and Alsemero's 'hidden malady' (I.i.23–5).
20 *If I can* Metrically amphibious.
21 *honest* (1) truthful; (2) honourable, chaste
22 *broad* (1) capable of too broad an interpretation (to be easily answered); (2) indecent (*OED* a. 10; 6c)

ALSEMERO

But that's not a modest answer, my lady:
Do you laugh? My doubts are strong upon me.

BEATRICE

'Tis innocence that smiles, and no rough brow
Can take away the dimple in her cheek.
Say I should strain a tear to fill the vault,
Which would you give the better faith to?

ALSEMERO

'Twere but hypocrisy of a sadder colour,
But the same stuff. Neither your smiles nor tears
Shall move or flatter me from my belief:
You are a whore.

BEATRICE What a horrid sound it hath!

It blasts a beauty to deformity;
Upon what face soever that breath falls,
It strikes it ugly. Oh, you have ruined
What you can ne'er repair again!

ALSEMERO

I'll all demolish and seek out truth within you,
If there be any left. Let your sweet tongue
Prevent your heart's rifling – there I'll ransack
And tear out my suspicion.

BEATRICE You may, sir –

'Tis an easy passage. Yet, if you please,
Show me the ground whereon you lost your love:

27 *strain . . . vault* weep enough to fill the heavens with water

29 *sadder* (1) more melancholy; (2) more sombre (*OED sad* a. 5; 8)

30 *stuff* cloth

32 *whore . . . hath* Recalling Desdemona's shocked reaction to her husband's use of the same word (*Othello*, IV.ii.160).
horrid full of horror, abominable (*OED* a. 2)

33 *blasts* blights, withers; brings infamy upon (*OED* v. 8 a–b)

37–9 *demolish, rifling, ransack* Alsemero develops the architectural metaphor latent in Beatrice's *ruined* and *repair*, picking up the play's recurrent identification of her body with the structure of the castle itself – see I.i.67, 216.

38–9 *Let . . . rifling* Let your honeyed tongue [do its best to] stop me plundering the secrets of your heart

41 *easy passage* easy way into my heart (carrying on the architectural metaphor); the audience are probably meant to hear an unconscious play on *easy* = sexually compliant (Williams, *Glossary*, p. 109)

41–2 *passage. Yet . . . / Show* ed. (passage, yet if you please. / Show Q)

42 *ground* grounds

My spotless virtue may but tread on that
Before I perish.
ALSEMERO Unanswerable –
A ground you cannot stand on, you fall down
Beneath all grace and goodness, when you set
Your ticklish heel on't. There was a visor
O'er that cunning face, and that became you;
Now Impudence in triumph rides upon't.
How comes this tender reconcilement else
'Twixt you and your despite, your rancorous loathing,
Deflores? He that your eye was sore at sight of,
He's now become your arms' supporter, your
Lips' saint.
BEATRICE Is there the cause?
ALSEMERO Worse: your lust's devil,
Your adultery.
BEATRICE Would any but yourself say that,
'Twould turn him to a villain.
ALSEMERO It was witnessed
By the counsel of your bosom, Diaphanta.
BEATRICE
Is your witness dead then?
ALSEMERO 'Tis to be feared
It was the wages of her knowledge: poor soul,
She lived not long after the discovery.
BEATRICE
Then hear a story of not much less horror
Than this your false suspicion is beguiled with:

43 *My . . . that* so that my spotless virtue may only [have the chance to] trample on it
47 *ticklish* (1) unsteady; (2) lecherous (Williams, *Glossary*: 'tickle', p. 308)
48 *became* (1) was becoming; (2) suited you because you were a hypocrite
49 *Impudence* Shamelessness
Impudence . . . upon't An allegorical construction – Alsemero imagines Impudence riding her chariot in a street pageant like those Triumphs of Fame, Fortune, Love, and Death popularised by Petrarch and widely illustrated in Renaissance art.
51 *your despite* one whom you despised
53 *arms' supporter* (1) the lover who supports your arm; (2) the heraldic figure who supports your coat of arms
53–4 *your . . . saint* 'that adored person to whom your lips pay devotion' (Frost) – i.e. by kissing. Cf. I.i.148.
54 *there* that
55 *Your adultery* i.e. the object of your adulterous passion
56 *It was* ed. ('Twas Q)

To your bed's scandal, I stand up innocence,
Which even the guilt of one black other deed,
Will stand for proof of – your love has made me
A cruel murd'ress.

ALSEMERO Ha!

BEATRICE A bloody one.
I have kissed poison for't, stroked a serpent:
That thing of hate – worthy in my esteem,
Of no better employment, and him most worthy
To be so employed – I caused to murder
That innocent Piracquo, having no
Better means than that worst, to assure
Yourself to me.

ALSEMERO Oh, the place itself e'er since
Has crying been for vengeance, the temple
Where blood and beauty first unlawfully
Fired their devotion, and quenched the right one –
'Twas in my fears at first; 'twill have it now.
Oh, thou art all deformed!

BEATRICE Forget not, sir,
It for your sake was done: shall greater dangers
Make the less welcome?

ALSEMERO Oh, thou shouldst have gone

63 *To . . . scandal* In reply to the scandal attaching to your marriage bed
I . . . innocence A slightly obscure turn of phrase, though the broad sense is clear: perhaps 'I stand here defiantly [as the very incarnation of] innocence'; Bawcutt interprets 'I stand up (set up, put forward) my innocence', but *OED* does not allow for a transitive use of the verb before the nineteenth century; Williams suggests that 'innocence' may have resulted from a misreading of 'innocent'.

65 *your love* my love for you

67 *stroked a serpent* The identification of Deflores as a *serpent* picks up the Fall motif; but the unconsciously erotic connotations of 'stroked' inevitably bring out the phallic suggestiveness of the metaphor (see Williams, *Glossary: serpent*, p. 273; *snake*, p. 280; *worm*, pp. 344–5).

74–6 *temple . . . devotion* Cf. I.i.1–2.

75 *blood* (1) Beatrice's aristocratic blood; (2) Alsemero's desire

76 *right one* i.e. devotion to God

77 *'Twas . . . first* Cf. I.i.2–4.
it i.e vengeance

78 *thou . . . deformed* Ironically Alsemero now recognises in Beatrice's the 'deformity' she once abhorred in Deflores (see e.g. II.i.43, 53; II.ii.40, 43).

79–80 *shall . . . welcome* Rather gnomic: Black suggests 'shall the greater dangers I have dared for you make my welcome less?'; but Beatrice seems to mean something more like 'shall greater dangers (i.e. those attendant on the murder) make lesser ones (i.e. those that would follow from my adultery) seem preferable?'

A thousand leagues about to have avoided
This dangerous bridge of blood – here we are lost.

BEATRICE
Remember, I am true unto your bed.

ALSEMERO
The bed itself's a charnel, the sheets shrouds
For murdered carcasses – it must ask pause
What I must do in this; meantime you shall
Be my prisoner only, enter my closet.

Exit BEATRICE. [ALSEMERO *locks her in the closet*]

I'll be your keeper yet. Oh, in what part
Of this sad story shall I first begin?

Enter DEFLORES

– Ha!
This same fellow has put me in – Deflores!

DEFLORES
Noble Alsemero!

ALSEMERO
I can tell you
News, sir: my wife has her commended to you.

DEFLORES
That's news indeed, my lord! I think she would
Commend me to the gallows if she could,
She ever loved me so well, I thank her.

ALSEMERO
What's this blood upon your band, Deflores?

DEFLORES
Blood? No, sure, 'twas washed since.

82 *bridge of blood* i.e. Piracquo's murder as the action that enabled Alsemero and Beatrice to unite in marriage
84 *charnel* place for storing the bones of the dead; cemetery
85–6 *pause/What* pause (to consider) what
88 *keeper* (1) custodian, warder (cf. Alibius and Lollio); (2) one who keeps a mistress (*OED* v. 1a; 4 – the latter sense is not recorded before 1676, but would be easily derived from *keep* v. 20b)
yet still
89 s.d. This edition (*after* l. 90 Q).
90 *put me in* intervened in my deliberations (and thereby given me a clue as to what I should do) (*OED* v. 45 h); *me* is probably an ethic dative.
96 *band* collar or ruff (*OED* n. 4a); Daalder suggests 'cuff' as a more likely alternative, but *OED* offers no clear example of this (*OED* n. 3)

ALSEMERO
Since when, man?
DEFLORES Since t'other day I got a knock
In a sword-and-dagger school – I think 'tis out.
ALSEMERO
Yes, 'tis almost out, but 'tis perceived though.
I had forgot my message: this it is,
What price goes murder?
DEFLORES How sir?
ALSEMERO I ask you, sir.
My wife's behindhand with you, she tells me,
For a brave bloody blow you gave for her sake
Upon Piracquo.
DEFLORES Upon? 'Twas quite through him, sure!
Has she confessed it?
ALSEMERO As sure as death to both of you,
And much more than that.
DEFLORES It could not be much more –
'Twas but one thing, and that is she's a whore.
ALSEMERO
It could not choose but follow. O cunning devils,
How should blind men know you from fair-faced saints?
BEATRICE (*Within*)
He lies! The villain does belie me!
DEFLORES
Let me go to her, sir.
ALSEMERO Nay, you shall to her! –
Peace, crying crocodile, your sounds are heard!
Take your prey to you – get you into her, sir.
Exit DEFLORES. [ALSEMERO *locks him in the closet*]

I'll be your pander now: rehearse again
Your scene of lust, that you may be perfect

98 *Since when, man* Metrically amphibious.
103 *behindhand . . . you* in arrears with her debt to you (*OED: behindhand* a. 1)
108 *that is she's* Bruster (that she's Q; Dyce: that she is)
109 *It* ed. (I Q)
113 *crying crocodile* According to the lore deriving from medieval bestiaries, crocodiles wept hypocritical tears before devouring their prey.

When you shall come to act it to the black audience
Where howls and gnashings shall be music to you.
Clip your adul'tress freely – 'tis the pilot
Will guide you to the Mare Mortuum,
Where you shall sink to fathoms bottomless.

Enter VERMANDERO, ALIBIUS, ISABELLA, TOMAZO, FRANCISCUS, *and* ANTONIO

VERMANDERO
O Alsemero, I have a wonder for you.

ALSEMERO
No sir, 'tis I – I have a wonder for you.

VERMANDERO
I have suspicion near as proof itself
For Piracquo's murder.

ALSEMERO
Sir, I have proof
Beyond suspicion, for Piracquo's murder.

VERMANDERO
Beseech you hear me. These two
[*Points at* ANTONIO *and* FRANCISCUS]
have been disguised
E'er since the deed was done.

ALSEMERO
I have two other
That were more close disguised than your two could be,
E'er since the deed was done.

VERMANDERO
You'll hear me! These mine own servants –

117 *black audience* i.e. of devils in hell; given that Alsemero is looking forward to their final judgement, *audience* may contain the secondary sense 'judicial hearing' (*OED* n. 3).

118 *howls and gnashing* Recalls the 'weeping [or "wailing"] and gnashing of teeth' to which the damned are condemned in the gospels (see e.g. Matthew 8:12, 13:42, 22:13, 24:51, 25:30; Luke 13:23).

119 *Clip* Embrace (*OED* v.[1]1a)
'tis May refer to Beatrice herself (Daalder) or to their embrace.

120 *Mare Mortuum* the Dead Sea – here punningly imagined as a place of the dead, and so as an entrance to hell (much as the River Styx marked the final threshold of the classical underworld).

121 *bottomless* Because the Dead Sea was rumoured to be bottomless, Rowley associates it with the 'bottomless pit' of hell.

ALSEMERO

Hear me! Those nearer than your servants,
That shall acquit them and prove them guiltless.

FRANCISCUS

That may be done with easy truth, sir.

TOMAZO

How is my cause bandied through your delays!
'Tis urgent in blood, and calls for haste;
Give me a brother alive or dead –
Alive, a wife with him; if dead, for both
A recompense for murder and adultery.

BEATRICE (*Within*)

Oh, oh, oh!

ALSEMERO Hark! 'Tis coming to you.

DEFLORES (*Within*)

Nay, I'll along for company.

BEATRICE (*Within*) Oh, oh!

VERMANDERO

What horrid sounds are these?

ALSEMERO Come forth, you twins
Of mischief.

Enter DEFLORES *bringing in* BEATRICE [*both wounded*]

135 *bandied* tossed aside (*OED* v. 2)

136 *urgent in blood* (1) pressing for prompt action through its effect on my blood (i.e. stirring up my passion); (2) urgent because of the blood that has been spilt. Dilke proposed 'urgent in my blood' – as it happens, a characteristically Middletonian locution (see Bruster, p. 9); however the line can be made to scan satisfactorily if the *r* in *urgent* is rolled.

137 *alive or dead* Bruster (p. 9) notes the occurrence of 'Dead or alive' in Middleton's share of *A Fair Quarrel* (II.i.121) – another indication of his possible involvement in this scene (see Introduction, p. x).

139 *adultery* Since betrothal was normally regarded as binding both in law and in the sight of God, Tomazo (who cannot yet know of her affair with Deflores) regards Beatrice's marriage to Alsemero as adulterous.

140–1 *oh* Beatrice's cries '*Within*', together with the offstage howls of the madmen (I.ii.185–91; III.ii.107, 160) and cries of 'fire' (V.i.68, 73) – like Deflores' 'work of secrecy' and Alonzo's concealed corpse – give theatrical reality to the idea of dangerous secrets hidden 'within' Vermandero's castle (I.i.159). Noting that Beatrice's cries echo those of Alonzo at III.i.28, and conjecturing that 'Alonzo is murdered in the same space that is later used to represent Alsemero's closet', Barker and Nicol suggest that 'the parallel . . . may be intended to emphasise the idea that Beatrice's murder is her punishment for Alonzo's death' (p. 12). Playing on the old idea of orgasm as erotic 'death', a number of productions, including the 1994 BBC version, have made Beatrice's shrieks sound disturbingly like groans of ecstasy.

140 *'Tis coming* i.e. the 'recompense' Tomazo has demanded

DEFLORES Here we are; if you have any more
To say to us, speak quickly, I shall not
Give you the hearing else – I am so stout yet,
And so, I think, that broken rib of mankind.

VERMANDERO
An host of enemies entered my citadel
Could not amaze like this. Joanna! Beatrice! Joanna!

BEATRICE
O come not near me, sir, I shall defile you:
I am that of your blood was taken from you
For your better health; look no more upon't,
But cast it to the ground regardlessly,
Let the common sewer take it from distinction.
Beneath the stars, upon yon meteor [*Points at* DEFLORES]
Ever hung my fate, 'mongst things corruptible,
I ne'er could pluck it from him; my loathing
Was prophet to the rest, but ne'er believed:
Mine honour fell with him, and now my life.
Alsemero, I am a stranger to your bed,
Your bed was cozened on the nuptial night,
For which your false bride died.

145 *I . . . yet* I am still strong enough (to listen)
146 *broken rib* Picks up the Fall motif – Eve having been created from Adam's rib (Genesis 2:21–3).
148 *amaze* Cf. III.ii.114; III.iii.71; IV.iii.98.
149 *O . . . me* Note the echo of Isabella at IV.iii.125.
150–1 *I . . . health* Blood-letting was perhaps the most common treatment in the regime of purgation by which early modern medicine sought to regulate the humoral balance of the body. *Blood* here includes both the 'blood' of aristocratic lineage, and the 'blood' of diseased passion; visually, it is linked to the actual blood coming from Beatrice's wound, and so to the bloodshed for which it is recompense.
153 *Let . . . distinction* The familiar analogy between castle and body underlies this figure – cf. the figure of purgation in Helkiah Crooke's anatomical treatise *Mikrocosmographia* (1618): 'the milt and the reins [bowels] do purge and cleanse the princely palace, and thrust, as it were, out of the kitchen, down the sink, all the filth and garbage' (p. 13).
154–5 *Beneath . . . corruptible* In the old concentric Ptolemaic universe, while the stars were thought to be 'fixed' in their spheres, eternal and unchanging, everything in the sublunary sphere was subject to mutability, corruption, and decay.
154 *meteor* By contrast with the 'fixed stars', the violent mobility of meteors and comets, 'shooting stars' that seemed to defy the sublime order of the other heavenly bodies, made them phenomena of ill omen. The figure is particularly appropriate to Deflores as an ambitious servant, conspicuously 'out of his place' (I.i.131).
155 *hung* ed. (hang Q)
160 *cozened* cheated. Daalder suggests a quibble on *cousin* = strumpet (*OED* n. 6); but *OED* gives no example of this usage before 1700.

ALSEMERO Diaphanta!

DEFLORES

Yes, and the while I coupled with your mate
At barley-break – now we are left in hell.

VERMANDERO

We are all there, it circumscribes us here.

DEFLORES

I loved this woman in spite of her heart;
Her love I earned out of Piracquo's murder.

TOMAZO

Ha! My brother's murderer!

DEFLORES Yes, and her honour's prize
Was my reward – I thank life for nothing
But that pleasure; it was so sweet to me
That I have drunk up all, left none behind
For any man to pledge me.

VERMANDERO Horrid villain!
Keep life in him for further tortures.

DEFLORES

No, I can prevent you: here's my penknife still;
It is but one thread more [*Stabs himself*] – and now 'tis cut.
Make haste, Joanna, by that token to thee –
Canst not forget! – so lately put in mind:
I would not go to leave thee far behind. *Dies*

BEATRICE

Forgive me, Alsemero, all forgive!
'Tis time to die, when 'tis a shame to live. *Dies*

163–4 *I . . . hell* Cf. III.ii.160.

164 *circumscribes* Cf. Marlowe's *Dr Faustus* (ed. Roma Gill, 2nd ed.) 'Hell hath no limits, nor is circumscribed / In one self place; for where we are is hell' (v.121–2).
us ed. (*not in* Q)

167 *honour's prize* capture of her honour (*OED: prize* n.³ 1); but the familiar sense of 'reward, trophy' is probably also present

171 *pledge me* drink a toast to me (*OED* v. 5). As Chakravorty (p. 161) points out, Deflores' line is adapted from Thomas Deloney's *The Gentle Craft*, where St Hugh, forced by a tyrant to drink the poisoned blood of St Winnifred, toasts the shoemakers: 'I drink to you all . . . but I cannot spare you one drop to pledge me.'

173 *prevent* forestall

175 *token* i.e. the wound he gave himself in the closet as a proof of his willingness to join her in death

VERMANDERO
Oh, my name is entered now in that record,
Where till this fatal hour 'twas never read.

ALSEMERO
Let it be blotted out, let your heart lose it,
And it can never look you in the face,
Nor tell a tale behind the back of life
To your dishonour; justice hath so right
The guilty hit, that innocence is quit
By proclamation, and may joy again.
[*To* TOMAZO] Sir, you are sensible of what truth hath done:
'Tis the best comfort that your grief can find.

TOMAZO
Sir, I am satisfied: my injuries
Lie dead before me, I can exact no more,
Unless my soul were loose, and could o'ertake
Those black fugitives that are fled from thence
To take a second vengeance; but there are wraths
Deeper then mine, 'tis to be feared, about 'em.

ALSEMERO
What an opacous body had that moon
That last changed on us! Here's beauty changed
To ugly whoredom; here servant obedience
To a master sin, imperious murder.
I, a supposed husband, changed embraces
With wantonness – but that was paid before;

180 *my name* Both Vermandero's family name and his personal honour are compromised by Beatrice's crime.
that record 'the heavenly record which lists criminal actions' (Frost) – or perhaps some imagined roll of dishonour (Daalder). Accent on second syllable of *record.*
182 *it* i.e. Beatrice's name
185 *so right* (1) in accordance with justice or righteousness; (2) with such precision (*OED* adv. 12; 5, 14, and cf. a. 4b 'right blow')
186 *quit* acquitted – obsolete past participle of 'quit' = acquit (*OED* v. 2b)
187 *proclamation* manifestation (*OED* n. 4) – i.e. because the guilty have been struck down by heavenly justice
188–9 *Sir . . . find* Although, as Daalder points out, these lines could be meant for Vermandero, they are more likely to be addressed to Tomazo, who appears to respond to them; *Sir* suggests a change of addressee, and its courteous tone is echoed by Tomazo (l. 190).
188 *sensible* conscious
196 *opacous* darkened, lying in (ominous) shadow (*OED* a. 1)
198–9 *servant . . . murder* Alsemero's language underlines the social subversiveness of Deflores' crime, in which murder is compounded by an assault on legitimate rank and authority.
201 *wantonness . . . before* i.e. Diaphanta, who has already paid for her offence with her life

[*To* TOMAZO] Your change is come too, from an ignorant wrath
To knowing friendship. Are there any more on's?

ANTONIO

Yes, sir, I was changed too, from a little ass as I was to a great fool as I am; and had like to ha' been changed to the gallows but that you know my innocence always excuses me.

FRANCISCUS

I was changed from a little wit to be stark mad,
Almost for the same purpose.

ISABELLA [*To* ALIBIUS] Your change is still behind,
But deserve best your transformation:
You are a jealous coxcomb – keep schools of folly,
And teach your scholars how to break your own head.

ALIBIUS

I see all apparent wife, and will change now
Into a better husband, and never keep scholars
That shall be wiser than myself.

ALSEMERO

Sir, you have yet a son's duty living –
Please you, accept it; let that your sorrow,
As it goes from your eye, go from your heart:
Man and his sorrow at the grave must part.

EPILOGUE

ALSEMERO

All we can do to comfort one another,
To stay a brother's sorrow for a brother,
To dry a child from the kind father's eyes
Is to no purpose, it rather multiplies:

206 *innocence* A play on the common use of 'innocent' to mean 'half-wit' or 'imbecile' (*OED* n. 3b)
208 *behind* to come (*OED* adv. 4)
211 *break . . . head* i.e. with cuckold's horns
215 *you . . . living* you can still count on my duty as your living son
220 *stay* appease, allay; comfort (*OED* v.[1] 28; v.[2]1b)
221 *kind* (1) behaving as a father naturally should; (2) loving (*OED* a. 1c; 6)
222 *multiplies* increases the grief

Your only smiles have power to cause re-live
The dead again, or in their rooms to give
Brother a new brother, father a child –
If these appear, all griefs are reconciled.

Exeunt OMNES

FINIS

223 *Your only smiles* Your smiles alone (addressed to the audience)
224 *rooms* place

APPENDIX: THE TEXT

(i) The 1653 Quarto

There exists only one seventeenth-century edition of *The Changeling* – a quarto printed early in 1653 by Thomas Newcombe for the bookseller, Humphrey Moseley. The printer can be identified from the ornament on Sig. B1; while the publisher is named on the title-page attached to thirteen of the surviving copies (see p. 1). Somewhat mysteriously, however, the imprint on the four remaining copies omits any reference to the publisher or his shop. Various explanations have been offered for this omission, but the reason for it remains obscure: Joost Daalder (p. xliii), arguing that Puritan hostility to the theatres in the interregnum meant that 'even the printing of a new play could get one into trouble,' speculates that Moseley commissioned a new title-page in order to avoid such unwelcome attention. There is, however, little evidence to support this hypothesis, and Douglas Bruster's more mundane conjecture that Moseley's address was deleted simply in order to facilitate sale by other booksellers seems more plausible. Indeed the fact that enough sheets survived from the original print-run to enable Moseley's widow to republish his edition with a fresh title-page in 1668 suggests that, having seriously overestimated his likely sales, Moseley might have had good reason to widen his market by wholesaling some copies to other retailers.

An editor's task is necessarily simplified by the fact Moseley's edition constitutes the only surviving early text of Middleton and Rowley's play; but it is also complicated by the fact that this edition appeared over thirty years after the play was first performed, more than a quarter of a century after the deaths of the authors. This means that the play appeared without the benefit of any input from the dramatists themselves or from the company which had once owned it. We also have no means of knowing the source and nature of the manuscript that Moseley supplied to Newcomb, though it probably came from reliable sources. A bookseller and publisher with marked royalist connections, Moseley did much to satisfy the continuing interest in drama during the interregnum years, from the outbreak of Civil War in 1642 to the Restoration of Charles II in 1660, when the London theatres were closed. He produced work by Shakespeare, Webster, and Fletcher, among others; and, in the same year in which he published *The Changeling*, secured his claims over fourteen other plays (including three more by Middleton) with a block entry on the Stationers' Register. In all likelihood Moseley acquired his rights to *The Changeling* – along with those for *The Spanish Gypsy* (1623), published later in the same year – from the financially embarrassed theatrical entrepreneur, William Beeston, the former owner of the Cockpit, where these two plays had originally been staged under the management of his father, Christopher. The Lord Chamberlain had confirmed both plays as William's 'propriety' in 1639. However, the fact that *The Spanish Gypsy*, which scholars nowadays credit principally to Dekker and Ford, appeared over the names of Middleton and Rowley alone, suggests that Moseley's connection with Beeston, who must surely have known the real authors, was not a close one.

Moseley's copy, perhaps acquired from Beeston along with the publication rights, does not appear to have been an authorial manuscript, since scholars are agreed that Q lacks many of the authorial spellings and linguistic habits peculiar to its two dramatists – though Rowley's fondness for ' 'um' as an abbreviation for 'them', for example, is as marked in the scenes usually attributed to him as ' 'em' in the scenes given to Middleton. But, if the manuscript supplied to Newcomb was non-authorial, what was its origin? In his 1958 Revels edition, N. W. Bawcutt, adducing the clear marking of entries and exits, as well as one or two theatrical-sounding stage directions, conjectured that 'the source of the printed text was probably a transcript from a theatrical prompt-copy' (Revels, p. xvi). While the term 'prompt-copy' may itself be misleading – as recent theatre-historians, aware of the physical difficulties of successful prompting in early modern playhouses have argued – it is clear that acting companies will have needed a working copy of the play-text in addition to the precious 'allowed copy' submitted for the approval of the Master of the Revels, and the individual 'parts' distributed to the actors. However, in the case of *The Changeling*, the evidence for the text's theatrical origins is rather slender – and Bawcutt himself seems to have abandoned his claim by the time he produced his facsimile edition fifteen years later. As Bruster and others have noted, Q's entrances are often marked late[1] – after a speaker has registered the entrant's presence on the stage – whereas in manuscripts marked up for playhouse use it was usual to mark an entrance early, so that the book-keeper could alert the actor in good time. Furthermore, Q's stage directions are generally sparser than we might expect from a theatrical manuscript; and, while some – notably the unique '*In the act-time* DEFLORES *hides a naked rapier*' at the beginning of Act III – must have been composed by someone with the material conditions of performance in a private theatre clearly in mind,

1 See Bruster, p. 2; Bawcutt (1973), p. 2.

there is no reason why that should not have been Middleton, whose experience in writing for these houses stretched back nearly twenty years to his work with the boy companies at the beginning of the century.

Another commonly recognised clue to a text's playhouse origins is evidence of cutting; and some scholars have been attracted by the possibility, first advanced by E. H. C. Oliphant, that two scenes may have been excised from the sub-plot in the text that has come down to us: on the one hand the characters of Antonio and Franciscus, the pretended fool and madman, are not only allowed to remain unnamed in the spoken text, but are introduced in a somewhat abrupt fashion, without any attempt to prepare the audience for their appearance in the madhouse; on the other hand, the wild dance of fools and madmen, meant to be performed by Alibius' inmates as part of Beatrice's wedding revels, never eventuates – even though it has promised to be the spectacular climax of the sub-plot.[2] If the dramatists were originally careful to fill these apparent gaps, then any excision must presumably have occurred as a result of theatrical cutting. However, even those, like Roger Holdsworth, who are attracted by Oliphant's thesis, admit that such carelessness about motivation and the naming of characters is relatively common in the period: Vermandero himself – as Bruster (p. 3) points out – remains anonymous for more than half the play, until Alibius names him in III.iii. As far as the 'madmen's morris' is concerned, it has, of course, been commissioned to wind up the wedding festivities on 'the third night from the first' (III.ii.249): this must be the night signalled by the arrival of Alibius and Isabella at the castle in the final scene (V.iii.121) just before the public indictment of Beatrice and Defores; so the time-scheme actually allows no opportunity for it to be performed, except via the rehearsal at the end of Act IV – though it is conceivable, I think, that this antimasque may have been repeated after the epilogue in imitation of those 'jigs' that traditionally rounded off performances in the outdoor theatres.

Moseley's text seems to have been printed with reasonable care by the standards of the time – though, in accordance with usual printing-house practice, it was proofed only in the course of printing, and then in a somewhat unsystematic way, with corrections made only to the outer formes of the B, D, and G gatherings. Most of these involve nothing more than obvious misprints – although there are two instances in which the proof-reader seems to have borne in mind the demands of sense and/or

2 This omission seemed serious to Tony Richardson, who chose to stage the masque in his 1961 Royal Court production, making it the occasion for exposing the imposture of Antonio and Franciscus.

metre (II.i.149; II.ii.131). Apart from a number of surviving misprints and occasional missing words, the main deficiencies of the Q text are in its treatment of the verse: there are numerous examples of mislineation (especially where two half-lines, or a line and a half have been crammed into a single line), verse is several times set as prose, and in a few instances prose is mistakenly set as verse. Such errors are particularly common in the scenes attributed to Middleton and seem, more often than not, to derive from the dramatist's manuscript habits, though sometimes the compositor may have been compelled to save space as a result of poor casting off. Where other kinds of lineation problem arise it is often difficult to be sure whether they result from faulty transcription by a scribe or compositor, or simply from the author's habits of composition. Rowley's madhouse scenes present particular difficulties, since they frequently involve dialogue in which some characters speak in verse while their interlocutors reply in prose: theatrical convention dictated that verse was normally used to mark the speech of characters of higher rank, while prose was assigned to their inferiors; but prose could also be used (as in *Hamlet*, for example) to signal the falling away from decorum entailed by madness. In *The Changeling* the result is that Alibius and Isabella speak almost entirely in verse; their servant Lollio is predictably a prose speaker; the pretended fool, Antonio, employs prose when in disguise, but reverts to verse when speaking *in propria persona;* while the pretended madman, Franciscus, mixes prose and verse in his imposture, but, like his rival, is naturally a speaker of verse. In the mixed dialogue that results, however, it is sometimes hard to be sure whether some of Isabella's lines, for example, are to be treated as incomplete verse or as prose, or whether (influenced by her interlocutors) she sometimes sinks to prose (see e.g. III.ii.42–3) – as she seems to do when herself feigning madness (see e.g. IV.iii.94–6); by the same token it is equally hard to know whether the iambic beat apparent in some of Lollio's lines is purely accidental, or whether, influenced by Isabella or Alibius, he occasionally rises to verse (see e.g. I.ii.17, 34). In addition to this, Rowley (who did not have a particularly subtle ear for the music of iambic verse) sometimes produces lines of such disconcerting metrical awkwardness that, if they are verse at all, can only be accounted for as crude syllabics (see e.g. I.ii.83–7). Middleton, by contrast, was a genuinely innovative dramatic poet, who treats the verse form with considerable freedom, not only making extensive use of feminine endings and hexameters, but sometimes composing lines that might be a syllable or two short (e.g. III.iii.137), or include one or more extra-metrical syllables (e.g. III.iii.139), without ever losing the rhythmic pulse. To complicate matters further, the Q text is marked by a fondness for contractions that sometimes overrides the requirements of metre – thus, for example, Q prints ' 'tis' at I.i.21 where the metre appears to require 'it is', just as it prints 'that's' for 'that is' at I.i.78, ' 'bout' for 'about' at II.ii.27, and ' 'Twas' for 'It was' at V.iii.56: it is possible that such seeming aberrations reflect the habits of whoever was responsible for the manuscript copy, but they may simply reveal the strength of the dramatists' shared predilection for idiomatic speech. The combined effect of all these metrical uncertainties was to license nineteenth-century editors like Dilke and Dyce to iron out perceived irregularities in the verse; a modern editor, however, must proceed more circumspectly, listening with particular care for Middleton's characteristically spiky rhythms, before deciding whether or not to emend the text.

(ii) Lineation

	This edition	**Q**
I.i		
146–7	O . . . thee / Your . . . ended	*one line*
162–3	Alsemero . . . son / Of . . . Alsemero	*one line*
164–6	He . . . wont / To . . . most / Unfeignèd	He . . . speaks / A . . . truth
210–11	He's much / Bound . . . sir	*one line*
212–13	As . . . want / My . . . else	*one line*
224–6	Here's . . . know / She . . . pair / Of . . . fingers	Here's . . . now / I . . . tanned / In . . . fingers
I.ii		
30–1	You . . . into't	*as verse* (You . . . by / One . . . into't)
33–4	Must . . . be / At home	*one line*
81–2	Ay . . . patient	*one line*
83–7	And . . . defrayed	*as verse* (And . . . commodious / To . . . sick / And . . . are / But . . . pieces / That . . . charge / Of necessaries / Fully defrayed.
89–90	Sir . . . hands	*as verse* (Sir . . . something, / The . . . hands
94	His . . . Tony	*as verse* (His . . . half / To . . . Tony)
166–7	Yes . . . Tony	*as verse* (Yes . . . say't; / Once . . . Tony)
193–4	There's . . . for't	*as verse* (There's . . . madman, / Was . . . Parmesan / Lost . . . for't)
II.i		
9–10	Than . . . him / For . . . choose	*one line*
52–3	Again! / This . . . me	*one line*
56–7	Soft . . . fair ! / I . . . now	*one line*
57–8	The . . . fixed / Thou . . . pool	*one line*
60–1	My . . . deliver / A . . . you	*one line*
61–2	What . . . since? / Do't . . . then	*one line*
64–5	Let . . . patience, / You . . . all	*one line*
66–7	Signor . . . lady, / Sole . . . Piracquo	*one line*

	This edition	**Q**
69–70	The . . . Alonzo, / With . . . Tomazo	*one line*
73–4	My . . . father / Charged . . . out	*one line*
74–5	Is . . . other / To . . . by	*one line*
75–6	It . . . luck / To . . . still	*one line*
121–2	May . . . ever / Meet . . . sirs	May . . . still: / You're . . . sirs
137–8	She . . . passions; / And . . . dangerous	*one line*
142–3	Nay . . . that / Be . . . enough	*one line*
II.ii		
5–6	This . . . well: / These . . . cabinets	*one line*
12–13	Were . . . like / In . . . borrow	*one line*
25–6	Pray . . . sir. / What . . . happy	*as prose*
48–9	I . . . sir: / The . . . side	*one line*
51–2	As . . . now, / Till . . . opens	*one line*
63–4	One . . . thousand – / Proves . . . royal	*one line*
69–70	And . . . here. – / Deflores	*one line*
72–3	What . . . done / To . . . physician	*one line*
77–8	Which . . . ago: / How . . . this	*one line*
79–80	Turn . . . see. / Faugh . . . perceive't	*one line*
81–2	Her . . . me! / She . . . amber	*one line*
83–4	I'll . . . this / Within . . . fortnight	*one line*
85–6	Yes . . . cure / I'll . . . other	*one line*
86–7	'Tis . . . pleasure / To . . . me	*one line*
87–8	When . . . used / To . . . unpleasing	*one line*
89–90	It . . . mends – / I . . . experience	*one line*
90–1	I . . . blest / To . . . on't	*one line*
93–4	It . . . manhood, / If . . . employment	*one line*
94–5	'Twould . . . seen, / If . . . it	*one line*
96–7	I . . . service / So . . . to	*one line*
97–8	We . . . you – / O . . . Deflores	*one line*
101–2	There . . . again, / The . . . on't	*one line*
106–7	For . . . yet / Beat . . . bosom	*one line*
109–10	Oh . . . freedom! / I . . . one	*one line*
112–13	Then . . . 'em / For . . . sight	*one line*
113–4	O . . . occasion! / Without . . . wishes	*one line*
115–6	In . . . Deflores? / There's . . . that	*one line*
116–17	Put . . . me: / It's . . . you	*one line*
120–1	If . . . knew / How . . . employed	*one line*
124–5	This . . . methinks; / Belike . . . such	*one line*
127–8	Possible . . . need / Is . . . thee	*one line*
130–2	That . . . ravishes	*as prose*
134–5	His . . . him: / He . . . more	*one line*
135–7	How . . . now / Dost . . . man / Dearlier rewarded	How . . . me! / Never . . . rewarded
144–6	I . . . rid / Myself . . . time: / Piracquo . . . dog-face	*as prose*
146–7	O . . . blood! / Methinks . . . already	*one line*
157–8	Thou . . . me / The . . . castle	*one line*
159–61	And . . . straits / Of . . . you, / I . . . lord	*as prose*
162–4	I'm . . . then. / 'Tis . . . rising / I'll . . . me	*as prose*
III.i		
9–10	Here . . . lord, / To . . . purpose	*one line*
11–12	All . . . anon / A . . . on	*one line*
13–14	I . . . glad / I . . . house	*one line*

	This edition	**Q**
20–4	Ay . . . awhile	*as prose*
25–6	Deflores . . . Deflores, / Whose . . . on	*one line*
26–7	Do . . . question / A . . . you	*one line*
III.ii		
29–31	If . . . fool	If . . . show / You . . . may / Call . . . fool
44–6	For . . . neither	For . . . mistress, / He . . . first; / The . . . Chambermaid / Yet . . . neither
47–51	Hail . . . poesy	*as prose*
53–5	O . . . kneels	*as prose*
62–3	Didst . . . poet	*one line*
67–8	Yes . . . ago	*one line*
77–83	Luna . . . sheep	*as prose*
87–8	Sweet . . . me: / Give . . . thee	*one line*
90–2	No . . . mouse-hole	*see Commentary*
119–25	Oh . . . strange! / Love . . . all	*one line*
135–6	Take . . . acquaintance / Of . . . within	*one line*
137–8	When . . . him, / I'll . . . time	*one line*
144–5	And . . . cousin; / I'll . . . morning	And . . . Valentine / Tomorrow morning
149–50	If . . . like / To . . . something	*one line*
151–3	Ay . . . six	Ay . . . begins / To . . . is/ Five . . . six
155–6	What . . . seven	What . . . is/ One . . . seven
166–7	How . . . freeze / Lives . . . alone	*one line*
172–4	How . . . that	How . . . Lipsius? / He's . . . harder / Questions . . . that
175–6	What . . . fear, / Having . . . smile	*one line*
184–5	Of . . . us, / Yet . . . lunatics	*one line*
217–18	What . . . fear, / Having . . . smile	*one line*
224–8	Becomes . . . not –' / [*prose*] And . . . on't	Becomes . . . more / Foolish . . . Lacedemonian. / Let . . . thing / About . . . on't
238–9	Fie . . . sweetheart / No . . . that	*one line*
270–1	You've . . . on't: / Madmen . . . commodity	*one line*
III.iii		
29–30	Why . . . more / Than . . . heart-strings	*one line*
48–51	It . . . sir. / Why . . . given / In . . . lady; / You . . . then	*as prose*
60–1	'Tis . . . then. / Look . . . florins	*one line*
68–9	I . . . hired / A . . . rate	*one line*
73–4	You . . . course / To . . . do	*one line*
89–90	How . . . sir? / This . . . well	*one line*
90–1	What . . . strange? / This . . . us	*one line*
94–5	Take . . . forgetfulness, / 'Twill . . . us	*one line*
97–8	I . . . you / Of . . . pain	*one line*
101–2	Oh . . . shall! / Speak . . . lose	*one line*
104–5	I . . . again / For . . . deed	*one line*
105–6	Soft . . . soft – / The . . . act	*one line*
124–5	I . . . it / With . . . modesty	*one line*
125–6	Push . . . yourself: / A . . . modesty	*as prose*
159–60	The . . . buy / My . . . me	*one line*
IV.i		
30–1	If . . . C	If . . . not, / Give . . . C

	This edition	**Q**
32–4	Where's . . . now: / [*prose*] and . . . not	Where's . . . child, / She . . . not
56–7	Would . . . cause / To . . . madam	Would . . . too. / Why . . . madam
81–2	Nay . . . madam, / Shall . . . maid	*as prose*
82–3	You . . . else, / Because . . . me	*one line*
102–3	And . . . doing, / I . . . it	*one line*
111–12	As . . . accident / Gives . . . another	*one line*
113–15	Ha . . . light! / At . . . pleasurable! / But . . . madam	Ha . . . pleasurable. / But . . . madam
115–16	Ay . . . tomorrow; / We . . . by't	*one line*
117–18	It . . . wench – / Most . . . now	It . . . Diaphanta / I . . . now
120–1	I'll . . . study / The . . . business	*as prose*
121–2	I . . . well, / Because . . . burden	*one line*
122–3	About midnight / You . . . gently	*one line*
IV.ii		
3–4	Nor . . . gentlemen / Are . . . who	Nor . . . absent / Tell . . . who
7–8	Some . . . Valencia	Some . . . Briamata, / Th'other . . . Valencia
17–18	You're . . . hot / Seek . . . here	*one line*
33–4	'Tis . . . fair / For you	*one line*
35–6	The . . . is, / There . . . on	*one line*
43–4	O . . . sir! / Methinks . . . him	*one line*
60–1	'Twill . . . reckon. / Sir!	*one line*
67–8	Your . . . you / Appear . . . strangers	*one line*
68–9	Time . . . swords / May . . . business	Time . . . acquainted; / This . . . business
73–4	You . . . look / To . . . sir	*one line*
74–5	Fear . . . not: / I'll . . . meeting	*one line*
85–6	This . . . on, / And . . . slowness	*one line*
97–8	Still . . . thee: / The . . . her	*one line*
104–5	Such . . . are. / Oh . . . earth	*one line*
110–11	Done charitably. / That . . . secret	*one line*
133–4	Sir . . . me – / I . . . composition	*one line*
143–4	Ha, ha, ha! / You . . . lord	*one line*
IV.iii		
80–1	Ay . . . la	Ay . . . out, / Vault . . . la
86–8	Marry . . . caper	Marry . . . yeomanry / Itself . . . stiffened, / There . . . caper
90–2	Very . . . Tony	Very . . . high, / Has . . . again, / You . . . Tony
94–100	Hey . . . had! / Stand . . . Dedalus, / And . . . labyrinth; / I'll . . . clew	Hey . . . way, / He . . . Icarus, / More . . . moons; / He's . . . up, / Thou . . . lower / Labyrinth . . . clew
V.i		
14–15	Hath . . . trust / A . . . woman	*one line*
30–1	Tush . . . quiet, / Or . . . all	*one line*
32–3	This . . . a-fire / Of . . . chamber	*one line*
33–4	How . . . sir? / That . . . house	*one line*
36–7	Push . . . aim / At . . . sure	*one line*
51–2	One . . . now: / Prithee . . . servants	*one line*
52–3	I'll . . . them, / Some . . . hurry	*one line*
76–7	Here's . . . loving! – / Oh . . . jewel	*one line*
78–9	Hie . . . chamber; / Your . . . you	*one line*
80–1	I . . . made / So . . . bargain	*one line*

	This edition	**Q**
83–4	When . . . you, / I . . . follow	*one line*
84–5	Th'art . . . sweetness! / The . . . dangerous	*one line*
95–6	Come . . . now; / Alas . . . cold	*one line*
105–6	O . . . virginity, / Thou . . . for't	*one line*
108–9	Now . . . flames / Are . . . sir	Now . . . are / Greedy . . . sir
110–12	Not . . . more, / I . . . you / In . . . us	Not . . . embrace / I . . . us
115–17	All . . . stifled	All . . . lords, / The . . . gentlewoman / How . . . stifled
124–5	He . . . be – / Deflores . . . me	*one line*

V.iii

14–15	How do I? / Alas . . . well	*one line*
40–1	You . . . sir – / 'Tis . . . please	*one line*
53–4	He . . . your / Lips' saint	*one line*
54–5	Worse . . . devil, / Your adultery	*one line*
56–7	It was witnessed / By . . . Diaphanta	*one line*
91–2	I . . . you / News . . . you	*one line*
142–3	Come . . . twins / Of mischief	*one line*
208–9	Your . . . behind, / But . . . transformation	*one line*